Edward Augustus Freeman

The Story of Sicily

Phoenician, Greek, and Roman. Third Edition

Edward Augustus Freeman

The Story of Sicily
Phoenician, Greek, and Roman. Third Edition

ISBN/EAN: 9783744693271

Printed in Europe, USA, Canada, Australia, Japan

Cover: Foto ©ninafisch / pixelio.de

More available books at **www.hansebooks.com**

THE STORY OF THE NATIONS

SUBSCRIPTION

EDITION

The Story of the Nations.

SICILY.

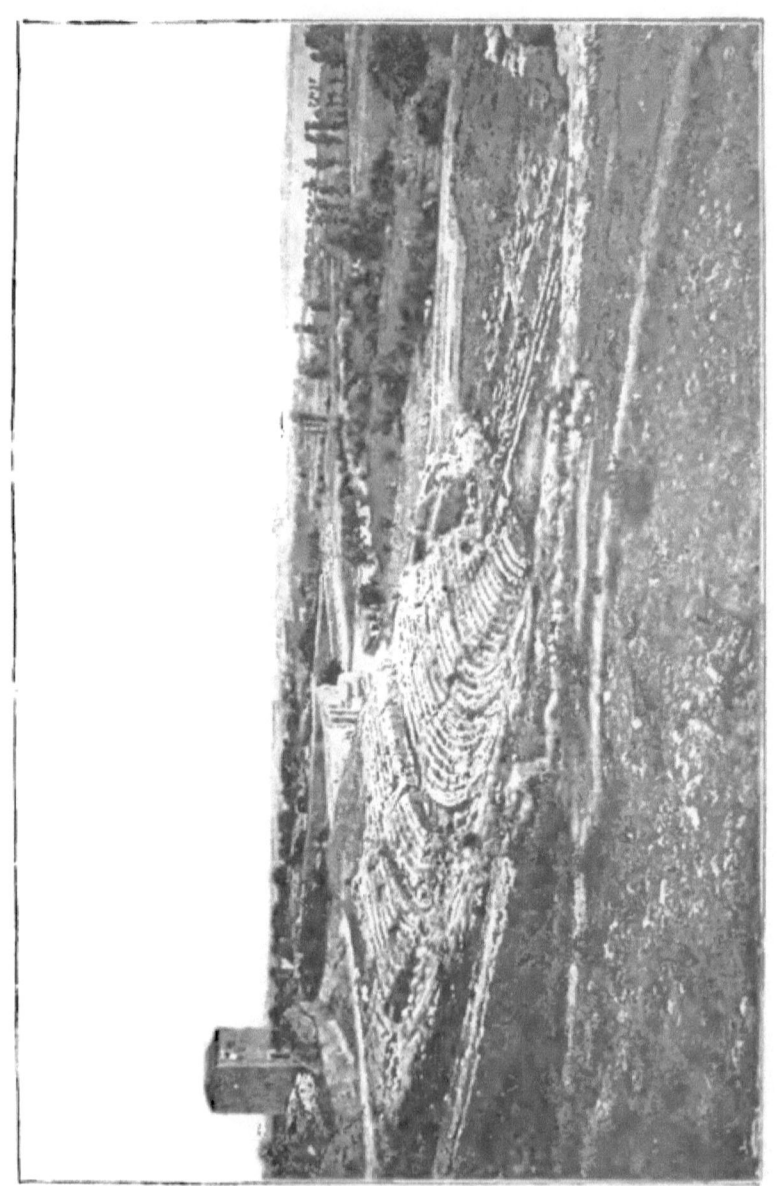

THE THEATRE, SYRACUSE. (See page 294).

SICILY

PHOENICIAN, GREEK, & ROMAN

BY

EDWARD A. FREEMAN, M.A., Hon. D.C.L., LL.D.

REGIUS PROFESSOR OF MODERN HISTORY, OXFORD, FELLOW OF ORIEL
COLLEGE, HONORARY FELLOW OF TRINITY COLLEGE, OXFORD

THIRD EDITION

PREFACE.

In undertaking "to contribute a short History of Sicily to the series called The Story of the Nations," Mr. Freeman says, in the Preface to his greater work on the same subject, that he did so "on the express ground that Sicily never was the home of any nation, but rather the meeting-place of many." The original suggestion had been that he should write a volume on Norman Sicily. But in view of the necessity of first introducing his readers to the earlier stages of Sicilian history, this suggestion finally ripened into the proposal to write the whole story of Sicily, from the earliest days of the Greek colonisation to the time of Frederick the Second.

The idea grew. It had for many years been a favourite saying of Mr. Freeman that "in order to write a small history you must first write a large one."

In this way the "Little History of Sicily" gave birth to the larger one, of which three volumes, reaching down to the time of the Athenian siege and the tyranny of Dionysios, have already been issued by the Clarendon Press. Besides this, there exist materials for a continuation of the larger history down to the period of the Roman Conquest and for a later volume on Norman Sicily. But, unhappily for his readers, he has not been spared to bring the work, either in its greater or lesser form, to completion.

With the exception of the headings from p. 297 onwards and the Index, which has been drawn up as far as possible on the lines of those made by the author himself for his greater work, the whole of the sheets had been passed for press by Mr. Freeman before he left England on his last journey—a journey to Spain, undertaken with a special view to the better understanding of the later parts of his great work. The present volume goes down to the end of the Roman dominion, and the last part of the book, which deals with Sicily as a Roman Province, covers a period which, in contradistinction to his usual practice, he had not yet written in the larger form. It had been his intention to add to the present a second volume, beginning with the coming of the Saracens, and which should, according to the hopes expressed in his greater work, have been at any rate carried on "till the Wonder of the World is laid in his tomb at Palermo," or, it may be, carried on yet further to the time when the "island story" should be merged in that of the new Italian Kingdom.

But it was not so to be. The "life and strength" that he had hoped for failed him before their time, and, in the language of the Psalmist, whose words were ever on his lips and in his writings, his strength was brought down in his journey, his days were shortened. He died at Alicante on March 16, 1892.

A. J. E. AND M. E.

CONTENTS.

	PAGE
PREFACE	vii

I.

CHARACTERISTICS OF SICILIAN HISTORY . 1–7

    Geographical position of Sicily—Strife of East and West—Summary of the History.

II.

SICILY AND ITS INHABITANTS 8–28

    Colonies in Sicily—Nature of Colonies—The older inhabitants—Phœnician and Greek Settlers—Shape of Sicily—Nature of the land—The Hill-towns—The Phœnicians—Phœnician Colonies in Sicily—Panormos, Motya, and Eryx.

III.

THE LEGENDS 29–38

    Héraklês—The Nether Gods—The Palici and the Goddesses—Arethousa.

IV.

THE GREEK SETTLEMENTS IN SICILY 39–56

    Foundation of Naxos—Foundation of Syracuse—Foundation of Leontinoi and Katanê—Foundation of Megara—Foundation of Zanklê and Gela—Kamarina, Himera, and Selinous—Foundation of Akragas—Foundation of Lipara.

V.

The First Age of the Greek Cities . . 57–75

The Syracuse *Gamoroi*—Tyranny—Phalaris of Akragas—Expedition of Dôrieus—The Samians at Zanklé—Wars of Hippokratés—Gelôn at Syracuse—War in Western Sicily.

VI.

The First Wars with Carthage and Etruria 76–86

Persia and Carthage—Invasions of Sicily and Old Greece—Battle of Himera—Death of Gelôn—Reign of Hierôn.

VII.

The Greeks of Sicily Free and Independent 87–103

Fall of tyranny at Akragas—All the cities free—Wealth of Akragas—Politics of Syracuse—Rise of Ducetius—Foundation of Kalé Akté—Great preparations of Syracuse.

VIII.

The Share of Sicily in the Wars of Old Greece 104–139

Sparta and Athens—Sikeliot appeal to Athens—Hermokratés at Gela—New War at Leontinoi—Appeal of Segesta to Athens—Hermokratés and Athénagoras—Recall of Alkibiadés—Battle before Syracuse—Alkibiadés at Sparta—The Athenians on the hill—Coming of Gylippos—Second Expedition voted—Coming of Démosthenés and Eurymedôn—Eclipse of the moon—Last battle and retreat—End of the Athenian invasion—Banishment of Hermokratés.

IX.

The Second Carthaginian Invasion 140–155

Expedition of Hannibal—Siege and taking of Selinous—Hannibal's Sacrifice—Death of Hermokratés—Siege of Akragas—Beginnings of Dionysios—Siege and forsaking of Gela—Treaty with Carthage.

X

The Tyranny of Dionysios . . 156-196

The tyranny of Dionysios—Revolt against Dionysios—Conquests of Dionysios—Fortification of Epipolai—Dionysios' double marriage—Siege of Motya—Foundation of Lilybaion—Sea-fight off Katanè—Carthaginian Siege of Syracuse—Defeat of the Carthaginians—Settlements of Dionysios—His defeat at Tauromenion—Wars in Italy—Destruction of towns in Italy—Taking of Rhêgion—Dionysios in the Hadriatic—War with Carthage—Death of Dionysios.

XI.

The Deliverers . . 197-232

Dionysios and his Son—Dionysios the Younger—Coming of Diôn—Diôn delivers Syracuse—Diôn and Dionysios—Diôn deprived of the Generalship—Return of Diôn—Recovery of the Island—End of Diôn—Timoleôn in Sicily—Recovery of the Island—New Settlement of Sicily—War with Carthage—Battle of the Krimisos—Last days of Timoleôn—Archidamos and Alexander.

XII.

The Tyranny of Agathoklés . . . 233-260

His early life—His rise to power—His conquests—Battle of the Himeras—He lands in Africa—His African campaign—Murder of Ophellas—Agathoklês king—End of the African expedition—Agathoklês and Deinokratês—Death of Agathoklês.

XIII.

The Coming of Pyrrhos and the Rise of Hierôn . . . 261-275

Various tyrants—Pyrrhos of Epeiros—Hellas, Carthage, and Rome—Conquests of Pyrrhos—He leaves Sicily—Exploits of Hierôn—Hierôn king.

XIV.

THE WAR FOR SICILY . 276–291

The Mamertines—Hierôn's alliance with Rome—Taking of Akragas—Roman taking of Panormos—Defence of Panormos—Hamilkar Barak—Battle of Aigousa—Carthage gives up Sicily.

XV.

THE END OF SICILIAN INDEPENDENCE . 292–318

Roman power in Sicily—The Hannibalian War—Death of Hierônymos—Slaughter of Hierôn's descendants—Taking of Leontinoi—Roman siege of Syracuse—Massacre at Henna—Epipolai in Roman hands—Punic force destroyed by pestilence—Taking of Syracuse—Exploits of Mutines—Outcry against Marcellus—Sicily an outpost of Europe.

XVI.

SICILY A ROMAN PROVINCE 319–354

Relations of cities to Rome—The Roman peace—First Slave War—Second Slave War—End of the Slave War—Prætorship of Verres—Death of Cæsar foretold—Peace of Misenum—War between Cæsar and Sextus—Cæsar master of Sicily—Third Slave War—Growth of Christian legends—Beginning of Teutonic invasions—Rule of Theodoric—Gothic War of Justinian—Connexion with East-Roman Empire—Constantine the Fifth.

INDEX 355

LIST OF ILLUSTRATIONS.

	PAGE
THE THEATRE, SYRACUSE	*Frontispiece*
OLYMPIEION, SYRACUSE	44
HÉRAKLÊS AND THE KERKÔPES (EARLY SCULPTURE FROM SELINOUS)	52
AKRAGAS, FROM THE OLYMPIEION	54
COIN OF SYRACUSE, TIME OF THE GAMOROI	60
TEMPLE OF ATHÊNÊ, SYRACUSE	61
COIN OF HIMERA, EARLY	64
COIN OF ZANKLÊ, SIXTH CENTURY	68
COIN OF NAXOS, c. 500 B.C.	68
COIN OF KAMARINA. EARLY	71
COIN OF SELINOUS. EARLY	75
DÂMARATEION	82
COIN OF GELA. c. 480 B.C.	85
COIN OF SELINOUS. c. 440 B.C.	85
TEMPLE AT AKRAGAS	88
AKTAIÓN AND HIS HOUNDS	97
COIN OF PANORMOS. c. 420 B.C.	102
COIN OF MESSANA. c. 420 B.C.	102
COIN OF SEGESTA. c. 415 B.C.	112
MAP OF SYRACUSE DURING THE ATHENIAN SIEGE	122

LIST OF ILLUSTRATIONS.

	PAGE
COIN OF AKRAGAS. c. 415 B.C.	126
SYRACUSAN PENTÊKONTALITRON (PRIZE ARMS OF ASSINARIAN GAMES)	134
SYRACUSAN STONE QUARRIES	135
COIN OF HIMERA. c. 430 B.C.	139
COIN OF KATANÊ. c. 410 B.C.	141
COIN OF SYRACUSE. c. 409 B.C. HEAD OF ARETHUSA	145
MAP OF AKRAGAS	148
SYRACUSE UNDER DIONYSIOS	162
PASSAGE IN THE CASTLE OF EURYALOS	164
APPARENT ARCH IN THE WALL OF ERYX	167
COIN OF MOTYA. c. 400 B.C.	168
MAP OF MOTYA AND ERYX	169
PHŒNICIAN CAPITAL FROM LILYBAION	172
TAUROMENION	174
COIN OF SYRACUSE. DIÔN'S TIME	205
COIN OF SYRACUSE. TIMOLEÔN'S TIME. ZEUS ELEUTHERIOS	223
TEMPLE OF SEGESTA	253
COIN OF AGATHOKLÊS, WITH NAME OF SYRACUSE ONLY. 317 TO c. 310 B.C.	260
COIN OF AGATHOKLÊS, WITH NAME ONLY. c. 310–306 B.C.	260
COIN OF AGATHOKLÊS, WITH ROYAL TITLE. c. 306–289 B.C.	260
COIN OF MAMERTINI AT MESSANA. c. 282 B.C.	262
COIN OF HIKETAS. 287–278 B.C.	263
COIN OF HIERON II. 275–216 B.C.	274
COIN OF QUEEN PHILISTIS c. 275–216 B.C.	275
PRETENDED TOMB OF THÊRÔN AT AGRIGENTUM	280

STORY OF SICILY.

I.

CHARACTERISTICS OF SICILIAN HISTORY.

THE claim of the history of Sicily to a place in the Story of the Nations is not that there ever has been a Sicilian nation. There has very seldom been a time when there was a power ruling over all Sicily and over nothing out of Sicily. There has never been a time when there was one language spoken by all men in Sicily and by no men out of Sicily. All the powers, all the nations, that have dwelled round the Mediterranean Sea have had a part in Sicilian history. All the languages that have been spoken round the Mediterranean Sea have been, at one time or another, spoken in Sicily. The historical importance of Sicily comes, not from its being the seat of any one nation, but from its being the meeting-place and the battle-field of many nations. Many of the chief nations of the world have settled in Sicily and have held dominion in Sicily. They have wrought on Sicilian soil, not only the history of Sicily, but a great part of their own history. And, above all, Sicily has been the meeting-place and battle-field, not only of rival nations and languages, but of rival religious creeds.

It follows from this that, while the history of Sicily has had a great effect on the general history of the world, it is still, in a certain sense, a secondary history. For some centuries past, and also in some earlier times, this has been true in the sense that Sicily has been part of the dominion of some other power ruling out of Sicily. But Sicily has not always been in this way a dependent land. In one age it contained the greatest and most powerful city in Europe. In another age it was the seat of the most flourishing kingdom in Europe. Yet its history has always been a secondary history, a history whose chief importance comes from its relations to things out of Sicily. The greatest powers and nations of the world have in several ages fought in Sicily and for Sicily. Their Sicilian warfare determined their history elsewhere.

In this way the history of Sicily is one of the longest and most unbroken histories in Europe. It does not belong, wholly or chiefly, either to what is called "ancient" or to what is called "modern" history. Of its two most brilliant periods, one belongs to what is commonly called "ancient," the other to what is commonly called "modern." And nowhere is it more hopeless to try to keep the two asunder; nowhere is the history so imperfect if we try to look at one period only. For the history of Sicily is before all things a history of cycles. The later story is the earlier story coming over again. That is to say, like causes have been at work in very distant times, and they have led to like results.

Now all these characteristics of Sicilian history come from the geographical position and the geographical character of the land. Sicily is an island. It is a great island, an island which, in the days when cities were powers, could contain many independent powers. And above all, it is a central island. It lies in the very middle of the great inland sea which parts and unites Europe, Asia, and Africa. That is to say, as long as the civilized world consisted only of the lands round the Mediterranean Sea, Sicily was the very centre of the civilized world. Its position invited settlement from every quarter, and its size allowed settlement from many quarters at once. Sicily therefore became the battle-field of many nations and powers; but it was so for many ages without becoming the exclusive possession of any one. And its position specially marked it out as the chosen battle-field of one particular form of strife. Sicily lies in the very middle of the Mediterranean. It forms a breakwater between the Eastern and the Western basins of that sea. We count it as part of Europe; but it comes nearer to Africa than any other part of central Europe. As it is a breakwater between the two seas, it is a bridge between the two continents. The question was sure to come, Shall the great central island belong to the East or to the West? Shall it be part of Africa or part of Europe?

On this last question the whole history of Sicily turned as long as Sicily played a great part in the history of the world. In the great strife between East and West, and between the religions which had been adopted in East and West, Sicily has at two periods of the world's history played a foremost part. The land has been twice fought for by Aryan and Semitic men, speaking Aryan and Semitic tongues, and professing and fighting for their several religions. In both cases the geographical relations of the struggle have been strangely turned about. In the strife between East and West, the East has become West, and the West East. That is to say, in the strife for Sicily, the Eastern side has been both times represented by men who have attacked Sicily from the West. Its enemies have been, not men coming straight from Asia, but men of Asia who had settled in Africa. In each case the representatives of the West (fighting from the East), have been men speaking the Greek tongue, and the representatives of the East (attacking from the West) have been men speaking a Semitic tongue. That is, they were first the Phœnicians, then the Saracens. In each case the strife has been made keener by difference of religion. In the first case it was the difference between two forms of heathendom, between the two very different creeds of Greece and Phœnicia. In the second case it was the keenest difference of all, the keenest because the two religions have so much in common, the strife between the two great forms of monotheism, Christianity and Islam. In both cases the strife has been waged in Sicily and for Sicily; in both cases the prize has in the end passed to the power which was at the time strongest in the neighbouring land of Southern Italy. That is, Sicily passed to the Romans in the first strife, to the Normans in the second. This forms the great cycle of Sicilian history; the main events of the earlier time seem to be acted over again in the latter.

This is the great characteristic of Sicilian history, but it is not quite peculiar to Sicily. The same kind of cycle, the same waging of the great strife of East and West at different times and by different actors, is to be found in the history of Cyprus and of Spain as well as in that of Sicily. But Cyprus is much smaller than Sicily; it lies in a corner of the Mediterranean, its revolutions did not affect the general history of the world in the same way as those of Sicily which lies in the middle. Spain is geographically much greater than Sicily; but Spain lies at what in early times was the end of the world, and the historical importance of Spain came much later, as it lasted much longer, than that of Sicily. Sicily, as the central land, was the truest centre of the strife. It is on its central position that the whole history of Sicily turns. As long as the lands round the Mediterranean were the whole of the European world, the strife for Sicily, the central land of them all, had an importance which none could surpass. So it was in the former time of strife, the strife between the pagan Greek and the Phœnician. By the second time of strife, the strife between the Christian Greek or Roman—we may call him either—and the Saracen, the boundaries of the European world had been enlarged. Sicily was no longer the centre of the world, and its fortunes, though still of great moment, are of less moment than before. In later times again, when the European world has spread over all parts of the earth, when the Ocean has become the central sea instead of the

Mediterranean, Sicily has altogether lost its central position and its importance. For some centuries Sicily has held only a secondary place in Europe, and it has commonly been dependent on some other power.

We may therefore sum up the history of Sicily in a very few words. It is the central land of the Mediterranean sea; it was the central land of Europe, as long as Europe meant only the lands on the Mediterranean sea. As such it became the battle-field of nations and creeds, the prize for Europe and Africa to struggle for. The first time of strife was between Greeks and Phœnicians, between representatives of West and East, between men of Europe and men of Asia transplanted to Africa. The end of this strife was the victory of Europe, but in the shape of the incorporation of Sicily into the dominion of Rome. Of that dominion Sicily remained a part for many ages, till the second time of strife came, the strife which was waged with the Saracen by men whom we may call either Greek-speaking Romans or Greeks under the allegiance of the Eastern Rome. The end was the establishment of the Norman kingdom of Sicily, which was for a short time the most flourishing state in Europe. After a while Sicily lost its central position and with it its special character as the meeting-place of the nations. But its history as such had kept it back from that form of greatness which consists in being the chief seat of some single nation. There has been no Sicilian nation. The later history of

Sicily has thus lost its distinguishing character. It has become an ordinary part, and commonly a subordinate part, of the general history of Europe, and specially of that of Italy.

In this way Sicilian history begins when the great colonizing nations of antiquity, the Phœnicians and the Greeks, began to settle in Sicily. Our first business therefore is to see what manner of people the Phœnicians and the Greeks were at the time of their first settlements, what manner of land Sicily was, and what earlier inhabitants the new settlers found in it. Then we shall go on with the history of the two colonizing nations in Sicily. In so doing we shall have to say again many things that have already been said in other parts of the Story of the Nations. Indeed the most part of the Story of Sicily must have been told already. But it has been told, as far as Sicily is concerned, piecemeal. Things have been told, not in their relation to Sicily, but in their relations to some other land or power. Here they will be told as parts of a connected Sicilian story, a story of which Sicily is the centre, and in which other lands and nations find their place only in their relations to Sicilian affairs.

II.

SICILY AND ITS INHABITANTS.

[It may be needful to explain that, during the present chapter and for some time after it, we have no contemporary, or even continuous, narrative to follow. In the very earliest times of course there could be none. The nearest approach to a narrative is the description of Sicily and its native inhabitants and of the Greek settlements there which Thucydides gives at the beginning of his sixth book. For the rest we have to put our story together from all manner of Greek sources. We have incidental notices of Sicily and the nation of Sicily in a crowd of Greek writers from the Odyssey onwards. Much is learned more directly from later Greek writers, as the geographer Strabo and the Sicilian historian Diodôros of Agyrium. If his work were perfect, we should have a continuous, though not a contemporary, Sicilian history. Something too may be got from Dionysios of Halikarnassos, the historian of Rome. All these preserve to us valuable notices from earlier writers, especially from the Sicilian historians Antiochos and Philistos. But they too were not contemporary. Of Phœnician authorities we unluckily have none. Among modern writers Adolf Holm has got together in his *Geschichte Siciliens* pretty well every scrap that can be found.

WE spoke in our first chapter of the way in which the geographical position of the island of Sicily, as the central island of the Mediterranean sea, allowed, and almost compelled it, to play the particular part in history which it did play. We have now to see how the history of the land was affected by its geographical character as well as by its geographical position. We must remember the general state of the world at the time when, first the Phœnicians and then the Greeks, began to plant colonies in Sicily and other lands. To such European nations as have already come, however dimly, into sight, the lands round the Mediterranean were the whole world, and the inland sea itself was what the Ocean is now. Europe contained no great kingdoms, like Asia; the more advanced a people was, the greater was its political disunion. The independent city was the accepted political unit. In Greece above all, the nature of the land, the islands, the peninsulas, the strongly marked inland valleys, fostered the separate being of each city in its fullest development. Every city either was independent or thought itself wronged if it was not so. It was only in the more backward parts of Greece that towns or districts in the early days grouped themselves into leagues. In Italy the growth of such leagues was the most marked feature. Outside Greece and Italy the other European nations had hardly got beyond the system of tribes, as distinguished alike from independent cities and from great kingdoms. Among the Asiatic nations the Phœnicians alone had at all fully developed the same kind of political system as the Greeks. With them too the independent city was the rule. They alone among barbarians knew anything of the higher political life. They were the only worthy rivals of Greece.

Now, as the world stood then, it was only nations like the Phœnicians and Greeks, whose political system was one of independent cities, that could in the strict sense plant colonies. We must distinguish colonies, as we now understand the word, from national migrations. In an early state of things nothing is more common than for a whole people, or a large part of a people, to leave their own land for some other. Their old land is left empty or much less thickly inhabited, and very often some other people steps in and takes possession of it. Both Greeks and Phœnicians and the other ancient nations of Europe and Asia must have come into their lands in this way. And the same thing went on again when the settlement of the present nations of Europe began, at what is commonly spoken of as the Wandering of the Nations. Then, for instance, the English settled in part of the isle of Britain, and gave it its name of England. The older England on the mainland of Europe was forsaken. So again in Greece, ever since the Greeks had settled there, there had been many movements of different divisions of the Greek nation, Dorians, Ionians, Achaians, changing their dwellings from one part of Greece to another, or going across into Asia. Real planting of colonies, as we understand the word, is something quite different from this. It is not the movement of a whole people or of so large a part of a people as to leave the old land at all forsaken or weakened. Part of the inhabitants of an established kingdom or city go forth to seek new homes in a new land; but the kingdom or city which they left still lives on. The two become what the Greeks called *metropolis* or mother-city and colony. And the Phœnician and Greek colonies, founded from cities, arose as independent cities from the beginning. The colony owed the metropolis honour and reverence, and colony and metropolis were ready to help one another in time of need. But, as a rule, a Phœnician or Greek colony was not politically subject to the metropolis which planted it. In later times colonies have been founded from kingdoms, and it has been held that a subject of a king, wherever he went, could not throw off his allegiance to his sovereign. Colonies have therefore been held to be part of the dominions of the king of the mother-country. They have from the beginning been dependent instead of independent; and when they have grown strong, they have often had to win independence by force of arms.

Now Sicily was in the early days of Europe one of the greatest of colonial lands. It was a chief seat for the planting of colonies, first from Phœnicia and then from Greece. It is the presence of these Phœnician and Greek colonies which made the history of Sicily what it was. These settlements were of course made more or less at the expense of the oldest inhabitants of the island, those who were there before the Phœnicians and Greeks came to settle. These oldest inhabitants were of three nations. Of these the names of two are so much alike that one is tempted to think that they must be different forms of the same name. And yet all ancient writers speak of them as wholly distinct nations. These are the Sikans (*Sicani*, Σικανοί) and the Sikels (*Siculi*, Σικελοί), each of which in turn was said to have given its name to the island. It was first *Sikania* (Σικανίη, Σικανία), then *Sikelia* or *Sicily* (*Sicilia*, Σικελία).

The Sikans claimed to be *autochthones*, sprung from the earth; that is, they were the earliest inhabitants of the land of whom anything was known. But the Greeks believed them to have come from Spain, and it is most likely that they belonged to that wide-spread non-Aryan race of southern Europe of which the Basques are now the survival. Nothing is known of the Sikan language, except so far as it is likely to survive in the names of places.

The Sikans no doubt came into the island by a progress of national migration, though in an unrecorded time. The other people whose name is so like theirs, the Sikels, certainly did so, and their settlement in the island is all but historical. Their tradition was that they had come into the island from Italy three hundred years before Greek settlement in it began, that is in the eleventh century B.C. And in a general way this belief seems quite trustworthy, though of course we cannot commit ourselves to exact dates. Of the Sikel language we know a good many words, and nearly all of them are closely akin to Latin. We may in short look upon the Sikel as an undeveloped Latin people. The Latins in Italy were able to develop a polity and a national life of their own; the Sikels could not do this, because at an early stage of their being they came across nations more advanced than themselves. In the fifth century B.C. there were still, as Thucydides witnesses, some Sikels left in Italy; but the great mass of the nation must have crossed into the great island. They came nearer than any other people to being the real folk of the land, and they gave the land its abiding name. The Sikans indeed appear in history as little more than a survival. They seem to have been driven into the western part of the island by the advance of the Sikels. And there they came under the dominion and influence both of Phœnicians and Greeks. Still they kept some towns, chiefly inland, and we hear of them as a distinct people as late as the fourth century B.C. The Sikels, on the other hand, play a great part in the history of the land to which they gave their name. But their story is mainly a record of the way in which they gradually became practically Greek. On the east coast they came for the most part under the dominion of the Greek settlers; but on the north coast and in the inland parts they kept many independent towns. These gradually came under Greek influence; they adopted Greek ways and spoke the Greek language, till in the Roman times they were reckoned as Greeks.

Besides Sikans and Sikels, there was a third people in the island, of whom we hear a good deal, but of whom we really know less than of either of the other two. These were the Elymians, who held the two towns of Segesta and Eryx in the north-west part of Sicily. They professed, like the Romans and some others, to be descended from the Trojans. This kind of claim always means that the people making it were an ancient settlement, but that they could not certainly connect themselves with any known city or land. In history the Elymians appear as so completely brought under Phœnician and

Greek influences that we cannot at all say what they originally were. We know nothing of their language. Their name is very like that of several other lands both in Europe and Asia; but it is always dangerous to make guesses because of mere likenesses of name. They are most famous because of their great temple on Mount Eryx, dedicated to a goddess in whom the Phœnicians saw their own Ashtoreth, the Greeks their own Aphroditê, and the Latins their own Venus.

It was in the land occupied by these nations, and largely at their expense, that, first the Phœnician and then the Greek colonists settled themselves. Both nations had already planted colonies elsewhere. The Phœnicians had settled in the Greek islands from which they had been driven by the Greeks, and also in Africa and Spain. The Greeks had settled in the islands and in Asia. But Sicily was a land in some things different from any of the other lands in which they settled. In Greece itself, and still more in the Greek islands, and afterwards in southern Italy, it was easy to occupy the whole land from sea to sea. On the other hand, most of the Greek colonies on the mainland, whether of Europe, Asia, or Africa, were settlements on the sea, holding a mere strip of coast with a barbarian background behind them. And whenever powerful kingdoms, like those of the Lydians and the Persians in Asia, grew up in that barbarian background, the independence of the Greek cities on the coast was threatened and sometimes destroyed. Among the Greek islands again some, as Crete and Euboia, were large enough to contain several independent cities; but none were of a size and geographical character to allow of any large inland region really far away from the sea. The Phœnicians also were used to much the same state of things. Their own land in Asia was a mere strip of coast between the sea and the mountains, studded with their famous cities, Sidon, Tyre, and others. And their colonies in Africa and Spain were of the same kind. They held the coast, but did not spread far inland.

In Sicily the Phœnician and Greek settlers found themselves under geographical conditions different from any of these. Sicily was an island; it was, according to the ideas of those times, a very large island. It approached to the nature of a continent. It was not only large enough to contain many cities; it was large enough to have its coast studded with sea-faring cities, and at the same time to leave a large inland region really away from the sea. Its shape, nearly triangular, is singularly compact; and it allows the greatest amount of coast to the greatest amount of inland country. In Sicily therefore a state of things followed unlike anything to be seen elsewhere. Phœnician and Greek settlers could occupy the coasts, but only the coasts; it was only at the corners that they could at all spread from sea to sea. A great inland region was necessarily left to the older inhabitants. But there was no room in Sicily, as there was in Asia, for the growth of great barbarian powers dangerous to the settlers. Neither Phœnician nor Greek was ever able to occupy or conquer the whole island; but neither people stood in any fear of being conquered or driven out, unless by one another.

But instead of conquest came influence. Both Phœnicians and Greeks largely influenced the native inhabitants. In the end, without any general conquest, the whole island became practically Greek.

We have said that the shape of Sicily is nearly that of a triangle. The ancient writers fancied that it was much more nearly a triangle than it is. It was thought to be an acute-angled triangle with a promontory at each of its angles, Pelôris to the north-east, Pachynos to the south-east, and Lilybaion to the west. The real shape of Sicily is that of a right-angled triangle, with the right angle to the north-east; the north-western angle is cut off, so as to form a short fourth side to the west. And the angles do not end in promontories. Lilybaion, now Cape Boeo, is not a promontory at all; it is the most western point of Sicily, but it is not high ground, and it is not an angle, but is in the middle of the short western side. Pelôris is now called Capo del Faro, after the *pharos* or light-house from which the strait itself between Sicily and Italy has taken the name of *Faro*. There are high hills not far off, but the actual angle is very low ground. And the only way to make a promontory of Pachynos is to make the island of Passero the promontory, and that is not at the angle but on the east side. But this notion of the triangle and the three promontories took possession of men's minds. When therefore they began to find sites for all the stories in the Odyssey, the little island of *Thrinakiê* spoken of there was ruled to be Sicily, and its name was improved into *Trinakria*, to give in Greek the meaning of *three promontories*. After all,

Sicily is really not far from being a triangle, and it is its triangular shape which makes it so compact. The north side runs very nearly east and west, the east side very nearly north and south; the longest side is the south-western. All three are much more nearly straight than most coasts; they are specially so as compared with the coasts of Greece. Compared with them, the Sicilian coasts are very little cut up with any large or deep inlets of the sea. But there are a good many smaller inlets which make excellent harbours, as above all at Syracuse, and also at Panormos or Palermo. Nor is the coast of Sicily surrounded by islands in the same way as the coast of Greece. There are a few very small ones near the coast, and there are two groups of some importance. The isles of Aigousa or the Ægates off the north-west corner are bold mountains in the sea. And to the north-east, between Sicily and Italy, are the volcanic isles of Lipara, the isles of Aiolos or of Héphaistos, which connect the volcanic regions of Ætna and of Vesuvius. The islands between Sicily and Africa, Melita (Malta), Gaulos (Gozo), and Kossoura (Pantellaria), are too far from Sicily to have had any continuous share in Sicilian history, though Melita is of importance at times.

Sicily is a very mountainous land, and even where there are no high mountains, it is full of hills and valleys. There are no large plains; that of Lentini or Catania on the east side is the chief. On the north side and part of the east, the mountains come near to the sea, sometimes quite close, forming very grand coast scenery. In the other parts the mountains keep much further inland, and the coast is mainly low, though at a few points on the south side the hills come down to make promontories. The great mountain of all is of course Ætna, the greatest volcano of Europe. It rises more than ten thousand feet above the sea, and it is so near to the sea that its whole height is seen. Yet its base is so vast and the slope so gradual that it needs the snow near the top to show how high it is. None of the other heights of Sicily come at all near it. The loftiest are to the north. The most striking after Ætna, though by no means the highest (for its height is not much more than two thousand feet), is Eryx (Monte San Giuliano) at the north-west corner. It comes nearer to the nature of a promontory at an angle than any of the supposed three. So hilly a land is naturally full of springs and streams, but there is no room for great rivers. There is no such thing in Sicily as a navigable river or an inland haven. The greatest river system is that of the Symaithos (or Giarretta) on the eastern side, where many streams, draining many valleys and the great Leontine or Catanian plain, run into the sea by a single mouth. Next in size is the Himeras or *Fiume Salso* on the south side. There is another river on the north side (now *Fiume Grande*) of the same name, and the two rise very near together, but the southern one has a much longer course. The rivers Halykos, Mazaros, Krimisos, and Orêthos, are of more importance as boundaries or from events that happened near them than from their size. Many of the streams of Sicily, specially on the north and north-west sides, are what are called *fiumare;* that is, in winter they are torrents, rushing fiercely into the sea, while in summer their beds are nearly dry.

Sicily has been always famous for its fruitfulness, and not without reason. The few wide plains, the lowlands between the mountains and the sea, and many of the inland valleys, are wonderfully rich in their growth. Even on hilly and stony ground rich patches of corn will grow between the stones. Men believed that wheat first grew in Sicily, as the gift of the goddesses of the island, and in the plain of Catania it was said to be still growing wild. However this may be, it is certain that no land has ever received more vegetable gifts from other lands than Sicily; olives, vines, oranges, the American prickly pear, all flourish. But the sugar-cane and the Egyptian papyrus have vanished, or nearly so; cotton is grown only in a few places; the palm grows, but its fruit does not reach perfection. But while fruit-trees of all kinds are abundant, there is a strange lack of what we call forest-trees. There were plenty of them in times past, but now there are very few. The hillsides are mostly quite treeless, and a valley which looks thickly wooded has often nothing but olives, almonds, and such like. Sicily was in old times famous for its horses and its sheep; the traveller is now more struck with the asses, mules, and goats; but there are more sheep inland than there are near the coasts. The seas abound in fish, specially the great tunny. In all ages the richness of the land has been dwelled upon with pride. As a Roman province, Sicily was the chief granary of Rome, and before and after, in the days of the Greek cities and of the Norman kings, it was the most flourishing land in Europe.

Some of the present customs of Sicily seem to have come down from the earliest times. The traveller is struck by the general absence of villages and country-houses; the mass of the people live in towns, and, except on the coast, the towns are mainly on the hill-tops. This fashion, common to most nations at an early stage, is spoken of as specially characteristic of the Sikans; it has gone on to this day, because the country has at many times, and in modern times till quite lately, been made unsafe by plunderers by land or sea. Many of the hill-towns, both Sikan and Sikel, are thus dwelled in to this day, and some of the Sikel sites play a great part in Sicilian history. Such specially are the inland towns of Agyrium (afterwards San Filippo d'Argirò), and Centuripa (afterwards Centorbi), both on high hills, and above all Henna, the seat of the great goddesses of Sicily, of whom we shall presently speak. This is now called *Castrogiovanni*; but it has not really changed its name; the name has nothing to do with any *John*. The Saracens corrupted *Castrum Hennæ* into *Casr-janni*, and that was misunderstood and translated into *Castrum-Johannis*. Cephalœdium (now Cefalù) is a wonderful Sikel site on the north coast. The old town, with some precious Sikel remains, stood on a high hill overhanging the sea; below are Sikel walls, joining in to the sea, almost like the Long Walls of Athens. The Sikan sites are of less importance, but we shall come across some of them, and the Elymians have left us Eryx and Segesta. Among these nations, who were in the island before recorded history begins, came the settlers from the two great colonizing nations, who, at this stage of their history, had come to build their cities on the coast, not commonly on the high hills, and never very far inland. We must first speak of the Phœnicians and then of the Greeks.

The Phœnicians then, the foremost of barbarian nations, the only real political rivals of the Greeks, came into Sicily and other western lands from the narrow strip of land at the east of the Mediterranean, between Lebanon and the sea, where were their old and famous cities of Sidon, Tyre, and Arvad. The name by which we call them (Greek Φοῖνιξ, Latin *Pœnus, Punicus*) is not their own name, but one which perhaps marked their land as the land of palm-trees. They called themselves and their land *Chna* or *Canaan*. For of a truth they came from the Canaan of the Old Testament; they worshipped the gods of Canaan, Baalim and Ashtaroth, with their foul and bloody rites, burning their children in the fire. Their tongue was the same as the Hebrew, and a very little knowledge of Hebrew will explain many Phœnician names. Thus the most famous of all, *Hannibal*, is the Grace of Baal, just as the Hebrew *Hananiah* is the Grace of Jehovah. Turn it round, and it is *Jehohanan, Johannes*, our familiar *John*. To the Greeks the Phœnicians were of course *barbarians*, a name given to all who did not speak Greek. It no doubt implies a certain degree of contempt for those who did not speak Greek; but it proves nothing as to the measure of civilization reached by the people so called, or even as to the degree of distance between their tongue and the Greek. The Phœnicians were the boldest sea-faring people in the world and the most cunning traders. In this way they spread themselves over a great part of the coast of the Mediterranean, founding in some places mere factories, in others actual colonies. They occupied many points in the island of Cyprus and many of the Ægæan islands, and seemingly points on the Greek coast itself. At this early time, to which we can give no exact date, they were far advanced in material arts above the Greeks and all other Europeans; but they are said not to have been an inventive people, but rather to have spread abroad the inventions of others. Certain it is that the Greeks learned much from them in the way of material culture; and they learned a much more precious gift, namely the alphabet. All the various forms of written letters now used in Europe have come in different ways from the letters which the Greeks first learned of the Phœnicians. The name *alphabet* shows it; it comes from the first two Phœnician letters, *aleph* and *beth*, in Greek *alpha* and *beta*.

Yet, with all this, the Greek was a Greek and the Phœnician was a barbarian. The superiority of the Asiatic was in material inventions; what the Greek learned, he developed and improved as no barbarian ever did. It is the art, the polity, the language, of Greece, not that of Phœnicia, which has influenced the world for ever. In time the Phœnicians were glad to copy Greek arts, to take back their own gifts in a shape in which they could hardly have known them. But at this early time the Phœnicians were the more advanced people, above all in everything to do with trade and a sea-faring life. While the Greeks hardly ventured to stir beyond their own Ægæan and the islands just off Western Greece, the Phœnicians sailed everywhere in the Mediterranean, and even made their way into the Ocean. And at least one Phœnician colony was planted on the Ocean itself, outside what men called the pillars of Héraklès, the heights on each side which seem to guard the entrance to the Mediterranean. This was Gadeira or Gades, said to be the oldest settlement of all. And so it well may be; for one great object of Phœnician trade was the gold of Spain (Tharshish, Tartèssos), then the land of gold; the nearer colonies were posts on the way. Gades, hardly changing its name in the modern *Cadiz*, though never a ruling city, has been a flourishing haven of trade through all the ages till now.

But the chief land of Phœnician settlement was Africa, and that brings us round to our own Sicily. Many Phœnician cities were planted in Africa, Hippo, Utica, and others, and above all Carthage. But Carthage, which grew to be the greatest of all Phœnician cities, was the youngest of the African settlements. Its name (Καρχηδών, *Kartaco, Carthago*) means the New City, like Greek *Neapolis* or English *Newton*. The first syllable is the word for city, which we see in many Old Testament names, as *Kirjath*-jearim. But we have nothing to do with Carthage as yet. Carthage at a later time plays so great a part in Sicilian history that we are tempted to bring it in before its time, and to fancy that the Phœnician colonies in Sicily were, as they are sometimes carelessly called, Carthaginian colonies. This is not so; the Phœnician cities in Sicily did in after times become Carthaginian dependencies: but they were not founded by Carthage. We cannot fix an exact date for their foundation, nor can we tell for certain how far they were settled straight from the old Phœnicia and how far from the older Phœnician cities in Africa. But we may be sure that their foundation happened between the migration of the Sikels in the eleventh century B.C. and the beginning of Greek settlement in the eighth. And we may suspect that the Phœnician settlements in the east of Sicily were planted straight from Tyre and Sidon, and those in the west from the cities in Africa. We know that all round Sicily the Phœnicians occupied small islands and points of coast which were fitted for their trade, but we may doubt whether they anywhere in Eastern Sicily planted real colonies, cities with a territory attached to them. In the west they seem to have done so. For, when the Greeks began to advance in Sicily, the Phœnicians withdrew to their strong posts in the western part of the island, Motya, Solous, and Panormos. There they kept a firm hold till the time of Roman dominion. The Greeks could never permanently dislodge them from their possessions in this part. Held, partly by Phœnicians, partly by Sikans and Elymians who had been brought under Phœnician influence, the north-western corner of Sicily remained a barbarian corner.

Of these three settlements which the Phœnicians kept in Western Sicily, Motya has the shortest history.

It was the settlement nearest to Africa, planted on a small island in a sheltered bay, a little to the north of Lilybaion, the most western point of Sicily. There was as yet no town of Lilybaion. But in the time of Carthaginian dominion, in the fourth century B.C. Motya was forsaken, and a very strong town arose on Lilybaion, now the modern Marsala. Motya has never been rebuilt, but large remains of its Phœnician walls may be seen.

The other two Phœnician towns are on the north side of Sicily, where the coast makes a bend so as to form a bay looking to the east. On the rocky hill which forms the southern shore of this bay stood the Phœnician town of Solous, Soluntum, Solunto, said to be so called from *Sela*, the rock, a name which is found in the Old Testament. It was the most important Phœnician outpost against the Sikels, and afterwards against the Greeks, to the east. So its site is not, like those of the other Phœnician towns, close on the sea, but on the inland side of the hill, with the sea at its foot. The site is now forsaken; there are large remains of the town, but they date only from Roman, not from Phœnician times.

But the greatest of all Phœnician settlements in Sicily lay within the bay of which the hill of Solous is one horn, but much nearer to the other horn, the hill of Herkté, now Pellegrino. Here the mountains fence in a wonderfully fruitful plain, known in after times as the *Golden Shell* (Conca d'oro). In the middle of it there was a small inlet of the sea, parted into two branches, with a tongue of land between them, guarded by a small peninsula at the mouth.

There could be no better site for Phœnician traders. Here then rose a Phœnician city, which, though on the north coast of Sicily, looks straight towards the rising sun. It is strange that we do not know its Phœnician name; in Greek it was called *Panormos*, the *All-haven*, a name borne also by other places. This is the modern Palermo, which, under both Phœnicians and Saracens, was the Semitic head of Sicily, and which remained the capital of the island under the Norman kings. The ground has been quite changed. The two branches of the All-haven have become dry land, and the modern port of Palermo has moved away from the old city. This must be borne in mind; because the city which we shall have to speak of down to the Norman times is still the old Panormos planted on the fork of the two havens, quite unlike the Palermo that now is.

Thus in Sicily the East became West and the West East. The men of Asia withdrew before the men of Europe to the west of the island, and thence warred against the men of Europe to the east of them. In the great central island of Europe they held their own barbarian corner. It was the land of Phœnicians, Sikans, and Elymians, as opposed to the eastern land of the Greeks and their Sikel subjects and pupils. We must remember also that the Phœnicians were settled in Africa and Spain, and that they gradually occupied the islands, great and small, around Sicily and to the west of it. Into all these lands the Phœnicians brought their tongue and their creed. The gods of Canaan were worshipped in Sicily. Men at Panormos and Motya made their children pass through the fire, and whatever the temple on Eryx was at first, it became the house of Ashtoreth. The strife between the Greeks, who had at least a nobler form of heathendom, and the Phœnicians was therefore something of a crusade or holy war from the beginning, and men clearly felt that it was so. But we must remember that the Greeks had but little warfare with the Phœnician settlements in Sicily as long as they were independent; the great strife began when Carthage rose to dominion.

We have thus gone through those nations that were in Sicily before the Greeks. That is the primitive inhabitants, Sikans, Sikels, and Elymians, and the Phœnician colonists who settled among them. All of them together have left but small traces of their presence. The chief are the tombs hewn in the limestone rocks, which abound in many parts, specially in the deep valleys on the south-east. These are doubtless mostly Sikel, but they may have been Sikan before that. We have spoken of the Phœnician walls at Motya; they may well be Old-Phœnician; the work at Eryx and Lilybaion is Carthaginian. And we have mentioned the Sikel building at Cefalù. There is very little more, except the tombs of two Phœnician women in the Museum at Palermo. There are Phœnician coins with Phœnician legends; of the other nations we have no coins, till they came to coin after Greek models. Of the Sikan and Elymian tongues we can say nothing; the Sikel tongue, we have seen, was near akin to the Latin. But we have no writings or inscriptions in any of them. The Phœnician language and all about the Phœnicians is well known, but not by reason of their presence in Sicily. All these nations, the Phœnicians themselves among them, make only a preliminary part of our subject. The real history of Sicily, as a land playing a great part in the affairs of the world, begins with the coming of the Greeks.

III.

THE LEGENDS.

[Here, even more than in other parts of the story, we have to pick up scraps of knowledge where we can. Our nearest approach to anything continuous is in the fifth book of Diodôros, where he is dealing with the legendary times of Greece, and brings in many of the stories of his own island. About the Palici we learn most from the late Latin writer Macrobius, who has collected a great deal about them from many sources; but Diodôros has something to say too. The account of Hadranus comes chiefly from two notices in the History of Animals by the late Greek writer Elian. The legend of Démétér and Persephoné is scattered over the whole range of Greek literature; but in its special relation to Henna it comes out wholly in Latin writers. It begins in the great speech of Cicero against Verres, and goes on in the poets Ovid and Claudian.]

In the history of Sicily, perhaps even more than elsewhere, we must take special heed to distinguish genuine tradition, that is history in an imperfect shape, preserving the memory of real events, from two forms of untrustworthy statement. There are some tales which are sheer invention, devised with a purpose. There are also legends which have grown up, one hardly knows how, tales which are not true, but in which there is no conscious purpose to deceive. Thus the tale of the Sikel migration from Italy is a piece of genuine tradition, recording a real event.

The tale of the Trojan origin of the Elymians is a piece of sheer invention. Round both of these stories, as statements of fact or supposed fact, legendary details have grown. And legendary details have grown also where there is not so much groundwork of fact or supposed fact as this. Many tales grow up out of some local worship or are meant to explain some local phænomenon. Of all these kinds of stories we have plenty in Sicily. We have tales which grew up among the Greeks themselves after they came into the island. And we have tales which the Greeks took over from the Sikels, and tricked out according to their own fancy.

One class of stories arose out of the supposed necessity of finding real sites for all the places spoken of in the Odyssey. This the Greeks, above all in Sicily, looked on as a kind of duty. For Odysseus had sailed to the West; he must therefore have visited Sicily. We have already mentioned how the little island of *Thrinakiê*, where the oxen of the sun grazed, was held to be Sicily, and how the name was improved into *Trinakria*. The poet of the Odyssey may or may not have meant some real isle; he may have meant some corner or peninsula of Sicily, mistaken for an island—as some said that Mylai or Milazzo was the place—he assuredly did not mean Sicily itself as a whole. On the other hand, we cannot doubt that the picture of Skylla and Charybdis sprang up out of tales told by sailors, very likely Phœnician sailors, about the wonders of the strait. Then the monstrous giants of the Odyssey, Laistrygones and Kyklôpes, were quartered in Sicily.

A whole crop of legends therefore grew up about Polyphêmos, the nymph Galateia, and her other lover Akis. Others, as Ætna came to be better known, changed the giant shepherds into giant smiths, who forged the thunderbolts of Zeus and had Héphaistos to their master. These are all purely Greek stories, into which little or nothing of native belief or tradition has crept in.

We have said that the Trojan origin of the Elymians was sheer invention with a purpose. The story must have been of Elymian invention, but invented after the Elymians had learned something of Greek legend. It took several forms, and legendary details grew about it. But it concerns us most that it clearly, among the Greeks at least, displaced an older Greek story, which also looks very like invention with a purpose. The Greek hero Héraklês got mixed up with the Phœnician Melkart, and in that character he was sent on various errands in the West, as far as the Ocean. Many stories arose about him in Sicily, about his driving away the oxen of Géryonês, about their crossing the strait, and how the hero first received the worship of a god in the Sikel town of Agyrium, where the hoof-prints of his oxen were to be seen. All this last the historian Diodôros, who was a man of Agyrium, takes care to tell us at length. But above all Héraklês wrestled with Eryx, the *epônymos* of the mountain and town so-called, and overthrew him. He thus gained a right to his land, but he left it to him on a kind of lease, to hold till a Herakleid should come and claim it. This last part at least of the story was clearly made up in the interest of certain Herakleids who, as we shall see in time, did come to claim Eryx. But it is plain that the story of Héraklés at Eryx before the war of Troy upsets the story of the Trojan origin of the Elymians. And men were driven to strange shifts in trying to reconcile the two.

The story of the famous mythical artist Daidalos coming to Sicily is of quite another kind. Here we can see traces of real native legend, though greatly tricked out by Greek fancy. Daidalos, having offended Minôs, the powerful king of Crete, flies to Sicily, or rather, as we are specially told, to *Sikania*. There he is entertained by the Sikan king Kôkalos— every pains is taken to point out that he was Sikan and not Sikel—for whom he builds the strong city of Kamikos. He does also many other wonderful works in all parts of the island; among others, he builds the temple on Eryx. That is, as usual in such cases, all wonderful works were attributed to him. Presently Minôs comes with a great fleet to Sicily to punish Daidalos; but he is killed in a bath by the daughters of Kôkalos. His followers, or some of them, settle in Sicily, and build a town of Minôa where they first landed, with a tomb of Minôs and a temple of Aphrodité. Here we have both Phœnician and Greek elements. The story had put on a Greek shape; but the bringing of Minôs into the story was most likely suggested by a Phœnician settlement at Minôa. But King Kôkalos and his town of Kamikos must be true Sikan tradition. Nobody had any interest in inventing them. And Kamikos was a real town, which plays a part in

Sicilian history, though a small one. It has been placed on the site of the mountain town of Caltabellotta near Sciacca, and it must at any rate have been not far off.

This is perhaps our only bit of Sikan story; the Sikels have left us much more. We have already seen at Agyrium a Greek story fixed on a Sikel site. But we have a large amount of Sikel belief and tradition which made its way into the mythology of the Greeks. As was natural in Sicily, a land so full of volcanic phænomena of all kinds, the Sikel religion was a worship of the powers of nature, and above all of the powers under the earth. The corn itself, growing up from the earth, was looked on as a gift from the nether powers. Then there was the great burning mountain of Ætna, and several smaller volcanos which threw up only mud, as at Maccaluba near Girgenti; there were the hot springs at Termini and near Sciacca. There were volcanic lakes, deep holes in the earth, and many things which fitted in with the worship of the nether-gods, gods, in Sikel belief, awful but kindly. Some bits of Sikel religion have come down to us almost untouched; others have been so worked into Greek legends that we cannot even guess their native shape. Thus there was a Sikel goddess Hybla, whom the Greeks looked on as the same with several goddesses of their own mythology, here with one, there with another. Three towns in Sicily were called after her, one in the south-eastern part of the island, now Ragusa, another on the coast north of Syracuse, near the place where the Greek colony of Megara was afterwards planted.

This gave its name to the Hyblaian hills not far off, famous for their honey ; but there is no hill strictly called Mount Hybla. The third Hybla is inland, not far from Catania, and is now called Paternò. The worshippers of the goddess here were specially skilled in the interpretation of dreams. Just below her temple is a mud volcano and some mineral springs, showing plainly enough that Hybla was a goddess of the nether-world. Then there was the Sikel fire-god Hadranus, who had a temple near Ætna, not far from Paternò, where a town Hadranum, now Adernò, was afterwards built. In his temple fire was ever burning. The story goes that in it were kept a thousand great dogs, who knew and welcomed good people when they came to worship, while the bad they drove away or tore in pieces, according to the measure of their sins. They also guided travellers who had lost their way, in which we may see some training like that of the dogs of Saint Bernard. More famous than these is the Sikel holy place which plays the greatest part in Sicilian history. This was the temple and lake of the Palici, the Great Twin Brethren of Sikel worship. Their temple stood in a plain north of the hill-town of Menænum, now Mineo. There were anciently two volcanic craters ; now there is only one, within which the water bubbles up in several places. An oath taken here was the most binding of all oaths, and it was held that its breach was always followed by some fearful judgment. The Palici were clearly gods of the earth ; in their story they came out of the earth. They were kindly gods also, who gave special shelter to slaves. Here we have an almost untouched Sikel worship; the Greeks did nothing, save, after their manner, to invent parents for the Sikel gods, to say that the Palici were sons of Zeus and a nymph Thaleia, or, more fittingly, of the fire-god Hadranus or their own Hêphaistos. In the old Italian religion, of which the Sikel creed was one form, the gods had no parents.

But in the most famous of all seats of Sikel worship we see how a story which had grown up in Greece was carried bodily into Sicily, how it was fitted to sites and phænomena there, and so fully took possession of them that, amid the rich adornments of Greek fancy, it is not easy to see what the original Sikel belief was. This is the story of the special patronesses of Sicily, the goddesses of Henna, the powers of the earth that sent up the fruitful corn. Their Sikel character, whatever it was, has been quite lost in the Greek story of Démétèr and her daughter Persephonê, called specially *Korê*, the Maid, and how the Maid was carried off by Aïdôneus, the god of the nether-world. The tale was carried to Sicily, and fixed at Henna and the neighbouring lake Pergus. It grew on Sicilian ground, and reached its height in the hands of the Latin poets. In the oldest form of the tale, in the Homeridian hymn to Démétèr, there is no thought of Henna or of Sicily at all. Later on, as in the odes of Pindar and in various other notices, the goddesses appear as special goddesses of Sicily, but without any mention of Henna. It is by the Greek poet Kallimachos, in the time of the second Hierôn, that Henna is first spoken of as having anything to do with the goddesses. Then the Latin writers

Cicero and Livy describe Henna as the specially holy place of the goddesses, and fix the story to its neighbourhood. Lastly, in the Latin poets, specially in Ovid and Claudian, we find the tale told at length, as happening at Lake Pergus and other places in Sicily. The maiden Persephonê, with her playmates the nymphs, is gathering flowers by the lake; as she goes to pluck a wonderful narcissus with a hundred heads, Aïdôneus comes up through one of the holes by the lake, with his chariot and his black horses, and carries off the Maid. In the plain by Syracuse, the nymph Kyana rebukes him and bids him let the Maid go. Kyana is turned into the fountain that bore her name, and Aïdôneus carries off his prize to the nether-world. Then come the wanderings of Dêmêtêr in search of her daughter, just as in the version that knows nothing of Sicily. In the end Zeus settles that Persephonê shall stay half the year with Aïdôneus as queen of the nether-world. But she receives Sicily as a wedding-gift, and she is to stay the other half year with her mother as one of the two great goddesses of the island.

Here is the local belief of Sikel Henna so adorned by Greek fancy that we do not, as in the case of the Palici, see what it was that the story started from. Last of all, we have another very famous story, which arose out of physical phænomena in Sicily, but which seems to be wholly a Greek story, devised after the Greeks had settled in the island. In the island of Ortygia, on which the town of Syracuse began, was a spring of fresh water very near to the sea. Hard by, in the sea itself, was another fresh spring, bubbling up in the midst of the salt water. The two things, it was thought, must have something to do with one another. So the story grew that the maiden Arethousa, over the sea in Elis, was pursued by the river-god Alpheios. She prayed to her mistress Artemis, who turned her into a fountain. Her waters ran under the sea till they turned up again in Ortygia, and her lover Alpheios also followed her with his stream through the waves. Both in Old Greece and in Sicily men were well used to rivers running under the earth and coming up again. So it did not seem impossible that they might run under the sea also; and grave writers like Strabo and Pausanius go into scientific arguments whether so it could be. Here then we again see the powers of the nether-world, only this time under the sea and not under the earth. We see them this time also in a purely Greek shape, as there is no reason to think that Arethousa has anything to do with any Sikel worship or story. It can be shown that the legend grew out of the local worship of Artemis in Elis. It was simply carried to Sicily to explain the local wonders of Syracuse.

Thus we have purely Sikel beliefs, as in the stories of Hybla, Hadranus, and the Palici. We have, as in the story of Dêmêtêr and the Korê, a Greek tale fitted to a Sikel sanctuary, and practically displacing the old Sikel worship. Lastly, we have, in the story of Alpheios and Arethousa, a Greek story simply carried over to a Sicilian site. Thus the Greek influenced the Sikel and the Sikel influenced the Greek. It will always be so when two nations meet which are near enough to each other, as any two

European nations are near enough, to influence one another. The Sikels were kinsfolk of the Greeks who had lagged behind. They were not savages, nor had they, like the Phœnicians, a civilization of their own quite different from that of the Greeks. We have now to tell what came of the meeting of these nations and of their influence on one another. The way in which the Sikels became Greek, that is, how Sicily became Greek, is the great feature of old Sicilian story. That story we shall begin to tell in our next chapter.

IV

THE GREEK SETTLEMENTS IN SICILY.

B.C. 735–580.

[Of the Greek settlements in Sicily we have the precious sketch at the beginning of the sixth book of Thucydides, in which some say that he followed the Syracusan writer Antiochos. The books of Diodôros in which he must have described them more fully are unluckily lost, save some fragments. A good deal may be learned from Strabo, from whom we see that there were often several stories current about the same foundation. And there are casual notices in many places, in Plutarch's lesser works and elsewhere.]

THE Western Greeks at least had some vague notions of Sicily and the Sikels as early as the time of the Odyssey. We there hear of a land called *Sikaniê*, which can only mean Sicily, and of a people called Sikels, who may be those either of Sicily or of Italy. With them the Greeks seem to have carried on a brisk trade in buying and selling slaves. The suitors threaten to sell Odysseus to the Sikels, and old Laertês is waited on by a Sikel woman. But such a trade, carried on along the coast, as all intercourse between Greece and Sicily still was ages afterwards, carried on too most likely in Phœnician vessels, does not prove much intercourse between the people at the two ends. It is plain that Greek notions of Sicily were still very vague when settlement in Sicily began. It is said that the Phœnicians spread tales likely to frighten any other people from settling there.

For a long time Greek settlement was directed to the East rather than to the West. And it was said that, when settlement in Italy and Sicily did begin, the earliest Greek colony, like the earliest Phœnician colony, was the most distant. It was believed that Kymê, the Latin Cumæ in Campania, was founded in the eleventh century B.C. The other plantations in Italy and Sicily did not begin till the eighth. Kymê always stood by itself, as the head of a group of Greek towns in its own neighbourhood and apart from those more to the south, and it may very well be that some accident caused it to be settled sooner than the points nearer to Greece. But it is not likely to have been settled three hundred years earlier. Most likely it was planted just long enough before the nearer sites to suggest their planting. Anyhow, in the latter half of the eighth century B.C. Greek settlement to the West, in Illyria, Sicily, and Italy, began in good earnest.

It was said that the first settlement in Sicily came of an accident. Chalkis in Euboia was then one of the chief sea-faring towns of Greece. Theoklês, a man of Chalkis, was driven by storm to the coast of Sicily. He came back, saying that it was a good land and that the people would be easy to conquer. So in 735 B.C. he was sent forth to plant the first Greek colony in Sicily. The settlers were partly from

Chalkis, partly from the island of Naxos. So it was agreed that the new town should be called Naxos, but that Chalkis should count as its metropolis. So the new Naxos arose on the eastern coast of Sicily, on a peninsula made by the lava. It looked up at the great hill of Tauros, on which Taormina now stands. The Greek settlers drove out the Sikels and took so much land as they wanted. They built and fortified a town, and part of their walls may still be seen. As the first Greek settlers in the land, they set up an altar and statue of Apollôn *Archêgetês*, the Leader and Beginner. It stood outside the town of Naxos, and became the religious centre of the Greeks of Sicily, the *Sikeliots* as distinguished from the *Sikels*. Hither all who went from Sicily to any of the great festivals of old Greece came first to sacrifice to the common god of all Sikeliots.

Naxos, as the beginning of Greek settlement in Sicily, answers to Ebbsfleet, the beginning of English settlement in Britain. The oldest of Sikeliot towns, it never became one of the greatest, and about three hundred years after its foundation it was altogether swept away, and has never since been rebuilt. Its settlers, Chalkidian and Naxian, belonged to the Ionian division of the Greek nation. In the very next year, it is said, in 734 B.C., a Dorian city was founded in Sicily, which has a much greater history. Corinth on the isthmus, with its two havens looking east and west, was one of the greatest sea-faring cities of Greece, and sent out colonies both ways. A joint enterprise to Sicily and the Illyrian coast was now decreed, and two famous Corinthian colonies, Korkyra and Syracuse, arose as twin sisters. Chersikratés founded Korkyra and Archias founded Syracuse. Corinth seems to have claimed a measure of authority over her nearer colonies which was not usual on the part of a Greek metropolis. In the case of Korkyra this led to a War of Independence, and to bitter hatred between the mother and the daughter city. But no such authority was claimed over more distant Syracuse. Here therefore the metropolis and the colony were always on the best of terms, and the relations between them form the most pleasing story in Greek political life.

Kymê was planted on a high hill overlooking the sea; Naxos was planted all but in the sea, on a low peninsula. Syracuse was planted altogether in the sea on a low island. This shows how the Greeks had advanced since the days when all towns were built on inland hill-tops. The Greeks had caught up the Phœnicians. The island was that island of Ortygia which contains the spring of Arethousa. It lies close to the coast, so near that it was afterwards joined to it, sometimes by a mole, sometimes by a bridge. Running north and south, and with the peninsula called Plêmmyrion opposite to it to the south, the two fence in an inlet of the sea with a comparatively narrow mouth, which forms the Great Harbour of Syracuse, great as a harbour, though small as a bay. North of the island is another smaller harbour, so that Syracuse, like her mother Corinth, had two havens, though they were much nearer to each other than those of Corinth. A little to the north again is a long hill at its east end which rises sheer from the sea, and which stretches inland till it ends in a point. It thus looks down on the Great Harbour and on another bay to the north, with another peninsula, Xiphonia, stretching south to match Ortygia, and another small and low peninsula, Thapsos, in the middle of the bay thus formed. On the south there is a piece of low ground between the island and the hill. And there is a wide stretch of low and swampy ground between the Great Harbour to the east, the Syracusan hill to the north and the higher inland hills to the west and south. Through this low ground runs the river Anapos and its tributary Kyana, of which we have heard in a legend. The topography of Syracuse is of the greatest importance for its history.

When the Corinthian settlers came, the Island and the whole land were held by Sikels; but it is quite possible that Phœnicians had a factory for trade. The first Greek town arose on the Island. Syracuse grew by spreading on to the mainland and climbing up the hill. But it would seem that the settlers had, from the beginning or from a very early time, more than one outpost on the mainland to defend the land which they occupied. They had one post called *Achradina* on the east end of the hill overlooking the sea, and another called *Polichna*—we might say in English *Littleton*—on a small hill in the low ground just west of the Great Harbour. Here arose the *Olympicion*, the famous temple of Olympian Zeus. And there was most likely another outpost on the south side of the hill, where was a temple of Apollôn, called *Temenités*. Each of these outposts protected

OLYMPIEION. SYRACUSE.

one of the chief roads leading to Syracuse. Achradina and Temenités were afterwards taken into the city, but Polichna never was. From the time of Archias till now, Syracuse has always been an inhabited city; but for ages past it has shrunk up again within its first bounds on the Island. No part of the hill is at all thickly inhabited. From the Island the Sikels were of course driven out, and in so much land as the Greeks gradually took to divide among themselves, they were brought down to the state of villainage. The origin of the name Syracuse (*Syrakousai* in various spellings) is not clear. It never was the name of the Island as such; it was the name of the city on the Island, and spread as the city grew.

By the foundation of Syracuse Dorian Greeks had occupied the best position on the east coast of Sicily. This seems to have stirred up the Ionians of Naxos—they are commonly called Chalkidians, from their metropolis Chalkis—to found two new cities between Naxos and Syracuse. This was in B.C. 729. Theoklês himself founded Leontinoi, the only Greek city in Sicily on an inland site. But it was placed on a point needful to hold, as commanding the way from the inland hills to the plain of Leontinoi, the largest and most fruitful in the island. The town lay in a valley between two hills, with two *akropoleis*; it still lives on and keeps its name as *Lentini*. The other Chalkidian settlement at this time was Katanê, *Catina, Catania*, founded on a site close by the sea, but not actually in it, like Naxos and Syracuse. This town has been destroyed many times by earthquakes and by the lava of Ætna, but it has been rebuilt as often as it has been destroyed, and it is now a far greater town than Syracuse. The working of the lava has given rise to both pagan and Christian legends. The tale went that at the first eruption after the foundation of Katanê, the lava parted to spare the Pious Brethren, Amphinomos and Anapios, who were carrying off their parents on their shoulders. This became a very favourite story, and the brethren are often seen on the coins of Katanê. Of two other Chalkidian towns, Euboia—so called from the island where Chalkis stands—and Kallipolis, the sites are unknown; they must have been somewhere to the north of Naxos.

Almost at the same time that the Chalkidians were thus advancing in Sicily itself, there came a new Dorian settlement from Old Greece. This was from Megara, which, like Corinth, is a city on the isthmus with two havens, and was then one of the chief sea-faring and colonizing cities of Greece. In B.C. 726 the Megarian settlers, under their founder Lamis, set forth to seek a home on that part of the east coast of Sicily which lay between Syracuse and the Chalkidian towns. There they met with some strange adventures. It is remarkable that they seem never to have tried to settle on the peninsula of Xiphonia, a site which seems the best after Ortygia, and where now is the town of Augusta. First, they tried to settle a little to the north of Xiphonia, at a place called Trôtilon, where the river Pantakyas, Pantagias, or Porcari, runs into the sea with a wide mouth, hardly a mile or two from the place where it is a tumbling brook in the meadows. Thence they moved to take a share in the newly-founded Chalkidian settlement of Leontinoi. Theoklés, so the story goes, had planted his colony by agreement with the Sikels, and Greeks and Sikels lived together in Leontinoi as fellow-townsmen. Now no Greek held that he owed any duty to a barbarian, unless he was bound by special agreement, and both towards Greeks and barbarians an agreement was often kept in the letter and broken in the spirit. Theoklés told the Megarians that he and his Chalkidians could do no harm to the Sikels, because they were bound by a promise, but that the Megarians were not so bound, and that they might do what they chose. So the Megarians drove out the Sikels, and dwelled in Leontinoi along with the Chalkidians. Presently Theoklés began to devise another trick against the Megarians. The Chalkidians, when warring with the Sikels, had vowed an armed procession to the Twelve Gods. It was now time to fulfil the vow; but the Megarians had no right in it. The Chalkidians went through their ceremony, and then a herald proclaimed that every Megarian must leave the town before sunset. The unarmed Megarians could not stand against the armed Chalkidians; so they set forth to seek a third home, while the Chalkidians kept Leontinoi to themselves, without either Sikels or Megarians. Then the Megarians tried a winter on Thapsos, where Lamis died. Lastly they settled on a point of the bay between Thapsos and Xiphonia, near the greater Hybla. As is not very uncommon in such stories, they are said to have been helped by a Sikel prince who betrayed his own people. His name is Hyblôn, called after his town, as we shall find some other men. The wanderers at last founded a town on the coast, which they called after their metropolis, Megara, in which Hybla was pretty well swallowed up. Megara is no longer an existing town, but considerable remains may be seen.

According to our dates, Greek settlement in Sicily must have stopped for about forty years after the foundation of Megara, and it is certain that for a while Italy rather than Sicily was chosen as the land to be settled. But one famous city seems to have been founded not long after Megara. This is Zanklê, afterwards called Messana, which still keeps its later name in the form of *Messina*. It seems to have been first settled in an irregular way by pirates from Kymê. This would not give their town the rights of a regular Greek colony; but it was afterwards founded again in a more orderly way from Kymê and Chalkis, with a founder from each. It was a wonderful site, on the strait at the foot of the hills, with a noble harbour, fenced in by a narrow strip of land in front of it. *Zanklê*, or rather *Danklon*, is said to have meant a reaping-hook in the Sikel tongue; hence the name. The settlers at Zanklê presently turned the north-east corner of Sicily, and made themselves an outpost on the northern coast. This was on the peninsula of Mylai or Milazzo, which one legend called the grazing-place of the oxen of the sun in the time of Odysseus. Zanklê or Messana has always been a prosperous city, but in Greek times it never held at all a foremost place among the cities of Sicily.

The foundation of Zanklê completed the Greek possession of the eastern coast of Sicily. By far the greater part of that coast was now occupied by Greek settlements; but, unless we count the Zanklaian outpost at Mylai, no Greeks had as yet attempted to occupy either the northern or the southern coasts. About B.C. 689 Greek settlers began to occupy the southern coast also. These were Dorians from the island of Rhodes, with some companions from Crete, and some perhaps from other islands. The new colony was planted near the march of the Sikans and Sikels, on a row of low hills between the sea and a rich plain fenced in by mountains. It was close by the river *Gelas*, so called in the Sikel tongue from the coldness of its waters, which shows how near the Sikel tongue was to the Latin *gelu* and *gelidus*. The new settlers first occupied a point of the hill, which they called *Lindioi*, after one of the Rhodian towns; as the new city grew, Lindioi became the akropolis of *Gela*, so called from the cold river. Gela became a famous city, but it has neither wholly perished like Naxos nor yet has it lived on like Messina. It was destroyed after a life of several centuries; and after many more centuries, the present town of Terranova was built on part of its site.

There is little doubt that the foundation of Gela, the first Greek town on the south coast of Sicily, stirred up Syracuse to enlarge her borders. No town was so well suited as Syracuse to be at once a land and a sea power. Her object was to occupy the whole south-eastern corner, and to have a sea-board on the southern coast as well as the eastern. To this end she worked steadily but slowly, advancing both inland and along the coast. She had outposts at Helóron on her own coast and at Neaiton or Netum inland. Netum is *Noto;* but the present town is nearer the sea. Next Syracuse struck further inland, clearly aiming at the south coast. In 664 she occupied inland Akrai, now Palazzuolo, a hill full of Sikel tombs. In 644 she went on to Kasmenai, now Spaccaforno, on a hill some way inland, but looking down on the southern sea. Lastly in 599 she planted Kamarina on the southern sea. Syracuse now held the whole south-eastern corner of Sicily, with a long sea-board round the corner and an unusually large inland territory to enable her to hold the sea on both coasts.

What followed was as instructive as the relations between Corinth and Korkyra. All these Syracusan towns were doubtless meant to be, not separate commonwealths, but outposts of Syracuse, held by Syracusan citizens. At this time none of them coined money. And we hear of no disputes between Syracuse and any of them, except one. Kamarina was well suited to be a separate city and it sought for independence. A war followed, in which each side found allies, Greek and Sikel. In B.C. 553 the men of Kamarina were defeated, and their town was swept from the earth by its offended metropolis.

Meanwhile there was no Greek settlement on the north coast westward of the Zanklai outpost at Mylai. But presently, about 648 B.C. Zanklé went on to found a real colony much farther to the west, namely Himera, long the only Greek city on the north coast. Cephalœdium and other Sikel points lay between it and Zanklê, and towards the west it stood right in the teeth of the Phœnicians. It stood on a not very high hill near the sea, by the mouth of the northern river of its own name. It lived only two hundred and forty years, and now it is wholly forsaken. But it had an outpost towards the Phœnician territory, the Hot Baths (*Thermæ*, Θερμαί) of Himera, which the legend said were thrown up by the nymphs to refresh the wearied Héraklês after his wrestling at Eryx. The baths still remain, and the modern town keeps its name as *Termini*.

We must now go back a little. While Syracuse and Zanklê were working round their several corners, after the foundation of Himera, but before that of Kamarina, in 628 B.C. the Megarians of Sicily planted Selinous on the south coast, the most western of Greek cities in the island. It answers to Himera on the north side, as being planted as an outpost of Hellas on the very march of Phœnicians, Sikans, and Elymians. It had an outpost on the river Mazaros, the furthest Greek post in the island. The akropolis stood on a hill above the sea, between the rivers Hypsas and Selinous, and the temples and other buildings spread over that hill and over another hill on each side, a wonderful group. Selinous, like Himera, is now quite forsaken, but its ruins are the grandest in Sicily.

Between Selinous and Gela a large gap still lay without any Greek city. This in 599 B.C. was filled up by the foundation of Akragas, *Agrigentum, Girgenti,*

HÉRAKLES AND THE KERKÔPES.
(Early Sculpture from Selinous.)

which has always lived on without any real change of name. This was a foundation of Gela, which could thus endure to plant an independent colony on her own borders. Greeks from other places, especially from Gela's own metropolis of Rhodes, joined in the settlement. The new city was not so close to the sea as most of its fellows. It stood on a hill between two rivers in their valleys, Akragas and another Hypsas. The akropolis arose on a lofty and almost isolated point of the hill, from which the town gradually spread down, as Syracuse spread up. And, like Syracuse, the modern town has shrunk up again into its oldest part; the present Girgenti is only the akropolis of Akragas. But though the city spread, it never reached the sea; its small haven remained at a little distance. Akragas had a great trade with the opposite coast of Africa; but it never became a real naval power like Syracuse. But it grew rich and powerful in many ways, and was certainly the second Greek city in Sicily, as Syracuse was the first. The lower city is now forsaken, but nowhere can there be seen so many temples more or less perfect, besides the fallen one of Zeus Olympios, the greatest in Sicily.

Thus in about 140 years, the greater part of the coast of Sicily was occupied by Greek settlements. The Phœnicians and their neighbours kept their own barbarian corner. Independent Sikels kept the inland parts and a large part of the north coast between Mylai and Himera. But the east and south coasts were Greek. We shall come to see that Akragas was not the youngest Greek city in Sicily;

AKRAGAS, FROM THE OLYMPIEION.

but it was the last independent commonwealth settled from another independent commonwealth. It was not however the last attempt at such settlement. Soon after the foundation of Akragas, about 580 B.C., a body of settlers from Knidos and Rhodes, under the Knidian Pentathlos, strove to make a settlement in the heart of the Phœnician territory, near Lilybaion in the extreme west of Sicily. The new comers found a war going on between the Greeks of Selinous and the Elymians of Segesta :—we shall hear of several more such wars. The men of Segesta had Phœnician allies, while the new comers, Greeks and Dorians, naturally gave help to the men of Selinous, also Greeks and Dorians. But the Greeks were defeated, and Pentathlos was killed. His followers then sailed away round the north-west corner of Sicily to the isles of Aiolos; there they planted a colony on the largest of them, the isle of Lipara, which has ever since been an inhabited town. The new city of Lipara looked to Knidos as its metropolis, and reverenced the dead Pentathlos as its founder.

Thus the islands which lay between Sicily and southern Italy, two great lands of Greek settlement, themselves became Greek. The islands at the extreme west of Sicily, Aigousa and its fellows, naturally followed the fortunes of the neighbouring mainland, and the islands between Sicily and Africa were not touched by Greek settlement at any time. A time of nearly a hundred years now follows, which, as far as the Greek settlements were concerned, was a time of comparative peace and advance. We cannot say that there were no wars, either between Greeks and Greeks or between Greeks and Phœnicians; but there is much less war than usual for so long a time. In the course of the sixth century B.C. the independent Phœnician cities of Sicily began to come under the power of their great sister-colony Carthage. Soon after that time begins the first great war of any Sicilian Greeks with Carthage, the first time when Syracuse stood forth in her great calling as the champion of Europe against Africa. But during the greater part of the sixth century Phœnicians and Greeks in Sicily meddled but little with one another. The Phœnicians kept their own corner; the Greeks strengthened their hold on the parts which they had won, and extended their borders against neighbouring Sikans and Sikels. But Syracuse alone, in her south-western corner, held any considerable inland territory. By the time the great strife came, Syracuse, though not holding the same dominion over the other Greek cities as Carthage did over the other Phœnician cities, was as clearly the first among them. We must now go on to tell what little we know of the internal affairs of the Greek cities while this work of settlement was going on, and also what we know of the general affairs of the island from the completion of Greek settlement till the great war with Carthage. That will be, roughly, the history of the sixth century, B.C.

V.

THE FIRST AGE OF THE GREEK CITIES.

B.C. 735-480.

[For the whole period of this chapter we are still without any contemporary narrative; it is only quite towards the end that we have a continuous narrative of any kind. Then in his fifth and seventh books Herodotos tells the story of Dôrieus and of the reign of Hippokratês and the early days of Gelôn. The rest we have to put together from all manner of sources, mainly Greek writers who copied earlier ones. Aristotle tells us something in the Politics; so do Plutarch, Pausanias, Polyainos, and a crowd of other writers, among them Diodôros, whose continuous narrative is still missing, but who gives the laws of Charóndas out of their place. Perhaps no man in all Greek history or legend has more allusions made to him in Greek and Latin writers than Phalaris. But we have no narrative of his acts, beyond a few entries in the Parian Chronicle, short annals carved on stone in the third century B.C. The earliest reference to him is in Pindar, less than a hundred years after his time. It is perhaps needless to say that the Letters which were once believed to be his are a late forgery of no value whatever. On the whole, at this time we know very little of any of the Sicilian cities; but we know somewhat more of Syracuse than of the others.]

WHEN the Greek settlements in Sicily began, the old kingship of the Homeric times had everywhere passed away or had become nominal. The political tendency was to oligarchy. Thus the Bacchiads at

Corinth were a house which had been a royal house. By the time when Syracuse was founded, personal kingship had passed away, and the Bacchiads ruled as an oligarchic house, choosing magistrates from among themselves. The name *democracy* was not yet known; but the thing out of which it grew was forming itself. In all the old commonwealths citizenship could be had only either by descent or by special grant. Mere residence in a city, even from generation to generation, gave no political rights. Neither did residence go for anything in the old cities and boroughs in England and elsewhere; but there were commonly means of obtaining citizenship in other ways than by birth. In both cases the descendants of the old citizens kept their exclusive rights, while a large body of dwellers in the town grew up around them who were not citizens. The old citizens, who had divided the lands of the commonwealth among themselves or had kept them as common property, had no wish to share their rights with others. They intermarried among themselves; they kept all offices to themselves. Their numbers naturally grew smaller, while the numbers of the excluded class grew greater and greater. Thus these old citizens, once the whole people, forming what was really a democracy among themselves, gradually became an oligarchy, as concerned all the inhabitants who were not citizens. Then the excluded body wins political equality with the old citizens, either at once and by violence or by gradual stages. Then democracy begins. Such, with differences of detail arising out of the circumstances of different cities, was the story of the *patricians* of

Rome and the *eupatrids* of Athens. Such too was the story of the *Gamoroi* or *Landowners* of Syracuse. But mark the difference. At Rome and at Athens, the excluded class, the *plebeians* or *dêmos*, were a class of small landowners, for Athens and Rome were inland cities living by agriculture. At Syracuse, a city in the sea, the old citizens had all the land; the new comers would be traders in or near the town.

We do not know for certain what led men to leave Corinth or any other city of Old Greece, to settle in Sicily. Some may have left their homes through political discontent. We have a remarkable notice that many settlers went to Syracuse from the small town of Tenea in the Corinthian territory. Now the people of Tenea were a separate people from the Corinthians. They were said to be descended from Trojan captives, and long after, when Corinth was taken and destroyed by the Romans, the Teneats were received to favour. This looks as if the Teneat settlers hoped to better their political condition by emigrating. On the other hand, we know that at least one Bacchiad, the poet Eumêlos, went besides Archias. The circumstances of a colony are levelling; we may be sure that every free settler got at least a lot of land and a vote in the assembly of the new city. But it does not follow that the lots were all equal or that there may not have been distinctions in the disposal of offices. For a while, as long as the settlement was weak, they would welcome new citizens. When these were no longer needed, the tendency among the old citizens would be to closer equality among themselves and to sharper separation between themselves and new comers. We get one sign of political disputes among the *Gamoroi* themselves. When Himera was founded from Zanklé, we read that the Mylétids, banished from Syracuse in civil strife, took part in the settlement. This looks like the banishment of a whole *gens*, like that of the Alkmaionids at Athens and the Tarquinii at Rome; but we know not how it came about.

We know however enough to say, what we might have taken for granted without, that there was at Syracuse a general assembly of the whole body of the *Landowners*, and also a smaller senate, we know not

COIN OF SYRACUSE, TIME OF THE GAMOROI.

how chosen. We hear of the general assembly (like the *comitia curiata* at Rome) sitting as a court on a man named Agathoklés, who, when the temple of Athéné (now the great church of Syracuse) was building, defrauded the goddess of the stones that were meant for the work. And we hear of the senate in a story of a shameful quarrel between two young men of the ruling order, which divided the whole city and led to political disturbances. A wise old senator counselled that both should be banished before matters grew worse. But his advice was not followed, and the government of the Landowners was over-

TEMPLE OF ATHÊNÊ, SYRACUSE.

thrown. We must suppose that the excluded people took one side in the personal quarrel. They rose, and called in the help of the Sikel serfs or villains who tilled the lands of the Landowners. Between them they drove the Landowners out of the city, and held Syracuse for themselves. There was thus a new Syracusan people, and one not purely Greek; they formed the first democracy under that name that Syracuse had seen. The banished Landowners occupied the outpost of Kasmenai and held it as a separate commonwealth, much as the Athenian oligarchs held Eleusis after the Thirty were driven from Athens. We have no exact date for this revolution; but there can be no doubt that it happened in the first years of the fifth century B.C. We shall hear of the oligarchs at Kasmenai again.

We may be sure that something like this growth of an oligarchy out of a body of old citizens happened in other Sikeliot cities besides Syracuse. What distinguishes Syracuse is that, during all this time, about 240 years from her foundation to the driving out of the Landowners, she never saw a *tyrant*. We do hear very vaguely of one *king* at Syracuse; but the mere title of king went on in many Greek commonwealths, and of King Pollis we know only that he gave his name to a kind of wine. A tyrant of Syracuse there certainly was not as yet. In the Greek commonwealths the word *tyrant* had a definite meaning, and was not simply a name of reproach for an oppressive ruler. The tyrant was a man who put his own power instead of the law, one who took to himself the power, or more than the power, of a king in a commonwealth where there was no king by law. This he might do in various ways: if he could in any way get a bodyguard, that was enough. Sometimes he was a popular leader against the oligarchs to whom the people were foolish enough to vote a guard. Sometimes he was a magistrate or general who turned his lawful powers against the state. Sometimes he held some commission which put public money in his hands, and he spent it in hiring mercenaries. When he had got power in any of these ways, he commonly used it oppressively, but not always. The name *tyrant* does not of itself imply the oppressive use of power, but only the unlawful way of gaining it. Some tyrants were bloody and greedy and committed frightful crimes; others allowed the usual course of the commonwealth to go on whenever their own interests were not concerned, and were simply ready to step in with their spearmen whenever it suited them. The tyrants never, till a much later time, called themselves kings or put their heads on the coin; but they seem to have been pleased if anybody else would call them kings. They always tried to leave their power to their sons, and they often did; but the son seldom knew how to keep what the father had known how to gain.

Tyrants were more common in the Greek cities of Sicily than they were in Old Greece. The first recorded tyrant in Sicily is Panaitios of Leontinoi about B.C. 608. He is said to have been general in a war with Megara, the first recorded war, most likely not really the first war, between Greeks and Greeks in the island. He is said to have risen by means of dissension between rich and poor, most likely between old and new citizens. But we know nothing more about him and at this time nothing more of his city. Far more famous was another tyrant a little later, Phalaris of Akragas, who held power there from about B.C. 570 to 554. No man in all Greek history ever came to be more talked about and to have more stories told of him; but we have no real account of his actions. One thing is to be noticed, that he rose to power in Akragas only ten

HIMERA, EARLY.

years after the foundation of the city, when neither he nor any other grown man could have been born in it. A story which places him at Himera and makes the poet Stêsichoros warn the people, by the fable of the horse and the man, not to give him a body-guard, must belong to some other tyrant; stories of one tyrant are very often told of another. At Akragas he rose to power by taking public money that was in his hands and using it to hire mercenaries. He made conquests from the Sikans, but there is no sign that he ruled in any Greek city besides Akragas. He is most famous for keeping a brazen bull into which men were put, and roasted to death by a fire underneath the image, while their cries represented the roaring of the bull. The story is as old as the poet Pindar. No doubt cruelty of this kind was suggested by some Phœnician model; the worst Greek, as a rule, only slays, he seldom tortures. At last Phalaris was overthrown by a certain Télemachos, who perhaps restored liberty, perhaps only put a milder tyranny instead of that of Phalaris. The tyrant and his chief supporters are said to have been roasted in his own bull; but this sounds legendary.

Meanwhile at Katanè in the course of the same century we see the rule of one man in a better shape. When a Greek city was torn by disputes, the citizens sometimes gave extraordinary powers, for life or for a time, to one man whom they could trust. He was to settle everything by a code of laws. Such an one was Charòndas, who made laws for Katanè and for some other cities. These old lawgivers not only made political constitutions, but put forth rules ordering the whole life of the citizens. Some scraps of the laws of Charòndas have been preserved, which show much of the simple shrewdness of old times. Thus he allowed a man to put away his wife or a woman to put away her husband, but he added that in such a case they must not marry anybody younger than the person put away. And a story is told of his death, which is also told of more than one other lawgiver. The old custom, Greek and Teutonic, was to come armed to the assembly. This Charòndas forbade. One day, so the story ran, Charòndas had gone out of the city after some robbers, and of course went armed. While he was away, an assembly was held, and dispute rose high. Charóndas went in to quiet the people; but he forgot to take off his sword. One man cried out, " Charóndas, you are breaking your own law." " No," he said, " I will rather confirm it," and slew himself.

We hear of tyrants in other cities besides Panaitios and Phalaris, and some of these come in a story which makes a kind of appendix to the Greek colonization of Sicily. In the course of the sixth century B.C. the Phœnician towns in Sicily had become dependencies of Carthage. There was therefore still less hope of founding new Greek settlements in the barbarian corner than there had been at the time of the expedition of Pentathlos. The independent Phœnician towns had not been aggressive; but now that they are under the supremacy of the great ruling city, wars between Phœnicians and Greeks form a large part of Sicilian history. They began by an attempt to renew the enterprise of Pentathlos. This was made by Dórieus, son of the Spartan king Anaxandridas, about the year 510 B.C. He was disappointed of the succession to the kingdom, and went to seek a home elsewhere. After some other adventures, he was bidden by the Delphic oracle to go and recover the lands of his forefather Héraklés in Sicily, those lands of Eryx which Héraklés had left to be given up whenever a descendant of his should claim them. But Dórieus forfeited his right by not at once obeying the oracle. Instead of going straight to Eryx, he turned aside to war against Greeks, helping the men of Krotón in southern Italy against Sybaris. So, when he came to Eryx, he was defeated and slain with many of his men in a battle with the Elymians of Segesta and their Phœnician allies. Whether Carthage sent troops to the help of her dependencies we cannot say. But Elymians, Phœnicians of Sicily, and Carthaginians, were all alike concerned to hinder a Greek settlement in those parts.

So Dórieus failed to win back the lands of his forefather and to found a Hérakleia on Eryx. Still something came of his attempt. Euryleón, one of his officers, gathered the remnant of his followers, and went to help the people of Selinous against a tyrant called Peithagoras. In the war with him Euryleón occupied the post called Minóa, of which we have heard in the story of Kókalos and Minós, and set it up as a town called Hérakleia. So there was a new Hérakleia, though not on Eryx. But Euryleón, after overthrowing the tyranny of Peithagoras, made himself tyrant of Selinous. Presently the people rose and slew him.

But we are now coming to much more famous tyrants than these. A great line of rulers arose at Gela, but they did not stay there. All that we know of Gela in these times is that there were disputes in the city, and that at one time one party *seceded*, as it is called in the Roman history, to the town of Maktórion in the Geloan territory. They were brought back, neither by force nor by persuasion, but by the wonder-working power of some holy things of the nether-gods—perhaps of the two goddesses of

Sicily. These holy things, whatever they were, were in the hands of Télinês of Gela, a descendant of one of the first settlers. By their means, we are not told how, he brought back the malecontents. He was rewarded with the hereditary priesthood of the deities whom he served, and his descendants became great in Gela. About the year 505 B.C. the oligarchy in Gela was upset by the tyrant Kleandros,

ZANKLÊ. SIXTH CENTURY.

NAXOS. C. 500 B.C.

who was killed about seven years later, and his power passed to his brother Hippokratês. Hippokratês was, as far as we can see, the first man in Greek Sicily who aimed at being something more than the lord of a single city. He strove to found as large a dominion as he could, hiring mercenaries, Greek and Sikel, and taking towns both Greek and Sikel. Thus he won Naxos and Leontinoi and the lost Kallipolis and the Sikel Ergetioń. His dominion thus spread from the southern to the eastern sea, leaving Zanklé in possession of one corner and Syracuse of the other. His dealings with these two cities are the first piece of Sicilian history of which we know anything in detail.

Zanklé was now ruled by one Skythês, who is spoken of as king; perhaps the old kingship had gone on there. Rhêgion, on the other side of the strait, was ruled by the tyrant Anaxilas, the first Italian ruler who plays any part in Sicilian history. This was the time when the Persian king Darius was bringing back the Greek cities of Asia under his power, and many of their inhabitants were ready to seek new homes elsewhere. About the year 493 B.C. Skythês proposed to them to settle in a body in Sicily. They were to found one great Greek colony on the north coast where there was no Greek city but Himera, at a point called *Kalê Aktê*, the Fair Shore, between Cephalœdium and Mylai. Many Samians and some Milesians agreed to come, and set sail. Meanwhile Skythês was warring against Sikels, most likely with a view to the new settlement. But, when the Greeks from Asia were drawing near, Anaxilas sent a message to them, counselling them that, instead of taking the trouble to found a new city at Kalê Aktê, they should take possession of Zanklé. They would find the town undefended, while Skythês and his army were engaged in the Sikel war. The Samians and Milesians were not ashamed so to treat the man who had planned such a service for them, and when Skythês and his army came back, they found themselves shut out of their own town. Skythês then asked help of Hippokratês. The story reads as if Hippokratês were in some way his overlord; for, when he came, he put Skythês in prison for losing Zanklê. He then made a shameful treaty with the Samians in Zanklê. They were to keep the town, but they were to give up to him half the goods in it, and he was to take all the goods outside the walls. In all these cases the inhabitants are reckoned among the goods; and Hippokratês took possession of the whole army of Skythês as his slaves. Three hundred of the chief men among them he handed over to the Samians, bidding them put them to death. This they would not do; but we know not what became of them. Hippokratês thus got a great booty, and went back to Gela. We are glad to hear that Skythês contrived to get out of prison, and to escape to Asia to King Darius, by whom he was greatly honoured. Nor did the Samians keep Zanklê very long. For Anaxilas, who had first stirred them up, presently turned them out, and took the town to himself. He was thus lord of two cities, Rhêgion and Zanklê, on the two sides of the strait, the first, but not the last, ruler of Italy who also ruled in Sicily. And he is said to have now changed the name of Zanklê to Messana; but that change most likely came a little later.

Hippokratês now engaged in a war with Syracuse, hoping to add the south-eastern corner of Sicily to his dominions. He defeated the Syracusans in a battle by the river Helôros south of the city, and came as near to Syracuse as the Olympieion, near the Great Harbour. It is not easy to see why he did not go on further to attack the city. But somehow there was time for negotiations with distant powers. For Corinth the mother and Korkyra the sister of Syracuse forgot their differences when Syracuse was in danger. They joined in a mediation, and Hippokratès made peace with Syracuse on receiving the site and territory of Kamarina, the town which the Syracusans had destroyed. He now founded it afresh. All this is told without any exact date; but it was most likely during the last days of the rule of the Landowners at Syracuse, and it may have helped to bring about their fall.

Hippokratès died in the year B.C. 491, while he was

KAMARINA. EARLY.

besieging the Sikel town of Hybla, the Heraian Hybla or Ragusa, which lay conveniently between his new dominions and those of Syracuse. Like all other tyrants, he wished to hand on his power to his children; but his two sons were young and unable to keep it. The people of Gela would have nothing to say to them, and set up their commonwealth again. We now hear for the first time of a memorable man, Gelôn, son of Deinomenès. He was a descendant of that Tèlinès who had brought back the Geloan seceders from Maktòrion, and he was his successor in his priestly office. He was also the commander of Hippokratês' cavalry, and had played a great part in his wars. He was one of four brothers, Gelôn, Hierôn, Polyzêlos, and Thrasyboulos, of all of whom we shall hear again. Gelôn now professed to take up the cause of the sons of Hippokratês, and marched against Gela in their name. But instead of setting them up, he took the tyranny to himself. Here was a base act, but we are apt to blame it on the wrong ground. No wrong was done to the sons of Hippokratês, who had no right to the unlawful power of their father; but a great wrong was done to the people of Gela, whose newly restored freedom was destroyed again. Through life we shall find Gelôn quite unscrupulous in the way of gaining dominion. But he was a great and wise ruler, and founded a great power; and he was presently called to the noblest work that could fall to the lot of any Greek.

Gelôn thus held the dominion of Hippokratês, the greatest as yet seen in Sicily. He was soon both to enlarge it and to change its seat. The Landowners had now been driven from Syracuse, and they held Kasmenai. About B.C. 485 they prayed Gelôn to bring them back to Syracuse. So he did; but he made himself lord over both them and the commons. He was now tyrant of Syracuse as well as of Gela; he made Syracuse the head of his dominions, and gave himself to enlarging and strengthening it in every way. And some of the ways were strange enough. His advance was of course threatening to Hyblaian Megara, so near to Syracuse. The oligarchic government then made war on Gelôn without the consent of the commons. When he had the better in the war, the oligarchs were naturally in mortal fear, while the commons feared nothing, and most likely looked on Gelón as a deliverer. To all men's surprise, he sold the commons as slaves to be sent out of Sicily, while the oligarchs he took to Syracuse and made citizens. The town of Megara he destroyed, and joined its lands to those of Syracuse, keeping Megara only as a fortress. And he did exactly the same to the people of Euboia, the town whose site we do not know. The reason he gave for thus treating his friends ill and his enemies well was that he thought the commons a most unpleasant neighbour. But the commons of Syracuse he in no way oppressed, being most likely bound to them by some promise. And, when the men of Kamarina revolted and slew his governor, he pulled down the town and made the people come and live at Syracuse. At last he made one half of the people of his own native city of Gela remove to Syracuse in the like sort.

So Syracuse grew at the cost of the other cities of Sicily. As the population grew so greatly, the town itself needed to be enlarged. As yet the Island had been the city, while Achradina was only an outpost on the hill. Gelón now carried the western wall of Achradina down to the Great Harbour, thus taking Achradina into the city. But both it and the Island kept their separate defences. The *agora*, the meeting-place and market-place, which must have been at first in the Island, was now moved into the low ground between the Island and the hill, which had now become the lower Achradina. Gelón was now lord of the greatest city in Sicily, perhaps in all Hellas, and lord of the greatest dominion that had ever been in Sicily or anywhere in Hellas. As such he felt more like a king of Sicily than like an ordinary tyrant of Syracuse. He invited men from all parts who could be useful to him; he hired many mercenaries and gave them citizenship. Next in power to him was Thêrôn, tyrant of Akragas, a descendant of that Telemachos who had overthrown Phalaris. He had risen to power, like most tyrants, by a trick; but he used his power mildly and left a good name behind him. He and Gelôn were fast friends, and, like princes in later times, they made an alliance by marriage. Gelôn took Thêrôn's daughter Damarata to wife. Their alliance, which took in all south-eastern Sicily, was to some extent balanced by another in the north-east where Anaxilas of Rhêgion and Zanklê was closely allied with Terillos, tyrant of Himera, and married his daughter Kydippê. These two pairs take in all Greek Sicily, save two cities. One was Katanê, of which we hear nothing, but which could not have kept much real independence while Gelôn held Naxos and Leontinoi on each side of it. The other was Selinous, which we find a little time later as a dependent ally of Carthage.

Now how had a Greek city come into this last case? We do not know for certain; but we have dim hints of a war between Greeks and Phœnicians earlier than the great one of which we shall have to speak directly. We hear of a war to avenge the death of Dôrieus, in which Gelôn claimed to have taken a part, and said that he had asked for help in

Old Greece, but had got none. This could not have been after Gelôn became tyrant; but he may have acted as an officer of one of the earlier tyrants. It would seem that in this war the Carthaginians destroyed the new town of Hérakleia between Selinous and Akragas, and this must surely have been the time when Selinous was made to join their alliance. But Gelôn claims to have hindered the barbarians from coming further west, and to have ended the war by a treaty which gave some commercial advantages to all Greeks. Something of this kind must have happened to account for the state of things which we find a little later. But the story is told very darkly, and we can look on the war which followed the death of Dórieus only as a forerunner of the great and successful war with Carthage of which we have now to speak.

SELINOUS. EARLY.

VI.

THE FIRST WARS WITH CARTHAGE AND ETRURIA.

B.C. 480-473.

[We now at last have a continuous narrative of Sicilian history for about two hundred years. The books of Diodôros for all this time are extant. He copied from earlier writers, among them the Syracusan historians Antiochos and Philistos. Sometimes he seems to copy a piece nearly in full, and gives us a clear and vivid account of things; at other times he is very confused, and seems not to have understood his authorities. Still it is a great gain to have a continuous narrative of any kind. Of Gelôn's dealings with the Greeks at the Isthmus we have the account of Herodotus. And we now for the first time come to absolutely contemporary sources, though not in the form of narrative. The odes of Pindar, commemorating the victories of Hierôn, Thêrôn, and other Sikeliots, in the games of Old Greece are full of references to events in Sicily. And there are some also in the poems of Simonidês, who, like Pindar, was entertained by Hierôn. Coins too begin to tell us more than before, and in the legend on Hierôn's helmet we have a contemporary inscription recording a fact. We have also a dialogue composed long after by Xenophôn in the names of Hierôn and Simonidês, which at least shows the kind of tradition which was handed on to later times.]

THE fifth century before Christ commonly seems to us the most brilliant time in the history of Greece, and it is one of the times of which we know most. And yet its most brilliant deeds show that the Greek folk had in some sort gone back in the world. Herodotus speaks of a time when all Greeks were free. That time had come to an end when the Greeks of Asia passed under the power of the kings, first of Lydia and then of Persia. Hellas was thus cut short; and presently she had to defend herself in Old Greece also; she had to fight to beat back the Persian invader. And so in Sicily at the same moment the Greek cities had to fight to beat back the Carthaginian invader.

These two powers, Persia and Carthage, were such as the barbarian world had never seen before. The Persian dominion was the greatest in extent that had ever been seen in the East, and the Persians, in their beginning an Aryan people, had in them a strong and abiding national life beyond most Eastern nations. The Phœnicians again were the most advanced of barbarian nations and the most like Europeans. And Carthage was the model of the ruling city for all time. The world had never seen such a dominion by sea as she now had. And now these two great powers threatened the Greeks on both sides, and, there is little reason to doubt, threatened them in concert. They had easy means of communicating through the men of the old Phœnicia. Sidon and Tyre were now under Persian supremacy; but they were still separate states, keeping their hatred for all Greeks and their friendship for Carthage. So it was agreed that Persia should attack the Greeks of Old Greece, and that Carthage should attack the Greeks of Sicily. There was this difference between the two, that the Persian king could not attack Greece except by taking a vast army over a long march in the face of the world. But the Carthaginians, being so much nearer to Sicily and having a starting-point in their Sicilian dependencies, could send a force against the Greeks of Sicily almost at any moment. Yet it needed time to gather a force fit for the purpose by hiring mercenaries everywhere. So neither power hurried. At last the Persian king Xerxes set out on his great march. The Carthaginians were then planning their warfare in Sicily; but their actual coming seems to have been sudden, and its time and place were fixed by events which were happening in the island.

Thérôn, tyrant of Akragas, seemingly invited by a party in Himera, drove out Terillos, tyrant of that city, and held the town himself. A power was thus formed which stretched right across Sicily and barred the Carthaginian advance to the east. Terillos and his son-in-law Anaxilas of Rhêgion and Zanklê asked for help at Carthage. So their treason against Hellas somewhat hastened the Carthaginian attack, and settled in what part of Sicily it should be made.

Meanwhile in the year 480 B.C. Xerxes was marching against Old Greece, and the patriotic Greeks who met in council at the Isthmus sent envoys to Gelôn to ask for help. He had the best reason in the world for not sending help to Old Greece, namely that he needed all his forces to defend Syracuse and all Greek Sicily against the Carthaginians. But a wonderful set of speeches are given by Herodotus as having passed between Gelôn and the envoys. They are quite unsuited to the circumstances of the time, and they were evidently made up afterwards by some clever Syracusan, as a satire on the airs which the cities of the mother-country gave themselves towards the colonies. The Lacedæmonian and Athenian envoys are made to insult Gelôn in the very act of asking for help. It is enough to say that Gelôn sent no help, and could not send any. And another story told how he sent an agent to watch the state of things in Greece. If the King should be successful, he was to give him a great sum of money not to come against Sicily. This agent was one Kadmos of Kôs, who had been tyrant in his own island, but had given up the tyranny and had settled at Zanklê with the Samians. It was thought a wonderful feat of virtue that, when Kadmos found that the money was not wanted, he brought it back safe to Gelôn.

And now the blow which had so long been looked for fell suddenly. Thêrôn was at his new possession of Himera, Gelôn was waiting at Syracuse, when the great fleet sailed from Africa under the command of Hamilkar, one of the *Shophetim* of Carthage. These were the chief magistrates, who are compared to the Roman consuls and the Spartan kings; the name is the same as that of the Hebrew *Judges*. The Greek writers commonly speak of them as *kings*. Hamilkar set forth with a vast force. The ships that carried the horses and war-chariots—for the Carthaginians still kept the fashion of the old Canaan—were sunk on the voyage. The rest of the fleet reached Panormos, and thence the ships sailed and the land forces marched to Himera. There Hamilkar pitched two camps, one close to the sea, the other on the hill, west of the town. The east side towards the river, and the landward side seem to have been left open. We hear nothing of any action on the part of Anaxilas; but the Selinuntines were bidden, and they promised in a letter, to send their horsemen to the camp on a certain day. Meanwhile Thèrôn and his force made a sally and were defeated. So the Carthaginians held the country and plundered everywhere. But Thèrôn was able to send a message to Gelôn, who at once marched to his help with his whole force. He pitched his camp on the right bank of the Himeras, and his horsemen scoured the country and took many of the Punic plunderers. The hearts of the men of Himera rose.

The story goes that the letters from Selinous to Hamilkar fell into the hands of Gelôn, and that he settled to attack the Carthaginians on the day when the Selinuntine horsemen were looked for. That day was commonly said to have been the same as that of the battle of Salamis in Old Greece. The two fights were certainly fought much at the same time, in the autumn of the year B.C. 480. And there is nothing against the story that they were fought on the same day, except that the tale sounds too good to be true.

We have two quite different accounts of the great battle which followed. One, as it was told at Carthage, is given us by Herodotus. He says that the Syracusan version was different; that we get from Diodôros. In the Carthaginian story Hamilkar stands apart from the fight, like Moses or Samuel. All day, while the battle goes on, he throws whole burnt-offerings into the fire. At last, towards evening, news comes that his army is defeated; he then throws himself into the fire, as the most costly gift of all. For this he was honoured as a hero wherever Carthage had power.

This is a grand story, and truly Semitic, but it tells us nothing about the battle. In the Syracusan story also a sacrifice offered by Hamilkar has a chief place; but that is the whole amount of likeness. Gelôn is said to have sent horsemen who went to the camp by the sea, and passed themselves off for the Selinuntines who were looked for. As such, they were let in. They killed Hamilkar, as he was sacrificing—to Poseidôn, this story says—and many others, and set fire to the ships. Then, at a given signal, Gelôn attacked the land camp, but was kept in check by the bravery of the Iberian mercenaries. The day was at last settled by the coming up of Thêrôn with the garrison of Himera. The whole barbarian host was killed or scattered, a few only escaping to the ships that were still at sea. Those who fled hither and thither were gradually hunted down and made slaves; the Akragantines especially caught a vast number, and set them to work at Thêrôn's great buildings. Thus Greek Sicily was saved from the Carthaginian invader, as Old Greece was saved from the Persian. Only the Persian was driven out for ever, while after seventy years the Carthaginian came again.

Gelôn now went back to Syracuse, and was received with all honours, even with the titles of the gods, Benefactor (εὐεργέτης), Saviour (σωτήρ), and King (βασιλεύς). And indeed from this time he and his successors are spoken of by Diodóros as kings, and Pindar freely gives that title to Gelòn's successor Hierón, while he does not give it to Thèrón. Presently envoys came from Carthage, and seemingly from Anaxilas, asking for peace. Selinous must now have been set free from Carthage, as we presently hear of it as an independent city. The Carthaginians had to pay a large sum of money, and to build two temples at Carthage in honour of the Greek goddesses

DÂMARATEION.

of Sicily. But they were not disturbed in their possessions in western Sicily. And a story was told that Gelòn made it one of the terms of peace that the Carthaginians should give up the practice of human sacrifices. This cannot be true; for no people interfered in this way with the religion of another, and the Carthaginians certainly did not give up the practice. But they may have engaged not to sacrifice Greeks; in any case he who devised the story well understood the difference between Greek and Phœnician religion, and all that was implied in a struggle between the two nations.

Gelôn himself gave great gifts to the gods of his own people at Olympia and elsewhere. He built the temples of Démétér and the Koré on the south side of Epipolai, and he began another temple near Ætna which he did not finish. For he died two years after his great victory, in the year 478 B.C. He was buried with all honour, and commemorated by a stately tomb in the low ground between Epipolai and the Olympieion. He was reverenced at Syracuse as a hero and a second founder, and in after days, when the statues of all the other tyrants were taken down, those of the deliverer of Himera were spared.

Gelón left a young son and three brothers, Hierôn, Polyzélos, and Thrasyboulos. His power was to pass to Hierôn, but Polyzélos was to have the command of the army, and was to marry Gelôn's widow and take care of his son. This arrangement did not last. Hierôn reigned splendidly, and gained great fame by getting round him all the poets and philosophers of his time, Simónidès, Æschylus, Pindar, besides Epicharmos, the founder of Sicilian comedy. And above all, his chariots and horses won prizes in the games of Old Greece, and their victories were sung in the odes of Pindar. But his rule was suspicious and cruel. He set spies upon all the acts of the citizens of Syracuse, and he was specially jealous of his brother Polyzélos, who was much beloved. Him, it is said, he tried to get rid of in a war, perhaps in Italy, perhaps against the Sikels. Polyzélos fled to Thérôn at Akragas, and war broke out between Thérôn and Hierôn. Some say that the two tyrants were reconciled by the poet Simónidês. Another story told how the people of Himera, oppressed by Thérôn's son Thrasydaios, offered their city to Hierôn, who betrayed them to Thérôn. Then Thérôn, so well spoken of at Akragas, went to Himera, and slew many of his son's enemies. The whole story is told confusedly; but Thérôn and Hierôn were reconciled, and Hierôn married a niece of Thérôn.

The chief action of Hierôn within Sicily, that of which he was most proud, was hardly to his credit. He wished to be equal to his brother, to have the honours of a founder. To win them, he moved the people of Naxos and Katanê to Leontinoi. He then repeopled Katanê with new citizens from various parts; he enlarged its territory at the cost of the Sikels; he then changed the name of the town to Ætna, and gave himself out as its founder. He called himself a man of Ætna, and as Hierôn of Ætna he won some of his victories in the games. And though he never ventured to call himself king at Syracuse, he set up his young son Deinomenês as King of Ætna.

The best side of Hierôn is seen out of Sicily, where he carries on Gelôn's work as a champion of Hellas against barbarians. Gelôn hardly meddled in Italian affairs. Hierôn, early in his reign, in 477, was able, without striking a blow, to save Lokroi from a threatened attack by Anaxilas of Rhêgion and Zanklê. And in 474 he did a work which is placed alongside of the day of Himera. The Greeks of Italy were often hard pressed by the barbarians; above all, Kymê was threatened by the

Etruscans. Hierôn sent help to the Greeks, and the fleets of Syracuse and Kymê won a great victory, which did much to break the Etruscan power, and gave Kymê a time of peace and prosperity. But an attempt to plant a Syracusan colony on the island of Pithékoussa or Ischia failed. In the British

GELA. C. 480.

SELINOUS. C. 440.

Museum we may still see the helmet which Hierôn dedicated for the Etruscan victory won in his name.

Here Hierôn won real glory; but he did nothing to help other Greeks in Italy against other barbarians. Anaxilas was now dead, and the government of his two cities was carried on by his steward Mikythos on behalf of his two sons. Mikythos sent help to the people of Taras or Tarentum, who were threatened by the Messapians or Iapygians in the heel of the boot. This is almost the only time that we hear of that people as dangerous to the Greeks; but it sounds like a foreshadowing of the general action of the nations of southern Italy which was presently to come. The two Greek cities were utterly defeated by the Messapians, but Mikythos kept his hold on both Rhêgion and Zanklê.

We have thus had to speak of the wars of Greeks against barbarians, both in Old Greece and in Sicily and Italy. Great victories were won; but in Old Greece the barbarians were driven out for ever, while in Sicily they came again. In Old Greece again the wars were waged by free commonwealths, while in Sicily they were waged by tyrants. We have now to see the cities of Sicily get rid of their tyrants, and enter on a time, if not of great victories, yet of wonderful prosperity and of a nearer approach than usual to peace among themselves.

VII.

THE GREEKS OF SICILY FREE AND INDEPENDENT.

B.C. 472-433.

[Our main authority now is the continuous history of Diodôros. He alone gives us any account of Ducetius. Pindar still helps us a little at the beginning, as he has odes addressed to citizens of Himera and Kamarina after they had recovered independence. The acts of Empedoklês come from his Life by Diogenês Laertios, compiled from various earlier writers. There are notices in Pausanias and elsewhere, specially notices of Sicilian luxury in Athênaios. And we now begin to feel the use of inscriptions, though those that concern us as yet are very fragmentary, and were graven, not in Sicily, but at Athens.]

WE now come to a time which we might call the golden age of Greek Sicily. Its cities are both independent and free. The tyrants are driven out. No Greek is under a barbarian master, nor does any Greek city bear rule over any other. The cities are wonderfully rich and flourishing, and are able to raise great buildings. We cannot say that there is no war either against barbarians or between one Greek city and another. But there is much less war than there is in the times either before or after. And the most remarkable war is one waged between Greek

TEMPLE AT AKRAGAS.

cities and a Sikel prince who was striving to bring about the unity and dominion of his own people.

We have marked our dates from the beginning of deliverance, though it did not come all at once. In the year B.C. 472 Thêrôn of Akragas died. Whatever men thought of him at Himera, he left behind him a good memory in his own city. He had greatly enlarged the town by taking in the great slope of the hill between the two rivers. He had made the walls which are still to be seen, and he had begun the great range of temples. At his death he received the honours of a hero, and was buried in a stately tomb in the burial-ground west of the city. The tomb in another part which is shown as his is of much later date. His power passed to his son Thrasydaios, who had ruled so ill at Himera. He ruled just as ill in Akragas. When, on what occasion we are not told, he began a war with Hierôn, his power at once broke in pieces. Akragas and Himera, which had no tie but that of a common master, parted asunder, and became again independent commonwealths. Peace was made with Hierôn, and Thrasydaios fled to Old Greece. There the people of the old Megara put him on his trial and put him to death. One can see no reason for this, unless that a tyrant was looked on as a common enemy of mankind, who might be brought to justice anywhere.

Here was a great blow struck at the cause of tyranny in Sicily. And Hierôn hardly strengthened it when in 467 he stirred up the sons of Anaxilas to demand from Mikythos an account of his rule in Zanklé and Rhégion. The faithful steward gave in an account which satisfied everybody, and the young men asked Mikythos to go on managing things for them. But he would not stay where he had been suspected. He went to Old Greece, and died in honour at Tegea. The sons of Anaxilas now took the rule of his two cities into their own hands; but they could not keep it so well as Mikythos had done.

The next year the great stay of tyranny in Sicily was taken away. In 466 Hierôn died at his own city of Ætna. There his son Deinomenês went on reigning, and made offerings at Olympia in his father's name. But the power of Hierôn at Syracuse and in the rest of his dominions passed to his brother Thrasyboulos, the last of the four sons of the elder Deinomenês. But the people of Syracuse were now weary of tyranny, and they presently rose to upset the power of Thrasyboulos. But it was a hard matter to get rid of him. For he had many mercenaries in his pay, and the men of Ætna came to fight for the house of their founder. Between them they held the fortified parts of Syracuse, both the Island and Achradina which Gelón had joined on to it. The men of Syracuse were driven to besiege their own city from outside. But the cause of Syracuse was felt to be the cause of freedom everywhere. From all parts, Greek and Sikel, which had been subject to Hierôn or where men had dreaded his power, helpers flocked to Syracuse. The tyrant was defeated in two battles by land and sea, and he presently agreed to surrender everything and go away quietly. He went and lived at Lokroi, where the memory of Hierôn was doubtless honoured. At the same time or soon after, the sons of Anaxilas were driven out of Zanklê and Rhêgion. The cities which had been under the rule of the lords of Syracuse again set up for themselves; even fallen Kamarina rose again, this time not as an outpost of Syracuse, but as a free colony of Gela. Thus all the Sikeliot cities were again independent, and all were free commonwealths, save only Ætna, where Deinomenês still reigned. So the famous line of the tyrants of Gela and Syracuse passed away from both those cities, and we are surprised to find that it had lasted only eighteen years.

The cities were now free, with neither tyrants within nor masters from outside. But it was not easy to settle the state of the new commonwealths after so many changes. The tyranny had swept away the old distinctions. At Syracuse, the city of whose affairs we hear most, there are no signs of any more disputes between the old Gamoroi and the old commons. But new distinctions had arisen. In the first zeal of deliverance men set up the feast of the *Eleutheria* in honour of Zeus *Eleutherios*, the god of freedom, and they admitted the mercenaries and others to whom the tyrants had granted citizenship to the same rights as themselves. But the two classes did not agree, and after a while (463) the old citizens, being the greater number, passed a vote that those whose citizenship dated only from the time of the tyrants should not be able to hold magistracies. The excluded class flew to arms. If fewer in number, they were better at fighting, and they again held the

Island and Achradina against the old citizens. This led to another enlargement of the city. The suburb of Tycha, outside Achradina on the north side of the hill, was fortified by the Syracusan besiegers of Syracuse, and became part of the city. The war went on for about three years, and it is not clear how it came to an end. But at last (461) the mercenaries were got rid of somehow.

Something of the same kind, disputes between the old citizens and the new, must have been going on in other cities also. For a general vote was passed by all the Sikeliot commonwealths that all the mercenaries everywhere should be settled in the one territory of Messana. This implies that that territory was open to settlement. It is moreover the first time that the name *Messana, Messènè, Messina*, is given to the town which had hitherto been called Zanklé. The dates are confused; but it was certainly about this time that the last Messenian war was going on in Peloponnêsos. Many Messenians were scattered abroad, and one cannot help thinking that it was now that the Messenian settlement at Zanklé happened, and that the city changed its name. It was the first town that took that name. Messènè in Peloponnêsos had hitherto been the name of a land, and the town of Messènè there was not founded till a hundred years later. Messana had the most motley population of any town in Sicily, and its policy was the most given to change, as one or the other party had the upper hand.

In one city even now the house of the tyrants still reigned. But Greeks and Sikels joined to drive Deinomenês and the Hieronian settlers out of Ætna.

The Sikels were led by their famous prince Ducetius, of whom we shall hear again. Ætna once more became Katanê; the old citizens came back; the honours of Hierôn were abolished, and his tomb was destroyed. But his settlers, and doubtless their king with them, were allowed to occupy the Sikel town of Inessa, further inland and nearer to the mountain. Its name was also for a while changed to Ætna.

Thus the Greek cities of Sicily fell back, as far as they could, on the state of things which had been before the rise of the tyrants. Each city was again an independent commonwealth. Those cities which, like Syracuse and Akragas, had borne rule over others, now lost their dominion, and with it that kind of greatness which comes of dominion. They gained instead freedom at home. The constitutions of the cities were everywhere democratic, or more nearly so than they had been before. And the cities were wonderfully rich and flourishing. Above all, strange tales are told of the wealth and luxury of the rich men of Akragas. But, after so many shocks and changes, above all after so many movements of men from one place to another, there were many causes of dispute within the cities. Men in Old Greece contrasted the constant changes in Sicily with the stability of the older cities where the same people had lived for ages. It is only at Syracuse and Akragas that we get any details. At Syracuse there were, naturally enough, disputes about the rights of particular men to lands and citizenship. And, what no democratic forms can hinder, there seem to have grown up a kind of official class which kept affairs in its own hands. Thus there arose *demagogues*, leaders of the people. This name was in its origin perfectly honourable, marking a lawful and useful position, though one which might easily be abused. The demagogue commonly spoke against the administration of affairs at the time, and he could sometimes carry a vote of the people in opposition to the magistrates. And it marks an exclusive kind of feeling on the part of a governing class when we hear complaints that all the young men gave themselves up to making speeches. For this was the time when oratory was becoming an art. And it began to be so first in Sicily. The first teachers of rhetoric were the Syracusans Korax and Tisias, and after them the more famous Gorgias of Leontinoi.

There was always a certain fear that the demagogue might grow into a tyrant. He did so both in earlier and later times. At this time there were no tyrants in Sicily; but there were men who were suspected of aiming at tyranny. There were several such at Syracuse. Thus about the year 454 one Tyndariôn gave himself out as the champion of the poor, and his followers formed themselves into a voluntary body-guard. The body-guard was the very badge of tyranny. Tyndariôn was therefore charged with treason, and was sentenced to death. But his followers rose, and, instead of being lawfully put to death, he was killed in the tumult. Presently the Syracusans adopted a law in imitation of the Athenian *ostracism*. That name is often misused. At Athens it meant that, when the state was thought to be in danger, a vote was taken in which every citizen wrote on a tile (ὄστρακον) the name of any man whose presence he thought dangerous. If 6000 citizens named the same man, he had to leave Athens for ten years. He could hardly be said to be banished, and he was in no way disgraced. He kept his property, and at the end of the ten years he came back to his full rights. Indeed his friends were often able to carry a vote to call him back before the time. At Athens this law worked well for a season, while the democracy was weak. When the democracy was fully established, it became needless, and gradually went out of use. We know much less of the working of the same institution at Syracuse. There it was called *petalism*, because the name was written on a leaf (πέταλον). The time of absence was five years. We know nothing of the details, whether they were the same as those at Athens or not. We are told that it worked badly, and was soon abolished by general consent. For it is said that, while it was in force, the best men withdrew from public affairs and left them to the worst men in the city. There may be some truth in this; for, after so many changes, political differences were likely to be much more bitter at Syracuse than at Athens. But these accounts clearly come from writers hostile to democracy. And it is quite certain that Syracuse was at this very time very flourishing at home and could act a very vigorous part abroad.

The constitution of Akragas after the fall of the tyrants seem to have been less strictly democratic than that of Syracuse. What we know about it comes from the Life of the philosopher Empedoklês. About him there is a silly story, how he threw himself into the furnace of Ætna, that men might think that he had become a god. And, as so often happens, this silly story has stuck to his name rather than any of his real actions. There is something very strange about Empedoklês. He seems to have given himself out as having a divine mission, and his followers believed that he did many wonders, even to raising the dead. He was certainly a poet and a physician, and he most likely had a knowledge of nature beyond his time. He cleansed rivers and did other useful works. And he was the foremost man in the commonwealth of Akragas in that day. He refused the tyranny or supreme power in some shape; he brought about the condemnation of some men who were aiming at tyranny; he lessened the power of the senate, and so made the state more democratic. In after days, when the Athenians came into Sicily and warred against Syracuse, and when Akragas was bitterly jealous of Syracuse, Empedoklês helped the Syracusans against Athens. For thus preferring the interests of all Sicily to the passions of his own city, Empedoklês was banished from Akragas. He went to Old Greece and died, and was buried at the elder Megara.

One can believe that the jealousy between Syracuse and Akragas, between the first city in the island and the second, had been handed on from the days of the tyrants or earlier. But it was at least greatly strengthened by events in the wars of the time. For, though

AKTÆON AND HIS HOUNDS.

the time was comparatively peaceful, there were wars. In 453 the commonwealth of Syracuse undertook to chastise the Etruscan pirates, just as Hieron had done. A fleet went forth and ravaged the whole Etruscan coast. Much spoil was brought in, and it would almost seem as if the Syracusans made some settlements in the islands of Corsica and Elba; but, if so, they did not last. And there was a war in the west of Sicily, of which we can make out nothing distinctly; but it looks as if Akragas and Selinous won some advantages over the Phœnicians. In neither of these meagre accounts do we see Akragas and Syracuse coming across one another in any way, friendly or unfriendly. It was another war with barbarians in which we hear of them in both ways, and which led to a lasting jealousy between the two cities.

This sprang out of the last and greatest attempt of the Sikels to throw off the dominion of the Greeks in their own island. Many of the Sikels on the coast had been made bondmen; but their inland towns were independent, and had largely taken to Greek ways. But they were hampered and kept in the background in their own land, and the more they felt themselves the equals of the Greeks, the less would they abide any Greek superiority. They had now a great leader among them, that Ducetius of whom we have already heard as helping against the Hieronians at Katanê. He strove to unite his people, and to win back for them the full possession of their own island. His schemes must have been very like those of Philip of Macedon a hundred years later. He would found a state which should be politically Sikel, but which should have all the benefit of Greek culture. He would be King of Sicily or of as great a part of it as he could, with his royal throne in one of the great Greek cities. But Philip inherited an established kingdom, which he had only to enlarge and strengthen; Ducetius had to create his Sikel state from the beginning. He started about the year 459, by founding the town of Menaenum, now Mineo, on the hill above the lake of the Palici, the special gods of his people. There mighty walls are to be seen, most likely of his building. From that centre, in the space of six years, he brought together most of the Sikel towns, all, it is said, except the Galeatic Hybla, into an union of some kind under his own headship. Unluckily we can say no more; of the terms of union we know nothing. For the power thus called into being he founded in 453 a new capital close by the holy lake, and bearing the name of Palica. He then came down from the hills to the plain, just as Philip came down from Aigai or Edessa to Pella. This was a step in advance; his next step, if possible, would have been to the sea. But we may be sure that he wished above all things to put his state under the protection of the great Sikel gods.

As yet Ducetius had not attacked any Greek city. His first step in that way was to besiege and take Inessa, now called Ætna. Thither, it will be remembered, the Hieronian settlers in the other Ætna, that is, Katanê, were allowed to move. Ducetius himself had helped to place them in the Sikel town. No Greeks gave any help to the remnant of the friends of the tyrants, perhaps with Deinomenes still calling himself their king. It was otherwise when Ducetius attacked the Akragantine town or post of Motyon. Ducetius was now so powerful that Akragas had to seek help at Syracuse. Ducetius won a battle against the joint forces of the two Greek cities, and took Motyon. The Syracusan general was charged with treason and was put to death. The Syracusans then sent a greater force, and, while the Akragantines besieged and recovered Motyon, they defeated Ducetius in a second battle. Defeat was what a power like that formed by Ducetius could not bear. There was no tradition of union among those whom he had brought together. All gradually forsook him, and the man who had striven to found the unity of his people was left alone, and in danger of his life.

Ducetius now took a bold step. He would throw himself on the generosity and the religious feelings of his enemies. He rode to Syracuse by night; how he passed the gate we are not told; but in the morning all Syracuse saw the dreaded Sikel king sitting as a suppliant at the altars of the gods of the *agora*. An assembly was at once held. Some were for putting him to death; but there was a general cry of "Save the Suppliant." Ducetius' life was spared, but he was not allowed to stay in Sicily. The Syracusans sent him to their metropolis Corinth, under a promise to live there quietly on a maintenance which the commonwealth of Syracuse supplied him with.

The Akragantines were much displeased with the

Syracusans for thus sparing the common enemy. And they were the more angry at what presently happened. Ducetius no doubt learned a great deal by living in a great city of Old Greece, and he made friends there. Before long he gave out that the gods had bidden him to plant a colony in Sicily. He set forth with companions who must have been mainly Greeks, and began his settlement at the same place, Kalê Aktê on the north coast, where Skythês of Zanklê had once wished the Ionians of Asia to settle. The Akragantines said that this could not have happened without at least the connivance of the Syracusans. A war broke out in which each side had allies; we are not told who they were. The Syracusans had the better; peace was made; we are not told on what terms. But from that time Akragas always had a grudge against Syracuse.

This war gave Ducetius time to go on with his settlement. Many joined him, both Greeks and Sikels; he was specially helped by the neighbouring Sikel prince Archônidês of Herbita. His Greek name is worth marking, as distinguished from the evidently Latin name of Ducetius. The new town grew and prospered, and Ducetius was supposed to be again planning greater things. But the chances of the Sikels came to an end when he died of disease in 444. Many of the Sikel towns remained independent; but their only hope now was to make themselves Greek, which they gradually did. And Syracuse conquered some of those which were near her own territory. One was Trinacia, the town which had in some sort given its name to the island.

Another was Ducetius' own Palica, which was destroyed. Thus all the great schemes of the Sikel prince came to an end. But he had done something. He had at least founded three towns, two of which lived on for many ages, and one of which, Menænum, now Mineo, lives on still.

For several years after this time there is no Sicilian

PANORMOS. C. 420 B.C.

MESSANA. C. 420 B.C.

history. We hear only that about the year 439, or perhaps somewhat later, Syracuse began to make great preparations for something. She built a fleet; she doubled the number of her horsemen; she was thought to be aiming at the dominion of all Sicily. Nothing more is told us; but it is plain that we have here the beginning of the story which we shall have to tell in our next chapter. The Chalkidians of Sicily and Italy were thoroughly frightened, and they began to seek for allies in Old Greece. Till this time Sicily has been pretty well a world of its own, and for the last generation a very prosperous world. The Greek cities were free and flourishing. The failure of the plans of Ducetius showed what was the destiny of the native races. Carthage kept quiet. She was no doubt only biding her time, and, before her time came, we have to tell what happened when Sicily became mixed up in the wars of Old Greece, and when the destiny of the greatest powers of Old Greece was fought out in the waters of Syracuse.

VIII.

THE SHARE OF SICILY IN THE WARS OF OLD GREECE.

B.C. 433–409.

[We have now, for the only time in the history of Greek Sicily, the narrative of a contemporary historian of the first rank. Through the whole of this chapter, except a very short time just at the end, we have the guidance of the Athenian Thucydides. In his earlier books we have to pick out what concerns Sicily from the general story of the Peloponnesian war. In the sixth and seventh books Sicily is the main subject, and they are the noblest pieces of contemporary history ever written. In the eighth book we have again to pick out what concerns Sicily from the general narrative, and just before the end we lose Thucydides, and are left to the very inferior, but still contemporary, Xenophôn. When Thucydides is to be had, we are tempted to despise Diodôros; and, during the greater part of the story, his account is, strange to say, below the usual level of his Sicilian work. But in some places he gives us valuable matter which he has clearly copied from the contemporary Syracusan historian Philistos. Philistos was indeed more than a contemporary; in all the latter part of the war he was an actual eyewitness and actor. The earlier Syracusan historian Antiochos ended with the conference at Gela in B.C. 423. And we have some subsidiary contemporary sources. There are many references to things that concern us in the plays of the Athenian comic poet Aristophanês, and the Athenian Isokratês, though he lived so long that he seems to belong to a later time, was contemporary with the great siege, and he has left a remark or two about it. Among the Lives of Plutarch, too, those of Nikias and Alkibiadês, deal with this time, and they preserve many things from Philistos and other lost writers. And, as usual, we pick up things occasionally in writers of all kinds, as Pausanias, Polyainos, Athenaios. Altogether there is no time before or after for which we have so much and so good materials.]

WE have now come to a time in which the Greek cities of Sicily get mixed up, in a way in which they have not been before, with the disputes of the mother-country. The more part of the Old Greek cities were now divided into two great alliances. These were Sparta with her following, and Athens with hers. Sparta was the head of the Dorians, Athens of the Ionians. Sparta was old-fashioned, oligarchic, slow to act. Athens was fond of new things, democratic, daring in enterprise. Sparta was strong by land and Athens by sea. But though in their home governments Sparta represented oligarchy and Athens democracy, yet in her dealings with other cities, Sparta had made herself better liked than Athens. The allies of Sparta were willing allies who followed her by traditional attachment. The so-called allies of Athens were mostly cities which she had lately brought under her dominion and which paid her tribute. When she had any willing allies, they were almost always cities which joined her out of some grudge against Sparta or some other member of the Lacedæmonian alliance. Before many years had passed, men found that Sparta, as a ruling city, was much more oppressive than Athens. But as yet Sparta represented free alliance and Athens represented subjection. The Lacedæmonian cause was therefore popular throughout Greece.

At this moment the two great alliances were at

peace, under the terms of a truce for thirty years made in the year 445. Even before that time, perhaps even from the time of the Persian wars, Athens, looking for dominion and influence everywhere, began also to look towards the West. As early as 454, we find, as an inscription shows, Athens meddling in Sicilian affairs and making an alliance with the Elymians of Segesta against some enemy, perhaps the men of Sikan Halikyai. In 443 Athens took the lead in founding the colony of Thourioi, near the site of the old Sybaris. And the beginnings of the Peloponnesian war itself had a close connexion with Sicilian and Italian affairs. The Korkyraians, ever in dispute with their metropolis Corinth, asked for help of Athens, setting forth the importance of their own island, as holding the key of Italy and Sicily. This was in B.C. 433. And in this same year, the year of her alliance with Korkyra, Athens also concluded alliances with Leontinoi in Sicily and with Rhêgion close to it. That is the beginning of the whole story. It is plain that Syracuse, whom we left at the end of the last chapter, strengthening her fleet and horsemen, was beginning to attack, or at least to threaten, her Chalkidian neighbours. They betake themselves to the great Ionian city for help. And when the war actually broke out in 431, it seems taken for granted on both sides that Sicily had something to do with the matter, though for several years nothing really was done on either side. Athens, as we have seen, was the ally of Rhêgion and Leontinoi; but she did nothing for them for several years. And, at the very beginning of the war, the Lacedæmonians bade the

Dorians of Sicily and Italy, as if they were members of their alliance, to join in building a great fleet. But for four years no ships of war passed either way between Sicily and Old Greece. The allies of Sparta in Sicily thought they did enough by vexing the allies of Athens in their own island.

In the year 427 we begin to see things more clearly. Syracuse with her allies was warring against the Chalkidian Leontinoi and her allies. With Syracuse, we are told, were all the Dorian cities of Sicily except Kamarina—we hear nothing of Akragas—and Lokroi in Italy. With Leontinoi were the other Chalkidian cities—that is, Naxos and Katanê—Kamarina, and Rhêgion in Italy. We hear nothing of Messana; a little later it was in alliance with Syracuse. The Syracusan league was much the stronger, and Leontinoi was hard pressed. Then the men of Rhêgion and Leontinoi, as allies of Athens, sent thither to ask for some real help. The great orator Gorgias of Leontinoi was one of the envoys, and he is said to have made a great impression at Athens. It was specially expedient at that moment to hinder any Sikeliot ships coming to the help of Sparta, for Korkyra was torn with sedition and could not do much for her allies. But Athens did not choose to run any great risk at first. A small fleet was sent, mainly to see whether it was well to do anything more. For about three years the war went on in a small way till, in the year 425, Athens sent a greater fleet to Sicily.

Nothing really great was done even now; but we hear several things which tell us a great deal as to the state of affairs in Sicily. Messana was always changing sides, according as one party or another in its mixed population got the chief power. One time, in 426 two Messanian tribes, attacked by the Athenians at Mylai, joined the besiegers in winning over Messana itself to the Athenian side. Presently the city changed back again to the Syracusan side. In Rhêgion there was a party which acted with Lokroi against their own city. Kamarina, allied with Athens, wavered; dislike to Syracuse and general Dorian sympathies were forces that pulled two ways. And we hear something of the older nations of Sicily. The Elymians of Segesta renewed their alliance with Athens, a fact of which nothing came at the time, but a great deal afterwards. Among the Sikels we hear that King Archônidês, the friend of Ducetius, was, as he might expect, a firm ally of Athens. In Inessa, the Sikel town of which we have heard so often, we find a state of things such as often was seen in Greece itself in the Macedonian times. The town was a separate commonwealth, but it was controlled by a Syracusan garrison in its akropolis. And one story most curiously illustrates Sikel feeling. The Sikels had a special grudge against Naxos, as having been the beginning of Greek settlement in their land. But they hated Syracuse yet more, as being far more dangerous. So when the Syracusans and Messanians attacked Naxos, a large body of Sikels came to its help. The Messanians were so much weakened that they called in fresh citizens from Lokroi. This grew into an union between the two commonwealths of Messana and Lokroi. Presently a new revolution drove the Lokrians out again. All these things show how much more unstable things were in Sicily, and specially in Messana, than they were in Old Greece.

Before long all parties in Sicily grew tired of a war in which nothing of any moment was done on either side. In 424 a larger Athenian fleet came, and its commanders called on their allies for more vigorous action. The call seemed to turn men the other way. Kamarina and Gela, colony and metropolis, first made peace with one another, and then invited the other cities to join with her. A congress was held at Gela; and there we for the first time come across one of the most memorable men in Sicilian history. This was Hermokratês of Syracuse, the chief man in that city. He was suspected of not being a friend to the democratic constitution; but no city ever had a wiser or truer leader in war and all foreign affairs, and men trusted him accordingly. At Gela he made a most remarkable speech. It is essentially the speech of the statesman of a colony. He cares for more than Syracuse; he cares for all Greek Sicily. But he does not, as some few did, care for the whole Greek folk everywhere. His teaching is that the Sikeliot cities should, if possible, keep peace among themselves; but that, in any case, they should not let any one out of Sicily meddle in their affairs. They should all join together to keep any strangers out. He tells the Ionians of Sicily that the friendship of Athens is all a blind. Athens, like all other states, is simply seeking dominion where she can find it. It is the common business of them all to keep her from finding any in Sicily.

Two things may be noticed in this speech. Hermokratês speaks of all Greeks out of Sicily as *strangers*. He does not even except his own metropolis of Corinth. And he speaks as if all Sicily were a Greek land. No one would find out from his speech that there were any Phœnicians, Sikels, or Elymians in the island. That is to say, the speech is one made for that particular moment. Just then no barbarian power was threatening, and a Greek power was. And when he argued against keeping out Athenians, he could not ask to let in Corinthians. Hermokratês knew perfectly well, and he showed it when the time came, how precious the friendship of Corinth might be to Syracuse, and how the enmity of Carthage was only sleeping.

Hermokratês prevailed, and peace was made. Each city was to keep what it had at the time. If Athenians or other strangers came in a single ship, they were to be received, but not more. The peace was accepted by the Italiot cities also, save Lokroi, where hatred to Athens was too strong. And the Athenian commanders were forced to accept it also, for which they were fined and banished when they got home. Something was gained. There was general, if not perfect, peace in Sicily; there were disturbances, but only in a small part of the island; and the next time the Athenians tried to meddle, they could do nothing at all.

The next quarrel that broke out in Sicily is memorable because it became one of the occasions of the great Athenian invasion some years later. After the

peace, the people of Leontinoi thought good to
strengthen themselves by taking in a body of new
citizens. This they did, but when it was proposed to
give the new citizens lots of land, the oligarchic party in
Leontinoi grew angry. We can only guess how things
stood ; but most likely the lots were to be made out of
folkland, which the rich men may have occupied, just
as they did at Rome. The oligarchs asked for help
at Syracuse. Syracuse was a democracy, and should
not have helped oligarchs ; but the temptation to win
dominion or influence at Leontinoi was too strong.
A bargain was struck. The commons were driven
out ; the oligarchs removed to Syracuse and received
citizenship ; the commonwealth of Leontinoi was
merged in Syracuse, and the town became a Syracusan fortress, like Megara. Presently some of the
settlers at Syracuse repented, and joined the ex-
pelled commons in occupying a Leontine fort and one
of the two *akropoleis* of Leontinoi. Thus there was
again a shadow of the Leontine commonwealth, which
sought for help at Athens.

Athens was now, in 422, much less powerful than
she had been in 425. Instead of sending a fleet, she
sent only two ships carrying envoys, who were to try
and get up a league in Sicily to check the encroach-
ment of Syracuse, and specially to restore Leontinoi.
Several cities, as Akragas and Kamarina, hearkened,
but nothing was done. No one would stir, unless
the Athenians came with a powerful fleet. So
Athens had to leave Sicily alone for six years,
during which we hear nothing more of Sicilian affairs.
The Leontine remnant seem to have held out, and

presently a new source of quarrel began at the other end of the island.

This was one of the frequent border-quarrels between the Greeks of Selinous and the Elymians of Segesta. Besides boundaries, they quarrelled about rights of marriage. This shows that the two cities must have had the *connubium* or right of inter-marriage, and that shows that the Segestans must have largely adopted Greek ways. The Segestans first asked help of Carthage, the common enemy of all

SEGESTA. C. 415.

Greeks; getting none there, they remembered their alliance with Athens some years back. So in 416 Segestan envoys came to Athens to ask for help against Selinous, and with them came envoys from the remnant of the Leontines to ask for help against Syracuse. Athens and Sparta were just then nominally at peace; but there were many grounds of quarrel, out of which war might break out again at any moment. Athens had now fully recovered her power. She was full of hopeful spirits, eager for some bold enterprise, and not knowing how great an undertaking it was to wage a really effective war so far off as Sicily. Their leader was the famous Alkibiadês, the most dangerous of counsellors, brave, eloquent, enterprising, but utterly unprincipled and thinking first of all of his own vain glory. He strongly pleaded for helping Segesta and Leontinoi, looking forward, so he said afterwards, to the conquest of all Sicily and of Carthage, and to all manner of impossible schemes. He was opposed by Nikias, the most trusted general of the commonwealth, an honest man and a good officer, but by nature slow to act, and who knew better than Alkibiadês how vain all his schemes were. He had also had the chief hand in making the peace with Sparta, and he did not wish to run the risk of breaking it. In the first assembly in which the matter was debated at Athens, it was voted to send envoys to Sicily, to see how matters stood there, and specially to find out whether the Segestans had any money, as they boasted of having a great deal.

The story went that these envoys and the other Athenians who went with them were taken in at Segesta in a strange way. The Segestans took them to see the temple on Eryx and its wealth, where the envoys were deceived by taking silver-gilt vessels for solid gold. Then they got together all the gold and silver plate in their city, and all that they could borrow anywhere else, and asked the Athenians to a series of banquets, at which each man passed off all the plate as his own. So the envoys went back, thinking that Segesta was a very rich city, and taking with them sixty talents as an earnest. This was early in 415. And now, though Nikias argued as strongly as he could against it, the expedition to Sicily was decreed. Three generals were put in command, Nikias himself, Alkibiadês, and Lamachos. Lamachos was not a rich man or a political leader like Nikias and Alkibiadês; so he had not the same influence. But he was one of the two best soldiers in Athens. The other was Dêmosthenês, of whom we shall presently hear.

And now the greatest force that had ever sailed from any Greek haven set forth to help Segesta and Leontinoi. Besides the force of Athens herself and her subject allies, she had in this war several willing allies, specially Argos, and Korkyra, ready to fight against her sister. There were 136 ships of war, 5,100 heavy-armed, 1,300 light troops. But where Syracuse was strongest, Athens was weakest. Only 30 horsemen were sent to meet the famous cavalry of Syracuse.

When men heard in Sicily that this great force was coming, the more part disbelieved the story. But Hermokratês told the Syracusan assembly that the news was true, and that they must make ready in every way to meet the danger. They must make alliances in Sicily, Italy, and everywhere, specially at Sparta, Corinth, and even Carthage. But they were not without hopes. He knew that the most experienced of the Athenian generals disliked his errand, and he said that the very greatness of the force would frighten men, and hinder the Athenians from getting allies.

All this was perfectly wise and true, as was everything that Hermokratês said and did about foreign matters.

But his home politics were suspected; so the demagogue Athênagoras arose to answer him. In his speech he gave the best definition of democracy ever given. It is the rule of the whole people, as opposed to oligarchy, the rule of a part. In a democracy the rich men, the able men, and the people at large, all have their spheres of action. The able men are to devise measures, and the people at large are to judge of them. But even in the most democratic states a kind of official class often silently grows up, men who are put forward in all matters, and who sometimes seem to keep the knowledge of affairs to themselves. Athênagoras, the opposition speaker, talks as the representative of those who were kept in the dark. He will not believe that the Athenians are coming; the tale is got up by official men in their own interests. Here he was quite wrong, and his counsel was bad. But he was wrong simply through not knowing the facts. On his own showing, his speech is both sensible and patriotic.

It was as Hermokratês said. The greatness of the force frightened even those who were friendly to Athens. The fleet met at Korkyra and sailed along the Italian coast; but it was only at Rhêgion that they were received with the least favour, and even there they were not allowed to come within the walls. And now the Athenian generals found out how the envoys had been cheated at Segesta. All the money in the hoard of that city was only thirty talents, that is, half a month's pay for the Athenian fleet. The generals then debated what to do. Nikias simply wanted to get the fleet home again with as little damage as possible. He said that they were sent to settle the affairs of Segesta and Selinous. Let them go and bring those two cities to any kind of agreement; then let them sail round Sicily, show men what the force of Athens was, and then go home. Alkibiadês, who had much wider schemes and who wished to show off his own powers of diplomacy, said that they should first make all the allies they could; then let them call on Syracuse and Selinous to do justice to Leontinoi and Segesta; and, if they would not, then attack them. Lamachos, who looked at things simply as a soldier, was for attacking Syracuse at once. Their force, he said, was now in perfect order; the Syracusans were frightened and unprepared. If they waited, their own strength would lessen, the fear of them would go off, and the enemy would be ready to resist them. But the other generals did not agree to this. So Lamachos joined the opinion of Alkibiadês. The Athenians sailed about to seek for allies, while the Syracusans made ready for the defence.

The only allies they found at this stage were Naxos and Katanê. The Naxians were really zealous for the Leontines. At Katanê men were divided; but the more part were for Athens. By the accident of some Athenian soldiers making their way into the town while Alkibiadês was speaking in the assembly, the enemies of Athens were frightened away, and the rest accepted the Athenian alliance. Katanê now became the Athenian headquarters. Messana would only give a market outside the walls. Kamarina would receive one ship only, according to the treaty. All this caused the fleet to sail backwards and forwards. One time they sailed into the Great Harbour of Syracuse; they made a proclamation for the Leontines to join them, and then sailed out again. They did a little plundering and skirmishing, not always successfully. In all these ways the Syracusans got used to the sight of the great fleet going to and fro, and doing nothing. Their fear of it therefore wore off, just as Lamachos had said that it would.

At this point Alkibiadês was called back to Athens, to take his trial on a charge of impiety. The famous story of the Hermês-breaking and all that followed it, so memorable in the history of Athens, does not concern us in Sicily, except as it turned Alkibiadês from the general of the Athenians into the best counsellor of Sparta and Corinth against his own city. For he did not go back to Athens for his trial, but escaped to Peloponnêsos, where we shall hear of him again. Meanwhile the command of the Athenian force in Sicily was left practically in the hands of Nikias. Now Nikias could always act well when he did act; but it was very hard to make him act, above all on an errand which he hated. One might say that Syracuse was saved through the delays of Nikias. He now went off to petty expeditions in the west of Sicily, under cover of settling matters at Segesta. He really did nothing except take the one Sikan town of Hykkara on the north coast, which was hostile to Segesta, and sell all its people. Himera refused to join Athens; nothing was done at Selinous; the Athenians could not take the Sikel town of Galeatic Hybla near Ætna, the seat of the goddess so called. Then they went into winter-quarters at Katanè (B.C. 415–414). The Syracusans by this time quite despised the invaders. Their horsemen rode up to the camp of the Athenians at Katanè, and asked them if they had come into Sicily merely to sit down there as colonists.

But the great danger against which Hermokratès had warned his fellow citizens was not to pass away so easily as this. The invaders were still in the land, and their leader could act vigorously whenever he did act. By a clever stratagem, a false message which professed to come from the Syracusan party in Katanè, Nikias beguiled the whole Syracuse force to come out to a supposed attack on the Athenian camp. Meanwhile the Athenian army went on board the ships and sailed in the night into the Great Harbour. There they encamped near the Olympieion; but Nikias took care to do no wrong to the temple and its precinct. A battle was fought next day on the low ground by the Anapos. The Athenians had the better, but the Syracusan horsemen kept them from pursuing. Nikias made this an excuse for doing nothing more, saying that he could not act without more horsemen and more money. So the day after the battle the Athenian fleet sailed away again, and took up their quarters for the rest of the winter at Naxos. One asks which did most for the deliverance of Syracuse, Hermokratès or Nikias.

Hermokratès meanwhile bade his countrymen keep up their spirits. They had done as well in battle as could be expected; they only wanted discipline. And to that end it would be well to have fewer generals and to give them greater powers. So at the next election, instead of fifteen generals they chose only three, of whom Hermokratês was one. They then went and burned the empty Athenian camp at Katanê, and spent the rest of the winter in preparations and fresh fortifications. The city was now again enlarged by taking the Tememitês, the precinct of Apollôn, within the walls.

The winter (B.C. 415–414) was chiefly spent on both sides in sending embassies to and fro to gain allies. Nikias also sent home to Athens, asking for horsemen and money, and the people, without a word of rebuke, voted him all that he asked. A very instructive debate took place in the assembly of Kamarina, where envoys from both sides were heard. Hermokratês again preached Sicilian unity, and called on Kamarina to help herself by helping Syracuse. The Athenians, he said, did not care for the Leontines and their Ionian kindred. They only wanted dominion, and they would treat Sikeliot allies just as they treated their allies nearer home. While they were talking in Sicily about the freedom of the Chalkidians, they were holding their metropolis Chalkis in bondage. Then the Athenian orator Euphêmos answered that the Athenians did everywhere what suited their own interests. They made their allies subject or left them free, just as suited them. They had made some of their allies into subjects, because it suited their interest to do so; others they had left free, for the same reason. In Sicily, at that distance, it was their interest to have free allies. It was not Athens, he said, but Syracuse, that threatened the freedom of anybody in Sicily.

The men of Kamarina were mostly inclined to
Athens; but it seemed safer to be neutral. So they
voted that, as the Syracusans and Athenians were
both their friends, they could not help either of them
against the others.

The Athenians also sought alliances among
barbarians as well as among Greeks. Most of the
Sikels took their side, but not all. And their help
was valuable, as supplying horsemen. Horsemen too
came from Segesta. The Etruscans also, old enemies
of Syracuse, sent some help. But nothing came of
an Athenian embassy to Carthage. The Carthaginians, we may be sure, were already biding their
time for their great attack on Greek Sicily. But
they meant, whenever they made it, to make it for
their own profit, and not to strengthen so dangerous
a power as Athens.

But the most important embassy of all was that
which the Syracusans sent to Corinth and Sparta.
Corinth zealously took up the cause of her colony
and pleaded for Syracuse at Sparta. And at Sparta
Corinth and Syracuse found a helper in the banished
Athenian Alkibiadês, who was now doing all that he
could against Athens. He told them everything, true
and false, about the wonderful schemes of Athens at
the beginning of the war. He told the Spartans to
occupy a fortress in Attica, which they soon afterwards did, and a great deal came of it. But he also
told them to give vigorous help to Syracuse, and
above all things to send a Spartan commander. The
mere name of Sparta went for a great deal in those
days; but no man could have been better chosen

than the Spartan who was sent. He was Gylippos, the deliverer of Syracuse. He was more like an Athenian than a Spartan, quick and ready of resource, which few Spartans were. We shall see what he did presently; but he had no chance of doing anything just yet. We must remember that at this stage Peloponnesian help to Syracuse has not yet come, but is making ready.

And now at last, when the spring came (414) Nikias was driven to do something. He had again moved his headquarters from Naxos to Katanê. Money and horsemen had come from Athens, but their horses were to be found in Sicily. Meanwhile Lamachos—for it must have been he—planned an attack such as he had doubtless meant from the beginning. It is very strange that the strong point called Euryalos at the western end of the hill of Epipolai had never been fortified. Almost at the same moment Hermokratês determined to guard it and Lamachos to attack it. The Athenian ships now carried the army to a point in the bay of Megara as near as might be to the west end of the hill, and then took up its station at Thapsos. From the coast the Athenians marched with all speed and climbed up the hill. At that very moment Hermokratês was holding a review of the Syracusan force in the meadows of the Anapos. He sent 600 men to guard Euryalos, not knowing that the enemy were already there. So first the 600, and then the whole Syracusan force that followed, were driven back by the Athenians. The Athenians now occupied all that part of the hill which lay outside

SYRACUSE SHOWING THE ATHENIAN SIEGE.

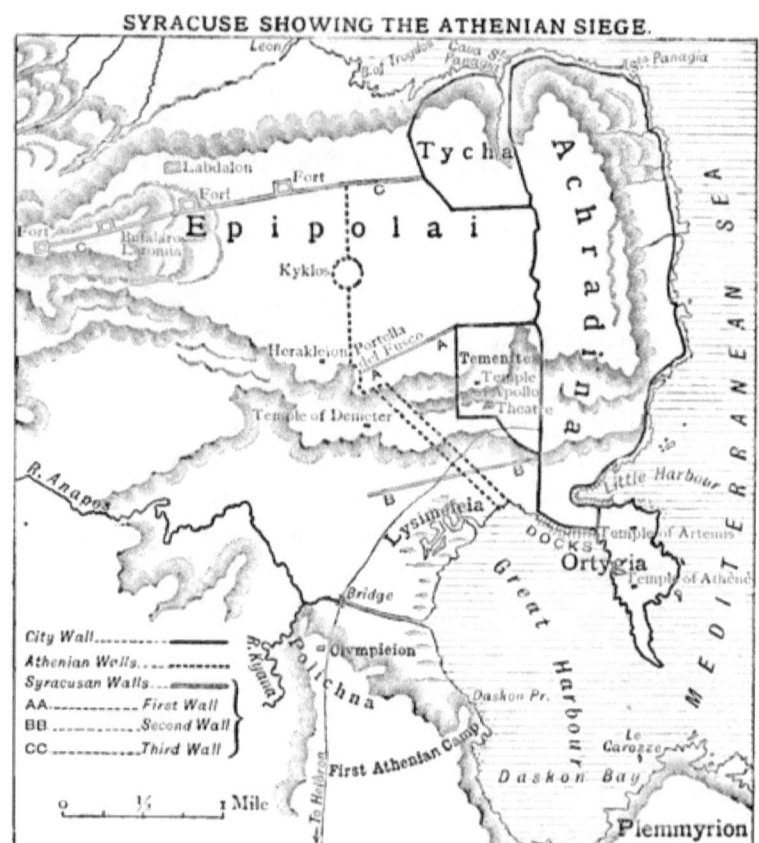

MAP OF SYRACUSE DURING THE ATHENIAN SIEGE.

the walls of Syracuse. They were joined by their horsemen, Greek and Sikel, and after nearly a year, the siege of Syracuse really began.

The object of the Athenians now was to build a wall across the hill and to carry it down to the sea on both sides. Syracuse would thus be hemmed in. The object of the Syracusans was to build a cross-wall of their own, which should hinder the Athenian wall from reaching the two points it aimed at. This they tried more than once; but in vain. There were several fights on the hill, and at last there was a fight of more importance on the lower ground by the Great Harbour. The Athenian wall had been carried down the south side of the hill; it was carried across the low ground in the shape of a double line, and it had nearly reached the water. The Syracusans were doing all that they could to stop it by means of a counter-wall. The Athenian army therefore went down, and a battle followed on the low ground by the Anapos. The Syracusans were defeated, as far as fighting went; but they gained far more than they lost. For Lamachos was killed, and with him all vigour passed away from the Athenian camp. At the same moment the Athenian fleet sailed into the Great Harbour, and a Syracusan attack on the Athenian works on the hill was defeated. Nikias remained in command of the invaders; but he was grievously sick, and for once in his life his head seems to have been turned by success. He finished the wall on the south side; but he neglected to finish it on the north side also, so that Syracuse was not really hemmed in. But the hearts of the Syracusans sank;

they grew wroth with Hermokratés and his colleagues and chose other generals. At last a party which had always been favourable to Athens prevailed so far that a day was appointed to discuss terms of surrender. It was at this darkest moment of all that deliverance came. On the very day that had been fixed for the assembly, a Corinthian ship, under its captain Gongylos, sailed into the Little Harbour. He brought the news that other ships were on their way from Peloponnêsos to the help of Syracuse, and, yet more, that a Spartan general was actually in Sicily, getting together a land force for the same end. As soon as the good news was heard, there was no more talk of surrender. That day was the turning-point of the whole war.

It was as Gongylos said. The Peloponnesian fleet was not large, hardly twenty ships, nearly all from Corinth and her colonies. And they were somewhat slow in coming; but they were at last on their way. Gylippos at first heard that Syracuse was altogether hemmed in. He gave up all hope for Sicily, but he thought of saving the Dorian cities of Italy. Nikias heard of their coming; but he only sent four ships to watch, and they were too late. For presently Gylippos heard that the Athenian wall was not finished on the north side, and that it was still possible to get into Syracuse by way of the hill. So he bade the Corinthians go on to Syracuse by sea; he himself sailed to Himera, and waited awhile, collecting troops, Greek and Sikel. Himera, Gela, and Selinous all sent help. The Sikel king Archônidês of Herbita, the friend of Ducetius, had lately died. He had been a firm ally of Athens;

but now Gylippos was able to win a large Sikel force to his side. Nikias heard all this; but he still loitered; the north wall was not carried to the brow of the hill. And one day the Athenian camp was startled by the appearance of a Lacedæmonian herald, offering them a truce of five days, that they might get them out of Sicily with bag and baggage.

Gylippos was now on the hill. He of course did not expect that the Athenian army would really go away in five days. But it was a great thing to show both to the besiegers and to the Syracusans that the deliverer had come, and that deliverance was beginning. Nikias had kept such bad watch that Gylippos and his troops had come up the hill and the Syracusans had come out and met them, without his knowledge. The Spartan, as a matter of course, took the command of the whole force; he offered battle to the Athenians, which they refused; he then entered the city.

The very next day he began to carry out his scheme. This was to build a group of forts near the western end of the hill, and to join them to the city by a wall running east and west, which would hinder the Athenians from ever finishing their wall to the north. Each side went on building, and some small actions took place. The Athenians also occupied the point called Plèmmyrion on the south side of the mouth of the Great Harbour. This served them both to watch the mouth and to secure a better station for their ships. To meet this stroke, the Syracusans occupied Polichna, and constant skirmishings went on between the two outposts. Gylippos too finished his forts and wall, and cut off the Athenians from all communication to the north. The whole stress of the war was now in the Great Harbour and the south side of the hill.

Another winter (B.C. 414-413) now came on, and with it much sending of envoys. Gylippos went about Sicily collecting fresh troops. All the Dorian cities, save Akragas, which remained neutral, now gave help, Kamarina among them. The cause of Syracuse was felt to be the common cause. Envoys were sent

AKRAGAS. C. 415.

to Sparta and Corinth, and at last a considerable force from various parts of the Peloponnesian alliance was got ready. The main part was very long in coming; but a few came more speedily; among them a gallant band from Thespia in Boiôtia.

Meanwhile Nikias wrote a letter to the Athenian people. This was an unusual step; hitherto he had sent only messages. He told the people that he wished them to know the exact truth, in how bad a case the army and fleet were. The ships were worn out; the men were deserting; Gylippos had come into Syracuse, and by his wall-building the besiegers were themselves more truly besieged. He did not say, perhaps he did not fully understand, how completely all this was his own fault. But he asked to be relieved of his command on the ground of sickness and long service. And he told the people that they must choose between two things. They must either recall the fleet and army before Syracuse, or else they must send out another force quite equal to that which they had first sent out two years before.

This letter came at a time when the Lacedæmonian alliance had determined to renew the war with Athens, and when they were making everything ready for an invasion of Attica. To send out a new force to Sicily was simple madness. We hear nothing of the debates in the Athenian assembly, whether any one argued against going on with the Sicilian war, and whether any demagogue laid any blame on Nikias. But the assembly voted that a new force equal to the first should be sent out under Dêmosthenês, the best soldier in Athens, and Eurymedôn. The people refused to relieve Nikias of his command, but ordered two of his officers, Menandros and Euthydêmos, to share it with him. Eurymedôn was sent out with this message, and with 120 talents in money; he then sailed back to join Dêmosthenês.

At Syracuse, since the coming of Gylippos, Hermokratês, though no longer general, was again listened to as an adviser. He and Gylippos were now exhorting the Syracusans to attack the fleet of the besiegers before the new Athenian force came out. He told them that the Athenians had not always been strong by sea; they had taken to it only at the time of the

Persian invasion; till then the Syracusans had had more to do with the sea than they. What the Athenians had done, the Syracusans might do also. And he said that the strength of the Athenians lay, not in their real power, but in their daring which frightened everybody. The Syracusans had only to meet them with equal daring. Thus stirred up, they made an attack on Plémmyrion by land and sea. At sea, after a hard fight, the Syracusans were defeated; but Gylippos took the Athenian forts on Plémmyrion, and the besieging fleet had now to go to the inner part of the harbour, to the small piece of coast between the two Athenian walls. Here they were pent up close to the Syracusan docks, and constant skirmishes went on.

Meanwhile the Syracusans were strengthened by help both in Sicily and from Peloponnésos. Their main object now was to strike a blow at the fleet of Nikias before the new force came. To this end the Corinthian officers taught them to make some changes in their naval tactics. The Athenian sailors did not think much of directly meeting an enemy's ship beak to beak. Their skill lay mainly in skilful manœuvres, sailing backwards and forwards, and attacking the enemy at any weak point. For this they had less room in the Great Harbour than in the open sea; so the Corinthians taught the Syracusans to make their beaks very heavy and strong for the direct attack. So taught, and skilfully guided by the Corinthian Aristôn, the besiegers attacked the besieging camp by land and sea. In the second day's fighting the Syracusans had the great delight of defeating the dreaded

Athenians on their own element. Their spirits rose high; Syracuse did indeed seem to be delivered.

It had been just when the Syracusans were most downcast that they were cheered by the coming of the Corinthians and of Gylippos. And just now that their spirits were highest, they were dashed again by the coming of Dêmosthenês and Eurymedón. A fleet as great as the first, seventy-five ships, carrying 5,000 heavy-armed and a crowd of light troops of every kind, sailed into the Great Harbour with all warlike pomp. The Peloponnesians were already in Attica; they had planted a Peloponnesian garrison there, which brought Athens to great straits; but the fleet was sent out to Syracuse all the same. Dêmosthenês knew what to do as well as Lamachos had known. He saw that there was nothing to be done but to try one great blow, and, if that failed, to take the fleet home again. The worst thing of all for the Athenians was the wall that Gylippos had built along the hill from west to east. Dêmosthenês first attacked it from the south side, but in vain. His next plan was to march all round the west end of the hill, and climb up by night at the point on the north side where the Athenians had gone up first of all. Dêmosthenês, Menandros, and Eurymedón, leaving Nikias in the camp, set out with provisions for five days, with masons and carpenters and all that was wanted, and marched round to the north side of Epipolai. The attack was at first successful, and the Athenians took two of the Syracusan forts. But the Thespian allies of Syracuse stood their ground, and drove the assailants back. Utter confusion followed. The moon gave light enough to see, but not to tell friend from foe. The watchword got known, and as there were Dorian Greeks, using the same war-cry, on both sides, the Athenians did not know Argeian friends from Corinthian enemies. At last the Athenians were driven over the hill-side, and many died by leaping or falling from the cliffs. The soldiers who had come first with Nikias, and who knew the country, for the most part escaped to the camp; the new comers lost their way, and were cut down in the morning by Syracusan horsemen.

The last chance was now lost, and Dêmosthenês was eager to go home. But Nikias would stay on; he said that he knew from his friends in Syracuse that the Syracusans were worse off than they were. He would not even agree when Dêmosthenês and Eurymedôn prayed him to move the camp to Thapsos or Katanê. But when sickness grew in the camp, when fresh help from Sicily and the great body of the allies from Peloponnêsos came in to Syracuse, he at last agreed to go. Just at that moment the moon was eclipsed. Few men then knew what an eclipse of the moon really was, and Nikias and his army were frightened at it as a warning against starting. Nikias consulted his soothsayers, and he gave out that they must stay twenty-nine days, another full revolution of the moon.

This resolve was the destruction of the besieging army. The object of Gylippos and the Syracusans now was to destroy the enemy in the harbour, lest they should get out and carry on the war from some other point. An attack was made by land and sea. The land attack was beaten back, chiefly by the Etruscan allies of Athens; but by sea the Syracusans had the better, and Eurymedon was killed. The hopes and spirits of the Syracusans grew higher than ever. They fully felt the greatness of their position, as the centre of the war which divided all Greece, with so many allies on their side, their mother-city Corinth, and the great name of Sparta herself. In the eyes of most Greeks at the time, Athens was the enemy of independence everywhere; let them destroy the armament now before Syracuse, and the enemy would be so weakened as to be no longer dangerous. The Athenians, on their side, had given up all hope of taking Syracuse; their only hope was to get home with as little damage as might be, and help their own city which was now so hardly pressed. It was felt on both sides that all would turn on one more fight by sea, the Athenians striving to get out of the harbour, and the Syracusans striving to keep them in it.

The Syracusans now blocked up the mouth of the harbour by mooring vessels across it. The Athenians left their position on the hill, a sign that the siege was over, and brought their whole force down to the shore. It was no time now for any skilful manœuvres; the chief thing was to make the sea-fight as much as might be like a land-fight, a strange need for Athenians. New devices were devised on each side. The Athenians tried grappling irons, called iron hands; the Syracusans covered their prows with leather to escape their grasp. Nikias, at his best now things were at the worst, went round exhorting all the

Athenian captains. He stayed on shore with the land force, while the other generals went on board.

The last fight now began, 110 Athenian ships against 80 of the Syracusans and their allies. Never before did so many ships meet in so small a space. The Syracusans had the great advantage of having the whole shore open to them, while the Athenians had only the small space between their walls. The Athenian ships sailed straight for the mouth of the harbour; the Syracusans attacked them from all sides. The fight was long and confused; at last the Athenians gave way and fled to the shore. The battle and the invasion were over. Syracuse was not only saved; she had begun to take vengeance on her enemies.

But there were still 40,000 men in the Athenian camp, and Hermokratês feared that they might gain some friendly point, Greek or Sikel, and might still be dangerous. But these 40,000 men were utterly broken in spirit; even the devout Nikias did not ask for the bodies of the dead. The men positively refused, when Dêmosthenês wished them to try one more chance by sea. There was therefore nothing for them to do but to seek some place of safety by land; and it was the object of Gylippos and Hermokratês to hinder them from so doing. But the day was a high day, a feast of Hêraklês, and in the maddening joy of the great deliverance men would not turn out to do any more work at least till the morrow. Hermokratês therefore sent a false message, in the name of Nikias' friends in Syracuse, saying that the roads were already stopped, and it was in vain to set out that night. By this means Gylippos found time to stop all the roads, bridges, and passes.

The Athenians waited one day, and then set out, hoping to make their way to some safe place among the friendly Sikels in the inland country. The sick had to be left behind, and the horsemen and heavy-armed had to carry their own provisions, for their slaves had all run away. In this strait Nikias, sick and weak as he was, did all that he could to maintain order and to keep up the spirits of his men. They marched along, but very slowly, as the Syracusan horsemen and darters harassed them at every step. It seldom came to hand to hand fighting. When it did, the Athenians still had the advantage. But when they got into a narrow and stony gorge which led to their first point, a gorge just beyond the present town of Floridia, they found it impossible to get on, because of the darters above and the heavy-armed who stopped the pass. On the sixth day, after frightful toil, they determined to change their course. They would now strike into the road to Helôron and march nearer the coast, till they could reach the inland country by going up the bed of one of the rivers. They hoped to find Sikel allies at the first of them, the Kakyparis or Cassibile.

They set out in two divisions, that of Nikias going first. Much better order was kept in the front division, and by the time Nikias reached the river, Dêmosthenês was six miles behind. But instead of Sikel friends, the banks were guarded by Syracusan enemies. The Athenians drove them off, their last success in the war. But they did not now think of trying the bed of the Kakyparis, but rather of some stream further on. They halted for the night by another stream, the Erineos. And in the morning a Syracusan force came up with the frightful news that the whole division of Dêmosthenês were prisoners. They called on Nikias to surrender also. A truce was made for Nikias to send a horseman to find out the truth, and he came back to say that the Syracusans had overtaken the division of Dêmosthenês in a difficult piece of ground, and had by many harassing

SYRACUSAN PENTÊKONTALITRON.
(*Prize Arms of Assinarian Games.*)

attacks brought them to surrender. Dêmosthenês made no terms for himself, but the Syracusans promised that of the 6,000 men that he had left none should be put to death either at once or by lack of food or intolerable bonds. They now called on Nikias to do the like. This he refused, but he proposed to Gylippos that the Athenian army that was left should be allowed to go free out of Sicily on condition of Athens repaying to Syracuse all the costs of the war, and leaving citizen hostages till the money was paid.

SYRACUSAN STONE QUARRY.

This was refused; the Athenians tried in vain to escape in the night. The next morning they set out, harassed as before, and driven wild by intolerable thirst. They at last reached the river Assinaros, which runs by the present town of Noto. There was the end.

The Athenians had doubtless meant to go up the bed of the river, and they did not expect to find so distant a stream guarded by Syracusan troops. But so it was. Yet the Athenians were so maddened by thirst that, though men were falling under the darts and the water was getting muddy and bloody, they thought of nothing but drinking. Then a body of Peloponnesians were sent down to slay them in the river bed. Nikias then prayed Gylippos to deal with him as he pleased, but to spare the slaughter of his men. No further terms were made; most of the horsmen contrived to cut their way out; the rest were made prisoners. Most of them were embezzled by Syracusans as their private slaves; but about 7,000 men out of the two divisions were led prisoners into Syracuse. They were shut up in the stone-quarries, with no further heed than to give each man daily half a slave's allowance of food and drink. Many died; many were sold; some escaped, or were set free; the rest were after a while taken out of the quarries and set to work. The generals had made no terms for themselves. Hermokratés wished to keep them as hostages against future Athenian attempts against Sicily. Gylippos wished to take them in triumph to Sparta. The Corinthians were for putting them to death; and so it was done.

So ended the Athenian invasion of Sicily, the greatest attempt ever made by Greeks against Greeks, and that which came to the most utter failure. It is wonderful that Athens could bear up as she did for several years after such frightful loss. In Sicily war still went on between Syracuse and the Chalkidians in the island; but the most notable result was that Syracuse and Selinous now repaid the help that they had received from Corinth and the whole Peloponnesian alliance by sending ships to serve against Athens (B.C. 412). Hermokratés and the Syracusans won special credit by their conduct in the war that was waging along the coast of Asia. The Spartans had now joined in an alliance against Athens with the Persian king Darius and his satrap Tissaphernes. They took pay from the barbarian and acknowledged him as master of all the Greek cities of Asia. Hermokratés did not directly refuse the alliance; but he withstood the satrap when he tried to cut down the men's pay, while the bribed Spartan officers connived at it. And when the people of Milétos pulled down the castle which Tissaphernes had built in their city, the Spartan commanders bade them be quiet and serve the King; but Hermokratés and the Syracusans stood their friends. The Sikeliot contingent was foremost in every battle, and they won themselves favour everywhere by their good conduct. But Hermokratés naturally drew on himself the bitter hatred of the satrap Tissaphernes.

Meanwhile party strife was going on at Syracuse. There, just as at Athens after the driving back of the Persians, the tendency of deliverance and victory was to make things more democratic. A popular leader named Dioklês had now the chief influence at Syracuse, and he is said to have drawn up a new code of laws. He was of course opposed to Hermokratês, and it was doubtless through him that (B.C. 409) a decree was passed deposing and banishing both him and the other generals who were in command in the Ægæan. This seems to us very unjust; but it is only fair to remember that the Sikeliot ships had been sent in the hope of a speedy overthrow of the power of Athens by the joint force of Peloponnêsos and Sicily. Nothing of the kind had happened, and there was doubtless sore disappointment at home. When the decree came out, the officers and seamen wished Hermokratês and his colleagues to keep their command in defiance of the orders from home. But they told their men to submit to the decree of the commonwealth, and consented only to keep the command till their successors came out. Then they withdrew. Many of the officers swore that, when they got back to Syracuse, they would do all that they could to bring about the restoration of Hermokratês and his colleagues. But he himself took other means to the same end which showed that the suspicions against him at home were not wholly without ground. Hated by Tissaphernes, he was on good terms with the rival satrap Pharnabazos, and from him he received a large sum of money to bring about his return to Syracuse how he could.

Meanwhile the Sikeliots in the Ægæan were able to show that they could do good service even without Hermokratês. They still kept up their character for bravery and good conduct. A strange adventure happened to some of them who were taken prisoners by the Athenians. They too were shut up in stone-quarries, to avenge the sufferings of the Athenians at Syracuse. But they contrived to dig their way out through the rock. Presently all the forces of Sicily were needed elsewhere. While the men of Selinous were warring on the coast of Asia, news came out that Selinous was no longer a city. The Sikeliots presently sailed back, being able to do the Peloponnesian cause one last service on the way. They helped to win back for Sparta the fort of Pylos, which Démosthenés had set up on Lacedæmonian ground in one of the earlier expeditions against Sicily. That was the last Sikeliot exploit in the eastern seas. There was reason indeed to call for every ship and every man of Greek Sicily for work in his own island. The news that had come from Selinous was true. A more frightful blow than the Athenian invasion threatened every Greek city in Sicily. The second Carthaginian invasion had begun.

HIMERA. C. 430 B.C.

IX.

THE SECOND CARTHAGINIAN INVASION.

B.C. 413-404.

[For this chapter our authority is almost wholly the narrative of Diodóros. He followed various earlier writers, and sometimes quotes them. Those available now were Philistos the contemporary Syracusan historian, Ephoros the general historian of Greece, and Timaios, the later Sicilian writer. This is one of the best parts of Diodóros' narrative, and it is plain that he must have made large use of Philistos; still it is a fall from Thucydides.]

CARTHAGE had been quiet, as far as concerned Sicily, all through the Athenian war. The schemes of Athens had threatened her; but nothing had come of the proposal of Hermokratés to seek Carthaginian help for Syracuse. After the defeat of the Athenians, there seems to have been perfect peace between Greeks and Phœnicians in Sicily. But two local wars were going on at the two ends of the island, out of one of which much was to come. The Athenian war was in a manner continued in the warfare which Syracuse was carrying on without much zeal against the allies of Athens, Katané and Naxos. And in western Sicily the story of the causes which led to the Athenian invasion were acting over again. Segesta and Selinous were still fighting on their borders, greatly to the advantage of Selinous. It was no use now for Segesta to ask help at Athens. Help was sought at Carthage, and, after some debates in the Carthaginian senate, it was granted. Segesta professed herself a dependent ally of Carthage.

The man at Carthage who was most eager for war was the Shophet Hannibal son of Giskon, grandson of Hamilkar who died at Himera. He could have had no spite against Selinous. In that town there was a

KATANÊ. C. 410.

party friendly to Carthage, and his father, banished from Carthage, had found shelter there. But the one passion of his soul was to avenge his grandfather. He hated all Greeks, specially those of Himera. Being made general with full powers, he first sent over a body of Africans, and took into pay another body of Campanians, who had been hired for the Athenian service, but had come too late. Had they been wandering about Sicily all this time? Hannibal contrived by subtle diplomacy to make Syracuse neutral; yet, when the Selinuntines asked for Syracusan help, it was voted, but not sent. But the dread of Syracuse caused Segesta to crave for further help from Carthage, and in the spring of the year B.C. 409, help came indeed.

Hannibal spent the winter in bringing together a vast army from all parts. Two things are to be noticed about it. A large body of Carthaginians gave their personal service, and Hannibal somewhere found Greeks who were not ashamed to take his pay against their brethren. With 60 triremes and 1,500 other vessels of all kinds, carrying 4,000 horsemen and all kinds of military engines, he sailed from Carthage to Lilybaion. He then left his ships at Motya, and marched straight upon Selinous. The news of his landing was brought to Selinous before he got there, or the city might have been taken unawares. As it was, there was no time to make ready for a siege. The Selinuntines were rich and prosperous; they feared their Segestan enemies so little that they had let their defences go out of repair. They were busy building the greatest of the temples which we now see in ruins, and Hannibal's coming kept them from ever finishing it. He advanced from the west; he took the Selinuntine outpost of Mazara; and he seems to have encamped on the western hill of Selinous. He then brought up his men and his engines, and attacked the central hill, the hill of the akropolis. Horsemen were sent to ask for help from Akragas and Syracuse, but the men of both cities were slow to march. Selinous, left alone, held out, we are told, for nine days of constant fighting. At last the Iberians made their way in; the rest followed; a general massacre took place for a while;

but some men escaped, and many women and children were spared as slaves. No such blow had ever before fallen on any Greek city of Sicily.

Those who escaped found a kindly shelter at Akragas. And presently a body of 3,000 Syracusans under Dioklês came, too late for any fighting. But Dioklês and Empediòn, the chief friend of Carthage at Selinous, who was among the refugees, made some kind of terms with Hannibal. Selinous ceased to exist as a city, even as a dependent city. It became part of the dominion of Carthage. Its walls were slighted; but the remnant who had escaped to Akragas were allowed to go back to the site. But it does not appear that Hannibal wrought any greater damage than was needed for his purposes. The destruction of the temples was clearly not his doing, but the work of an earthquake. But he had done all that his Segestan allies could have asked for. They would never again be threatened by the Selinuntines.

Hannibal had now seemingly done all that his commission from Carthage bade him do. But he had a further errand of his own; he came to avenge the death of his grandfather Hamilkar. Himera was not to be let off so easily as Selinous. There neither men nor stones were to be spared. With his whole force, strengthened by some Sikans and Sikels who had joined him, he marched on Himera, and attacked the town with his engines, and also with mines. The men of Himera bore up stoutly for the first day. At night help came. The force which Dioklês had led to Akragas had now grown to 5,000 and others were dropping in. A battle was fought beneath the walls, in which first the Greeks and then the barbarians had the better. At this moment, the Sikeliot fleet coming back from Asia, which had doubtless received orders on its voyage, came in sight of Himera. Then Hannibal cunningly spread abroad a false report that he was going to leave Himera, to march to Motya, to go on board his fleet, and to sail straight for Syracuse. Both Dioklês and the officers of the fleet fell into this trap; they thought their first duty was to save Syracuse. Dioklês marched back to Syracuse in such haste as to forget the sacred duty of burying the dead. Himera was to be forsaken; its inhabitants were to be taken by the ships in two parties to Messana. One party was taken safely; the rest kept up the defence for one day. The next morning, just as the ships came within sight to save the second party, the barbarians broke into the city, and all was over.

And now Hannibal had his own work to do. A massacre of course began; but a mere massacre was not what he wanted. He gave the spoil to his soldiers; the women and children were made slaves. Then all the men who were left, about 3,000, were taken to the place where Hamilkar had died. There they were insulted, tortured, and at last put to death as an offering to the ghost of Hamilkar. The walls of Himera were broken down; the temples were plundered and burned; the city, in short, was swept away. To this day there are mighty ruins at Selinous; but the hill of Himera stands empty.

So did Hannibal, with a mighty sacrifice, avenge

the death of his grandfather. He had cut Hellas short by two of her cities, and went back to Carthage with all honour.

And now we hear again of Hermokratês. He had two objects, to bring about his own recall at Syracuse, and to do something for the Greek cause in Sicily. With the money that Pharnabazos had given him, he built five triremes; he hired mercenaries; volunteers joined him; and at the head of 2,000 men he marched to Syracuse. But the people were afraid of

SYRACUSE. C. 409.   HEAD OF ARETHUSA.

him and would not vote his recall, and he did not wish to use force. He then thought of doing some exploit which should win him favour. With no commission from any commonwealth, he made war on the Carthaginians on his own account. He occupied the akropolis of Selinous, and rebuilt the wall, where his work is still to be seen. Men flocked to help him, and, with 6,000 men, he did what no Greek had done before, what no Greek since Dôrieus had tried to do. He marched into the very heart of the Carthaginian territory. The men of Motya were driven back into their island. He then went where no Greek soldier had ever been, into the land of Panormos, where he won battles and gathered the rich fruits of the Golden Shell. Pyrrhos, Atilius, and Robert Wiscard, all learned the way from Hermokratês of Syracuse. After this, many at Syracuse wished to recall him; but the vote could not be carried. He then made up his mind to do something which would still more strongly work on Syracusan feeling. He marched to Himera; he took up the bones of the men whom Dioklês had left unburied, and took them to Syracuse. The dead at last received their honours, and Dioklês was banished; but Hermokratês was not recalled.

Now at last he determined to use force. And well would it have been for Syracuse if he had come in, even as tyrant. As it was, he contrived to enter the city with a small party of Syracusans only; but the people withstood him and he was killed in the *agora*. Most of his followers were killed or banished. A few only escaped, those who were wounded and taken for dead. Among these was a memorable man indeed, Dionysios, son of another Hermokratês. We should hardly have looked to find him in the following of Hermokratês son of Hermôn. For the dangerous point of Hermokratês was that he was thought to be disloyal to the democratic constitution. No one doubted that he sought, first of all, the independence and greatness of Syracuse and then the independence and well-being of all the Greek cities. Dionysios professed attachment to democracy, but only as a means of getting power for himself.

About this time a new town was founded, which

came in some sort to represent the fallen Himera.
At the Baths of Himera the Carthaginians planted a
colony of Phœnicians and Africans. But it somehow
came again into Greek hands; so that the effect of
the destruction of Himera was that a new town, a
Greek town, though a dependency of Carthage, arose
nearer to the Phœnician strongholds than Himera
had been. Its name in Greek was *Therma Himeraia*,
and it still keeps the name of *Termini*, and has still its
hot baths. Its people are often spoken of as men of
Himera.

No one doubted that a general Carthaginian attack
on the Greek cities of Sicily would come before long.
And those cities, fewer by two than they had been,
were making every preparation. Syracuse got her
fleet ready, and found help in Italy and other quarters.
Akragas, expecting to be attacked first, strengthened
herself in every way, hiring mercenaries and getting
a Lacedæmonian commander named Dexippos, who
men hoped would be another Gylippos. Meanwhile
Hannibal was ordered to lead another host against
the Greeks. He had done his own work; he asked
to be let off on the ground of age; but he had to go,
only with his kinsman Himilkôn as a colleague. The
two set forth with a thousand ships of all kinds,
and an army of the usual kind, reckoned at 100,000—
some said three times as many.

The point aimed at was Akragas, but the Syracusan
fleet was afloat, and began the war with a successful
fight off the western coast. Then came the great
siege of Akragas. Hannibal pitched his camp on the

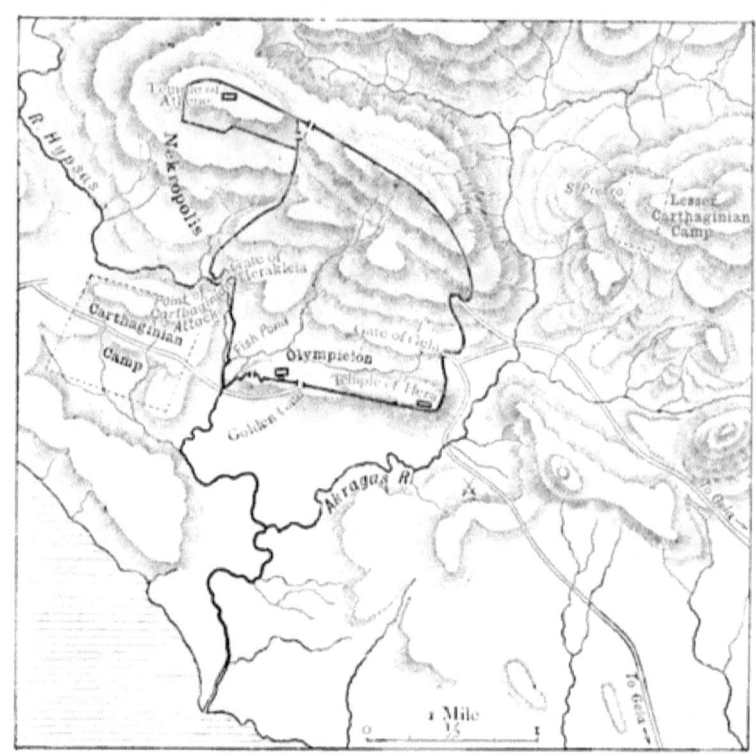

MAP OF AKRAGAS.

right bank of the Hypsas, near the south-west corner of the city, and planted a detachment on the heights on the left bank of the river Akragas to watch against any help that might come from Gela and the other cities to the east. Then he called on the men of Akragas to make peace with Carthage, and to join him against the other cities. When they refused, the siege began in the ravine west of the city. The Carthaginians destroyed the tombs of Théron and others. Presently a plague fell on them, of which Hannibal died, and which men looked on as the punishment of his sacrilege. But when Himilkôn satisfied the conscience of the army by burning his son to Moloch, they took heart again.

Meanwhile the Syracusan general Daphnaios was leading 30,000 men from Syracuse, Gela, Kamarina, and other cities, to the help of Akragas. The detachment on the heights came down to meet them, but they were defeated and driven to their main camp, and the allies took their post on the hill. Then the Akragantines called on Dexippos and their own generals to lead them out to battle, which they would not do. The people then streamed out of the city, and held an irregular military assembly, in which the allies seemed to have joined. Everybody believed that Dexippos and the Akragantine generals had been bribed. A tumult broke out; fear of Sparta protected Dexippos; but the Akragantine generals were attacked. Four out of five were stoned, and others were chosen in their place. Daphnaios now took the lead. He shrank from attacking the Carthaginian camp; but he cut off its supplies. But when Himilkòn brought his fleet from the west and cut off the corn-ships that were bringing food from Syracuse, the cry of bribery arose again, and now reached both Dexippos and the Syracusan officers. For one reason or another, all the allies marched off, and left Akragas to its fate.

Akragas, it must be remembered, was the second Greek city in Sicily in point of power, and perhaps the first in wealth and splendour. It was full of rich and bountiful men, and of noble buildings, among which the great temple of Olympian Zeus in the lower part of the city was fast drawing to perfection. Suddenly the Akragantine generals gave out that there was not food enough to go on, that the defence was to be given up, and the city itself forsaken. As many as 40,000 men, women, and children, many of them used to every luxury, had suddenly to leave everything and seek new homes. All who could not undertake the journey, the old and sick, were left behind. Some too would not go, among them Gellias, the richest and most bountiful man in Akragas, who sought refuge in the temple of Athênê on the akropolis. The flight was by night. Next morning the barbarians broke in, and slew and plundered. Gellias and his friends set fire to the temple and died in the flames. Himilkòn kept the town as winter-quarters for his army. He sent much spoil to Carthage, specially pictures and statues, for the Carthaginians had learned to value Greek art. So, after an eight months' siege, Akragas had fallen, though not so utterly as Selinous and Himera.

The alarm was great everywhere. The Akragantine refugees went to Syracuse, and accused the Syracusan generals of treason. They were strongly supported by Dionysios, who had so strangely escaped when Hermokratês was killed, and who had since made himself a name by good service before Akragas. In his speech he in some way broke the rules of the assembly, and the magistrates fined him. But a rich man, Philistos by name, paid the fine, and told him to go on; as often as the magistrates fined him, so often he would pay the fine for him. The people listened to Dionysios, and passed a vote, deposing the generals and choosing others, of whom Dionysios was one. Philistos was for a long while a firm friend of Dionysios, and he was one of the chief writers of Sicilian history. Unhappily we have only fragments of his writings.

Thus in the year B.C. 406, Dionysios took the first step towards making himself tyrant. The assembly now listened to him, and voted what he pleased. The Syracusans recalled the exiles, that is the friends of Hermokratês, and found quarters at Leontinoi for the refugees from Akragas. Two sets of people were thus attached to Dionysios. Every one now expected that the next attack of the Carthaginians would be on Gela. There was a Syracusan force there under Dexippos. But the Geloans asked for more help, and another body was sent under Dionysios. He threw himself into the political disputes of the city; he stirred up the popular party against the oligarchs, and procured the condemnation to death of the Geloan generals. Out of their confiscated goods he gave the soldiers double pay, thereby gaining more partisans. Then he went back to Syracuse to say that Himilkôn had tried to bribe all the Syracusan generals, and that he alone had refused the bribe. A vote was then passed, in the year B.C. 405, to depose the other generals and make Dionysios general with full powers. This was in itself a legal office. It did not mean that its holder was set above the laws, but only that, as a military commander, he could use his own discretion, without consulting colleagues or waiting for orders from home. But it was a power open to abuse, and, in the hands of Dionysios, it was only a second step towards the tyranny. He still wanted the body-guard. He did not venture to ask for it in Syracuse; so he marched to Leontinoi at the head of all the men under forty. There he held an irregular military assembly, and told them how traitors had sought to slay him. Then they voted him a guard of 600 men, which he presently raised to 1,000. He then dismissed and appointed officers as he pleased, and specially sent away Dexippos.

Dionysios now was tyrant. He had abused his legal office of general to win for himself a power beyond the law. He was now able to act as he pleased. He could hold assemblies, and men, under fear of his mercenaries, voted as he bade them. Thus Daphnaios and another of the deposed generals were put to death by what we should call a bill of attainder. Dionysios began to give himself something of the airs of a further prince. He married the daughter of his old captain Hermokratés. But as yet he had no strong castle: he lived in a house near the docks.

Meanwhile Gela, which he had been sent to defend, was besieged by Himilkón. On a hill outside the city was a famous temple and statue of Apollón. The Carthaginians, worshippers of their own Baalim and Ashtaroth, made war on the gods as well as the men of Greece, and they sent Apollón as a captive to their metropolis at Tyre. There he was heard of again seventy years later, when the Macedonian Alexander besieged Tyre. The men of Gela made ready for the defence. It was proposed that the women and children should be sent to Syracuse; but the women prayed that they might stay and share the fate of their husbands. Dionysios came to their help with a great force by land and sea, horse and foot, Sikeliot, Italiot, and mercenary. But he tarried so long on the road as to give great suspicion. And when he reached Gela and made an elaborate plan for attack on the Punic camp, the different divisions failed to act in concert, and the division which he himself commanded did nothing at all. Still greater suspicion was now awakened, and most of all when he gave out that Gela must be forsaken, and that its inhabitants must get to Syracuse how they could. And on the road he did the like by Kamarina. Not a Greek city was left along the whole southern coast of Sicily.

On the road indignation burst forth. The horsemen, the rich men of Syracuse, took the lead. They rode to the city with all speed, so as to be there before the tyrant could follow. They entered by the gate, no one suspecting them; but they disgraced a good cause by going to Dionysios' house and shamefully maltreating his wife, the daughter of Hermokratés.

It does not seem that the people in general took their side; they had not made a good beginning, and men may have thought that an oligarchy would be worse than the tyranny. Presently Dionysios was at the gate, which he found shut against him. But he made his way in by burning the gate with a great heap of tall reeds. He then slew and banished as he thought good, and was fully master of Syracuse. Some of the horsemen escaped to Inessa or Ætna. And the refugees from Gela and Kamarina were afraid to enter Syracuse and joined the Akragantines at Leontinoi. Two settlements of Dionysios' enemies were thus formed.

There can be no doubt that the suspicion against Dionysios was perfectly true. He who had complained so bitterly of the other generals had, even if his complaints were true, done worse than they. He had betrayed everything, including two Greek cities, to the barbarians. This at first seems strange, as in after times Dionysios was as ready as Gelón to make himself the champion of Hellas. But the matter became clear by the treaty which he presently made with Himilkôn. They two settled the fate of Sicily, and that on terms most of which must have been most galling to Dionysios, or to any Syracusan. Syracuse was cut short and hampered in every way, and Carthage was in every way strengthened. Carthage was to keep her old Phœnician dependencies, as also the Sikans, Selinous, Akragas, and the new town of Therma, as her immediate subjects. Gela and Kamarina were to be unwalled towns, paying tribute. Thus Carthage got the dominion of the whole south coast and an enlarged territory on the north. On the other hand, the Sikels were to be free; so was Messana; and Leontinoi, with its mixed population, was to be again a separate commonwealth independent of Syracuse. Syracuse was thus quite hemmed in with no means of advance in any way. But the price of all this was that Carthage gave Dionysios a guaranty of his dominion over Syracuse, of which one would like to see the exact words. It is plain that what Dionysios wanted was to have the support of Carthage till he had fully established his own power at home. Then he would cast the treaty aside, and win, for Syracuse and for himself, all that had been set free or given up to Carthage. And to a great extent he did so.

KAMARINA. C. 415.

X.

THE TYRANNY OF DIONYSIOS.

B.C. 405–367.

[The main authority for the reign of Dionysios is still the narrative of Diodôros. This part of his work is of very different degrees of value. Some parts are very good and full, evidently reproducing older writers, largely Philistos. In other parts he is very meagre and confused, and towards the end of the tyrant's life he tells us very little. We have also a little really contemporary matter from two Attic writers, the orator Lysias and the pamphleteer Isokratês. There is also a series of letters attributed to the philosopher Plato, dealing largely with Syracusan affairs, beginning in Dionysios' time. There is no reason to think they were really written by Plato; but they were most likely written by some one of his school not long after; so they may well give us Plato's views of things. Plutarch's Life of Diôn also begins in Dionysios' time. The fame of the tyrant was so great that the references to him and stories about him in later writers are endless, almost equal to those about Phalaris. And we begin to have some documentary evidence, in the form of Attic inscriptions with decrees in honour of Dionysios. But we unluckily have no documents from Syracuse of his age.]

DIONYSIOS was now tyrant of Syracuse, and he remained so for the rest of his life. Several attempts were made to get rid of him; but he kept his power for thirty-eight years, and he handed it on to his son. He knew how to keep power. He stuck at no cruelty or treachery that could serve his purposes, but he does not seem to have taken any pleasure in wanton oppression, and he strictly kept himself from the kinds of excess which overthrew many tyrants. As a ruler, he established a greater power than had ever been seen before in the Greek world. He was never lord of all Sicily; but he came nearer to being such than any man had ever done before, and his power reached far beyond Sicily. Syracuse he made at once the head of a great dominion, and in itself the greatest city of Hellas and of Europe. And his reign marks an epoch in the history of the world. He was the beginner of many things which were carried out more fully by the Macedonian kings. With him begins a wider and more complicated world than that of the separate Greek commonwealths, a world more like the modern world, with political powers of various kinds side by side. And his reign marks a great advance in the military art, both in the invention of engines of war and in the use of different kinds of troops in concert. He is at his best in his wars with Carthage. He is at his worst when he destroys Greek cities or peoples them with barbarian mercenaries. These were chiefly Italians, the foreshadowing of a time when Sicily was to pass under the dominion of an Italian city. His long reign covers a great space in Greek history. When he began, the Peloponnesian war was not yet ended; when he died, Philip of Macedon was growing up.

With Carthage he waged four wars, which enable us to part his reign into periods. During the first period, of eight years (405-397), he was strengthening his power in Syracuse and Sicily generally. He kept peace with Carthage; but he was evidently waiting till he could throw aside the galling treaty. His first act was to build a strong place for his own defence. To this end he turned the whole Island of Syracuse into a fortress. He built a new wall between it and the mainland; he built a strong castle on the isthmus and another at the extreme point of the Island. The former was his own dwelling. These strongholds he filled with mercenaries, and he allowed no one but his most trusted friends to live in the Island. The Island thus held the same place as the *akropolis* in other cities, and it is often, though incorrectly, so called. Men said that he had bound Syracuse down with chains of adamant.

He first broke the treaty by a Sikel war (404–403), which nearly brought about his overthrow. He marched against the Sikel town of Herbessus; but now that the Syracusans had arms in their hands, a large body revolted and made a league with the horsemen at Ætna. Dionysios gave up the siege of Herbessus; he went back to Syracuse, and there was besieged by the revolters. It was as in the time of Thrasyboulos, only Thrasyboulos had had no such stronghold as Dionysios had. The Syracusans again attacked the city from the hill, and they got ships from Rhêgion and Messana to attack the Island. They prevailed so far that many of the tyrant's mercenaries went over to them, tempted by offers of citizenship. This desertion seems to have quite broken Dionysios' purpose, and in a debate with his intimate friends, Philistos and others, he sought for means of escape. But Helôris, who is called his adopted father, answered, in words which were often quoted, that the robe of the ruler was a noble winding-sheet. Another friend bade him ride to the Campanians in the service of Carthage, who were quartered somewhere on the north coast. He took heart again; he did not ride to the Campanians, but he did send a message asking their help. Meanwhile he lulled his enemies to sleep by pretending to negotiate, offering to go away in five days with his private property. The besiegers were so foolish as to give up all watchfulness, and to send away the horsemen from Ætna. The Campanians and other mercenaries were thus able to come to the help of Dionysios, and he now went forth and defeated the disorderly besiegers in a battle. It was his policy to seem merciful; so he checked the slaughter and buried the slain. He then made a merit of this to the rest of his enemies who had escaped to Ætna. He invited them to come back on an amnesty, and some came. But others, when he boasted of burying the dead, answered that they hoped soon to be able to do as much for him.

The siege was now at an end. It was the Campanians who had won the victory for the tyrant. He did not trust them, but sent them away with great rewards. They marched towards the Carthaginian territory in the west, and were welcomed at the Sikan town of Entella, which was friendly to Carthage. But in the night they slew the men and took the town and the women to themselves. Entella became a Campanian town, the first place in Sicily, but not the last, which was seized in this way by Italian mercenaries. A new element was thus added to the mixed population of the island.

Sicily now began to be mixed up again with the affairs of Old Greece. The Peloponnesian War had ended in the utter destruction of the Athenian power. Sparta was now supreme in Greece, and the city which had professed to set all Greeks free was now holding down the towns everywhere under narrow oligarchies. It was the interest of Dionysios to attach himself as closely as might be to Sparta, and it was the interest of Sparta to support the power of Dionysios. But to support tyrants anywhere was against the policy of Corinth in any age. There was therefore a difference between Sparta and Corinth with regard to Syracusan affairs, and it is possible that this difference may have helped to bring about the open breach between Sparta and Corinth which took place some years later (B.C. 395). It is certain, though the story is told with a good deal of confusion, that, about this time, there were agents of both cities at Syracuse, the Spartan Aristos working for Dionysios and the Corinthian Nikoteles taking the popular side. We are further told that the Spartan brought about the murder of the Corinthian. At one stage no less a person than Lysandros himself came as Spartan envoy to Syracuse, and the alliance between the two oppressive powers was firmly settled.

Dionysios went on strengthening himself with more mercenaries and more fortifications. He now felt strong enough altogether to despise the treaty with Carthage, and to attack whom he would. And he used bribes quite as freely as arms. He drove away the refugee horsemen from Ætna, and then raised the old cry of Dorian against Chalkidian. Beginning in the year

B.C. 403, he attacked several cities, Greek and Sikel, Leontinoi, Henna, Herbita, but he did little more than harry their lands. Herbita was then ruled by a remarkable man, a second Archônidês. He founded a new city, Halæsa, on the same north coast where the other Archônidês had helped Ducetius to found Kalê Aktê. Sicily was then enriched by a new city; but meanwhile it lost an old one, and another was handed over to barbarians. One does not see that Dionysios had any ground of offence against either Naxos or Katanê, except that they were Chalkidian. But in 403 he got possession of both by treachery; and sold their people into slavery. Naxos, oldest of Greek cities in Sicily, he utterly destroyed and gave its lands to the neighbouring Sikels. The altar of Apollôn Archêgetês ceased to stand on Greek soil. Katanê he gave as a dwelling-place to his Italian mercenaries. The Leontines thought it was wise to surrender quietly, and they fared better. Leontinoi again ceased to be a separate city, and became once more a mere Syracusan outpost. But its people were not sold. They were taken to Syracuse and received citizenship, such citizenship as was where Dionysios was tyrant.

Thus was Hellas cut short in a way which had never before been known in Sicily. Greek rulers had destroyed Greek cities. Barbarians had occupied Greek cities. But no Greek as yet had handed over a Greek city to barbarians. Dionysios had given over Katanê to Campanians and the site of Naxos to Sikels. It is not always easy to understand his motives, the more so as he was all this time making ready for an enterprise for which one would have

thought that he would have been glad of the help and
good will of all the Greeks of the island. He had not
thought of keeping the treaty with Carthage one

SYRACUSE UNDER DIONYSIOS.

moment longer than he was obliged; he was planning
his first Punic war. But a Punic war was sure to bring
with it a Carthaginian attack on Syracuse; his first
object therefore was the strengthening of the city.

He had learned, both in the Athenian war and in his later war with the revolted Syracusans, how dangerous to the city was the undefended state of the hill. We know not whether any of the walls and forts built during the Athenian siege were still standing ; but, if any were left, they did not amount to a complete fortification of the hill. This great work Dionysios now, in the year 402, undertook, and he carried it out in a wonderfully short time. He carried on the north wall of Achradina and Tycha as far as the neck of Euryalos. There he built a strong castle, and carried the wall along the south side, seemingly to the point called *Portella del Fusco*. There the wall must have come down the hill into the lower ground, and it must have been carried down to the shore of the Great Harbour. It was a wonderful work, most carefully done, and a great deal of it is left. And this, unlike the fortification of the Island, was not a mere strengthening of his own power, but a real strengthening of the city. It was a work of which any lawful king or magistrate might have been proud. To such an end the people worked gladly along with the tyrant, and the work did something to make his tyranny less hateful.

Thus Dionysios made Syracuse, at all events in extent, the greatest city of Hellas and of Europe. He was now ready to wage war with the great barbarian commonwealth. We know not whether these events have anything to do with the fact that about this time he founded a new city at the foot of Ætna. This was close by the temple of the Sikel fire-god Hadranus. We know not whom he planted there, but

PASSAGE IN THE CASTLE OF EURYALOS.

the town took the name of the god, Hadranum, now Adernò, and its people looked on themselves as his special servants. As for the older cities, there was now, between Dionysios and the Carthaginians, only one free Greek commonwealth left in Sicily, namely Messana. And by this time the dread of Dionysios was spreading beyond Sicily. The Chalkidian town of Rhêgion began a war with Dionysios, which delayed his Punic enterprise somewhat. But as Rhêgion was but feebly supported by Messana, both cities were soon glad to make peace. And just then it suited Dionysios not to press hardly on them. To strengthen his interest in Italy, he thought of taking a wife there. But the Rhegines, whom he first asked, refused him. Some say that they added the insult that he might, if he pleased, take the hangman's daughter. But at Lokroi they gave him Dôris, the daughter of one of their chief men. On the same day that he married Dôris, he also married the Syracusan Aristomachê, both of them with all usual forms. For a man to have two wives at once was utterly against all Greek custom. But Dionysios kept them both; he had children by both, and treated them with equal honour.

All this time he was making ready for the war with Carthage. He hired mercenaries; he built ships of greater size than had been seen before, *quinqueremes*, with five banks of oars, as well as *triremes* with three. He invented the *catapult*, a machine for hurling great stones, and made various military improvements. His skill was shown above all in making troops of different kinds act in concert. By hiring the best soldiers of all kinds he was able to do this more thoroughly than generals of commonwealths who commanded only their own citizens. When all was ready, he gathered an assembly, and set forth the grounds for a war with Carthage. He would begin at once; for Carthage, he said, was just now weakened by a plague. Every one agreed. If they hated the tyrant, they hated the Carthaginians still more; and they thought that in war-time, with arms in their hands, they might find some chance of getting rid of him. Then he went through the form of sending an embassy to Carthage to declare war unless they agreed to set free all the Greek cities in Sicily. But, without waiting for an answer, he gave leave to the Syracusans to plunder the rich houses and stores of the Carthaginian merchants who were living at Syracuse. We see by this, as by some cases of intermarriage, that there was a good deal of intercourse between the Greek and the Phœnician city when they were not at war. And in the other Greek towns which were under Carthaginian dominion or supremacy, the people rose and put to death all the Carthaginians among them with insult and torture. Though a tyrant was at the head, it was a general rising of the Greeks of Sicily against barbarian enemies and masters.

And now the first Punic war of Dionysios began in the year B.C. 397. How and where to begin he had learned from his old captain Hermokratês. He carried the war at once into the Phœnician corner of Sicily. Never had any such force gone forth from any Greek city. When the lord of Syracuse made war, it was as if Athens had sent forth her fleet, and the Peloponnesian alliance its army, on the same errand.

APPARENT ARCH IN THE WALL OF ERYX.

With 80,000 foot and 3,000 horse, Dionysios marched along the south coast, while 200 ships sailed along in concert. The Greek towns on the road, which had just risen against the Punic yoke, added such forces as they could. He crossed the stream of Mazaros; then, finding that the Elymians of Eryx were ready to revolt against their Carthaginian masters, he marched thither and received them as allies. Then he began the great undertaking of this war, the siege of Motya.

Motya, on the western side of Sicily, was, like his own Ortygia on the eastern side, an island joined to

MOTYA. C. 400.

the mainland by a mole. But Motya, unlike Ortygia, was surrounded by its own haven, and the town had not spread on to the mainland. There was but little space on the island; so the houses of the rich men of Motya were of many stories, rising high above the wall. The citizens were stout-hearted, and there was a Carthaginian garrison, among whom, strange to say, there were some mercenary Greeks. They broke down the mole, and made ready for the defence.

The mole that was thus destroyed was merely a road. Dionysios began the siege by making it afresh and making it much wider, so that he could bring up his engines on it to play on the walls of Motya. He brought

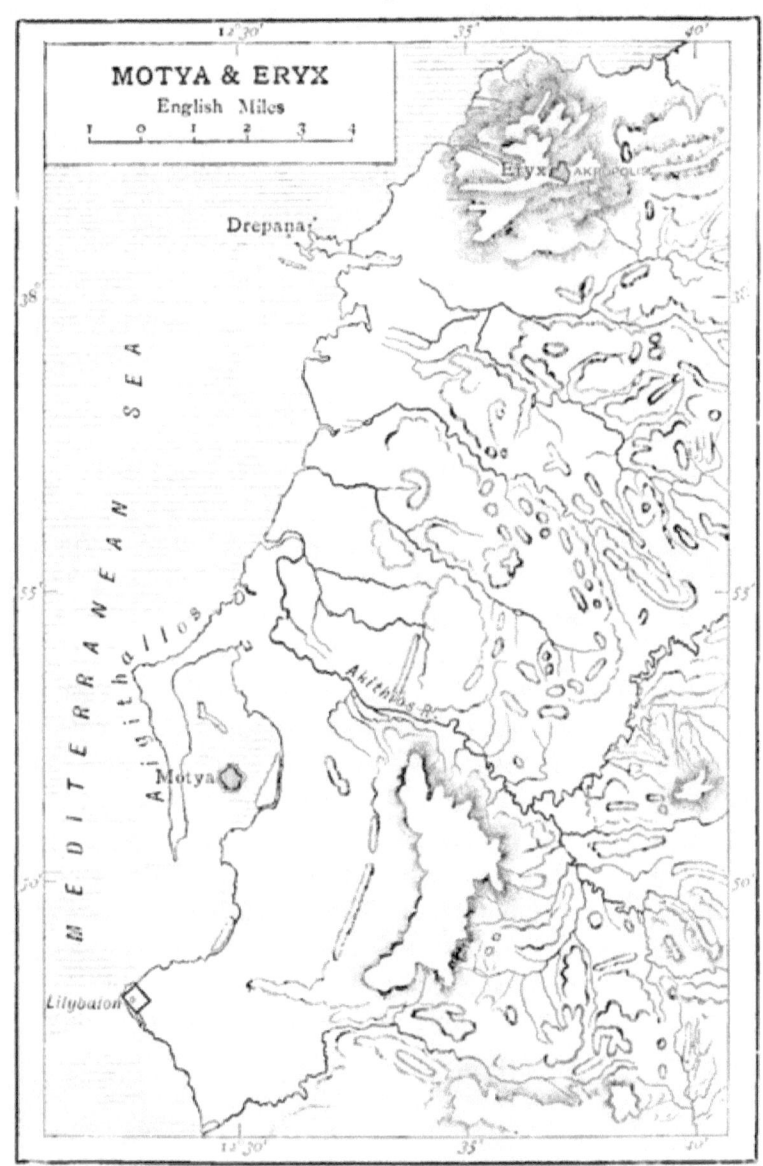

MAP OF MOTYA AND ERYX.

his ships into the harbour. There was then a long peninsula to the north-west of Motya, where there now are a number of islands; the ships were placed north of Motya by the isthmus. Meanwhile Dionysios went and made alliances with the neighbouring Sikans, and laid siege to Entella and Segesta which held out for the Carthaginians. The two Elymian towns, Eryx and Segesta, were thus on different sides. When the mole was finished, he went back to Motya. Meanwhile Himilkon tried to call off Dionysios from Motya by sending ten ships to make a dash on the Great Harbour of Syracuse. So they did, and destroyed such ships as they found in it; but nothing more came of the diversion. Then Himilkon made another sudden dash on the Greek ships in the haven of Motya. They were drawn up on land: but the engineers of Dionysios contrived to drag them across the isthmus. Then they were in the open sea, and sailed round to the north of the haven. But Himilkon did not care to attack a force that was stronger than his own, and Motya was left to its fate.

And now began the real fighting for Motya. It was like the Punic sieges of Selinous and Himera turned the other way. The distinctive thing at Motya was the tall houses. The engines of Dionysios were made of vast height to reach them. Bridges were thrown across, and men fought high in the air, many falling down from the height. This went on for some days. Every evening Dionysios called off his men, and the defenders took rest. This suggested a night attack; by that means the Greeks entered, and the city was taken. The Motyans fought on with true Semitic stubbornness; but the city was in the hands of the besiegers. Dionysios stopped the slaughter as soon as he could, that the people might be sold as slaves. To the Greek traitors who had taken service with the barbarians he was harsher. They were crucified, a piece of cruelty which the Greeks now began to learn from the Carthaginians. The rich spoil of the merchant city was given to the soldiers.

This was the greatest success that any Greek had ever won in Phœnician warfare. Yet in Sicily itself less came of the taking of Motya than might have been looked for. It may be that Dionysios found that such distant conquests could not really be kept. He left a garrison, chiefly of Sikels, in Motya; he left his brother Leptinês with the fleet to watch the coast, and he also left forces to go on with the sieges of Segesta and Entella. He himself went back to Syracuse for the winter. The next year (396) Carthage began to put forth her full strength for the war. Himilkôn, now Shophet, came with a vast army and won back all that Dionysios had gained. Leptinês could not hinder the Punic fleet from reaching Panormos. Eryx was taken by treachery; the siege of Segesta was raised; above all, Motya was won back by storm. Unluckily we have no details. And now Himilkôn determined to choose another point for the chief seat of Phœnician power in Western Sicily. He forsook Motya, and founded another town on the point of Lilybaion, where we wonder that no town had been founded before. Lilybaion became a wonderfully strong fortress, of which the

PHŒNICIAN CAPITAL FROM LILYBAION.

ditches and parts of the walls are still to be seen. Under the Arabic name of Marsala, it is the chief seat of the Sicilian wine-trade.

Having thus provided for the defence of the Carthaginian dominion, Himilkôn determined to attack the Greeks of Eastern Sicily. He took his fleet and army along the north coast to attack Messana. He did not even stay to chastise the men of Therma, but he sailed to Lipara and made the islanders pay thirty talents. Then he attacked Messana. The walls had been neglected, and the horsemen of the city were with Dionysios. So Messana fell into the hands of the Carthaginians; but most of the people escaped. Himilkôn's object now was to march against Syracuse, but, before that, he went through a solemn ceremony of destruction, which, though wrought only against stones and not against men, reminds one of Hannibal's sacrifice at Himera. He destroyed the town of Messana in a solemn and symbolic way, to mark his hatred of the Greeks. But he could build up as well as pull down, and, on his road, he struck a blow at Dionysios in this way also. This leads us to the foundation of another Sicilian town which came to be famous. The Sikels were now falling away from Dionysios, and Himilkôn wished specially to win over those Sikels to whom Dionysios had given the lands of Naxos. They were beginning to settle as a community on the neighbouring hill-side of Tauros. He gave them all help, and the new town of Tauromenion, in its origin a Sikel town, arose. Meanwhile Dionysios was building ships, strengthening fortresses, hiring mercenaries,

TAUROMENION.

doing everything for the defence of Syracuse. Among other things he persuaded the Campanians to whom he had granted Katanê to go inland and settle at Ætna. Of the state of Katanê itself at this moment we hear nothing; but was in some way under the power of Dionysios.

The great object on each side was of course to attack and to defend Syracuse. On the road thither it was a great object with Dionysios to attack the new settlement at Tauromenion, and with Himilkôn to defend it. It was made the meeting-place of the Carthaginian fleet and army. They were to go on in concert; but the land army was stopped in its march by a fresh outpouring of lava from Ætna, and they had to march all round the foot of the mountain to reach Katanê. Dionysios thus gained the start of them. He reached Katanê with his fleet and army, and brought on a fight between the two fleets while the land army of Carthage was still on its roundabout road. The fight was an utter defeat on the Greek side. Dionysios bade his brother Leptinês, who commanded the fleet, to keep all his ships together, because of the greater numbers of the enemy. Instead of doing this, he dashed on with thirty of his best ships far ahead of the rest. So, after much hard fighting, first his own division, and then the rest of the fleet, were overpowered by the Carthaginians. More than a hundred ships and 2,000 men were lost.

It was now clear that the Carthaginian force by land and sea would go against Syracuse as soon as Himilkôn brought up his land force. The Greek army generally was anxious to risk a battle by land.

But to Dionysios the safety of Syracuse was the first of objects. He therefore hastened back; but many of those who were Sikeliots, but not Syracusans, forsook him. He accordingly marched to Syracuse, and two days later Himilkôn reached Katanê by his roundabout march. He did not hurry; he gave his men of both forces a rest. He then tried in vain to win over the Campanians at Ætna, and then went on to Syracuse. Two thousand vessels of all kinds, 208 of them ships of war, sailed into the Great Harbour with all military pomp, like the fleet of Dêmosthenês and Eurymedôn twenty years before. The Carthaginian land-army marched round by the westward of the hill of Syracuse and entered the low ground by the Anapos. There, on Polichna and the flats near to it, the great camp was pitched. The worshipper of Melkart was not like the pious Nikias; Himilkôn made his headquarters in the sacred precinct of Zeus. Syracuse was thus again besieged, and by a far more terrible foe than her Athenian besiegers.

From the moment of his return to Syracuse Dionysios had begun to take every means for the defence. He sent off embassies to Sparta and also to Corinth—the war between the two cities had not yet broken out—at once to ask for help from his allies and to hire mercenaries in Peloponnêsos. Meanwhile Himilkôn began with an offer of battle which was declined. He then took to harrying the land and destroying its monuments. He came close up to the enlarged town, and plundered the temple of the goddesses of Sicily, Dêmêtêr and Persephonê. From that time, so the Greeks believed, success began to forsake him. His army was full of superstitious fears, and the Syracusans had the better in several sallies. He presently saw that the siege would be a long one; so he fenced his camp in with a wall, and built three forts on different points, one on Plemmyrion. But he sinned yet more in the eyes of the Syracusans by destroying the tombs of Gelòn and Damarata, which came within the circuit of his camp.

Meanwhile Polyxenos came back with thirty ships from the allies in Old Greece and Italy under the command of the Spartan admiral Pharakidas. A strange episode followed. Dionysios and Leptinês sailed out with some ships of war to convoy the provision ships of Syracuse. In their absence, the Syracusan ships, under whose command we are not told, defeated a part of the Carthaginian fleet, and the rest refused their challenge to come out and fight. Men's spirits were raised by this success: they began to think of getting rid of the tyrant; they did better against the enemy when he was away. In the midst of all this Dionysios came back, and he ventured to summon the people to a public assembly. This is one of many signs that, under his tyranny, though all things were done according to his will, yet the usual forms of the constitution went on. Dionysios praised the people for their exploit; he bade them be of good courage, and he would soon put an end to the war. Then, it is said, a speaker named Theodôros, a horseman and a man of renown in the city, ventured to make a long speech, denouncing all the acts of Dionysios. The people hoped that their allies would help them. They looked specially to Pharakidas, but he answered that he had no orders from Sparta to overthrow the power of Dionysios, but to help the Syracusans and Dionysios against the Carthaginians. The people were so wroth at this that Dionysios called for his mercenaries and dismissed the assembly.

This is a good example of the state of a city under a tyranny. If the legal course of things was likely to go against him, the tyrant could at once appeal to force. But Dionysios learned a lesson; he began to treat the Syracusans more mildly, and he presently had an opportunity of winning a worthier fame than he had ever yet won. The vengeance of the goddesses —so the Greeks deemed—now fell on the barbarians for the plunder of their temple. That is to say, a plague arose in the besieging army. It was autumn, and in autumn the swampy ground west of the harbour, where many of them were encamped, became deadly. Thousands died; at last the dead were left unburied. When the Punic army was seriously weakened, Dionysios laid his plans for a general attack by land and sea. He was zealously supported by his forces of all kinds, Syracusans and allies. But he had a band of turbulent mercenaries whom he wished to get rid of, and those he contrived to get slain by the swords of the Carthaginians. Otherwise the work of that day makes a thrilling and a glorious tale. The Punic camp was attacked on all sides by land and sea; Dionysios himself made a long march to make the attack from the west. The forts were taken; but the most stirring part of the story is where the Syracusan ships suddenly attacked the Carthaginians, who had no time to make ready. Many of their ships were sunk, many were set on fire; the old and young who had stayed in the city manned what ships they could, and came at least to share in the plunder. A great day's work was done; but the camp was not taken, and Dionysios took up his quarters for the night hard by the Olympieion in order to besiege it the next day.

Himilkôn perhaps knew that Dionysios had reasons of his own for not punishing the enemy to extremities. After some negotiations he and Dionysios secretly agreed that, on the payment of 300 talents, Himilkôn should go away with all the Carthaginian citizens in his army; the allies and mercenaries he was to leave to their fate. This suited the purposes of Dionysios, as it would hold up the Carthaginians to hatred throughout Sicily as men who betrayed their allies. The terms were agreed to. The money was paid, and the Carthaginians set sail in the night. The Corinthians, who knew nothing of the agreement, sailed after them and destroyed some ships. Then Dionysios led his army to attack the Punic camp. The Sikel allies of Carthage, knowing the country, had gone away in the night. The mercenaries were there still, but they were disheartened by the treachery of Himilkôn, and worn out by sojourn in the unhealthy ground crowded with dead bodies. The more part threw down their arms and only asked for their lives. They were taken and sold as slaves. The brave Spaniards stood to their arms, but offered peace and alliance to the tyrant. Dionysios knew their worth;

he took them into his service, and they helped him well on many later days.

No treaty followed the withdrawal of Himilkôn from the siege of Syracuse. Things stayed for several years as they practically were. Dionysios made no attempt on the Carthaginian possessions in Western Sicily. On the other hand, the Greek cities were at least delivered from Phœnician rule, though they had to accept the dominion or supremacy of the Syracusan tyrant instead. It seems strange that Dionysios did not press his advantage further. Carthage was grievously weakened by the war, by the plague, and by a revolt of the mercenaries in Africa. The Carthaginians thought that all this was the punishment for the sacrilege done against the Sicilian goddesses. So they built them a temple at Carthage, and learned of the Greeks who were among them what was the right way of worshipping them. Their consciences being thus satisfied, they plucked up heart, and were able to put down the revolt. It almost looks as if Dionysios, for his own ends, did not wish to press Carthage too hard.

The successful result of Dionysios' first Punic war seems to have largely spread his fame in Old Greece. A little later than the deliverance of Syracuse, the Athenians, now at war with Sparta and in alliance with Corinth, sought to win Dionysios to their side. It was soon after their great naval victory at Knidos (B.C. 394), and they were pressing their schemes in all quarters. They passed (B.C. 393) a decree in honour of Dionysios, of his brother Leptinês, and others of his friends. It was hard to find a way to describe him; he appears in the decree as "ruler of Sicily" (Σικελίας ἄρχων). An embassy was sent with the decree, one of whose members was the orator Lysias, a man of Syracusan descent. But Dionysios did not become an ally of Athens till he could be an ally of both Sparta and Athens at once.

Meanwhile Dionysios had much work to do in Sicily, and he had many difficulties. He too, like the Carthaginians, had to deal with a revolt among his mercenaries, and he had to give up to them the town of Leontinoi. And the people of Naxos and Katanê, driven out by himself, and the people of Messana, driven out by Himilkôn, were wandering about, seeking for dwelling-places. He restored Messana, but he did not give it back to its old inhabitants. He peopled it with colonists from Italy and from Old Greece. Some came from Lokroi, whence he had taken his Italiot wife. For her sake he always showed every favour to that city, while he in every way persecuted the Rhegines who had so deeply scorned him. He also planted a body of settlers from the old Messenian land in Peloponnêsos. But this gave offence to their enemies the Spartans, his most powerful allies, and this led to the foundation of a new Greek city, nearly the last that was founded in Sicily.

On the north coast, it will be remembered, there was only one of the old Greek settlements, that of Himera. That was now in a manner represented by the new town of Therma, which often took its name. Dionysios now took part of the territory of the Sikel town of Abacænum, between Cephalœdium and the Messanian outpost of Mylai. He there built a town on a high hill overhanging the sea, which forms the other horn of a bay between itself and Mylai. Here he planted 600 settlers from the old Messenia, and called the town Tyndaris, after the Great Twin Brethren of Peloponnêsos. The new city grew and flourished, and soon had 6,000 citizens. This kindled the wrath of Dionysios' enemies at Rhêgion. They seized on the opposite peninsula of Mylai, and there planted a body of those men of Naxos and Katanê whom Dionysios had driven from their homes. They tried to take Messana itself, but in vain. And it is to be noticed that their general was Helôris, a Syracusan exile. Was he the same as Helôris whom we have heard of as Dionysios' counsellor and adopted father? The new Messanians won back Mylai, and the Naxians and Katanaians were again wanderers. Thus the north-eastern corner of Sicily was held by men who were really attached to Dionysios. And he went on further to extend his power along the north coast. Sikel Cephalœdium was betrayed to him, and even, it is said, Phœnician Solous. The new Himera would naturally be friendly to him.

Dionysios had thus become a great power in Northern Sicily, and he was advancing in the central lands also. Henna itself was betrayed to him. The Sikel towns were now fast taking to Greek ways, and we hear of commonwealths and tyrants among them, just as among the Greeks. Agyris, lord of Agyrium, was said to be the most powerful prince in Sicily after Dionysios himself. He had gained dominion by slaying the chief men; but Agyrium was very powerful under him and numbered 20,000 citizens. With him Dionysios made a treaty, and also with other Sikel lords and cities. This seems to have been going on at the same time as the war at Messana, and Dionysios was specially anxious to chastise the Rhegines. But there were several difficulties in his way, specially the new Sikel town of Tauromenion, which he hated above all things. It was now (B.C. 394) winter, and the hill of Tauros was covered with snow. Greek citizen-soldiers were not fond of winter warfare; but the mercenaries, if well paid, would doubtless go anywhither at any time. Dionysios accordingly led his force in person to attack the new city. He seized, we are told, one akropolis, that is most likely the hill where the theatre is. He thence got into the town; but the people rose, and not only drove out the assailants, but sent them tumbling down the hill-side. Dionysios himself escaped, but he was very nearly taken alive.

This discomfiture at Tauromenion checked the plans of Dionysios for a while. Several towns threw off his dominion. We hear specially of Akragas, now free from the Carthaginians, and doubtless wishing to be free from Dionysios also. And the Carthaginians also began to stir again. In B.C. 393 their general Magón, seemingly without any fresh troops from Africa, set out from Western Sicily to attack Messana. Unlike the Punic commanders generally, Magón tried to win friends in Sicily by good treatment. Most of the Sikels therefore joined him, specially those of Abacænum, at whose cost Dionysios had founded his town of Tyndaris. But Dionysios marched against him, defeated him in a battle, and himself crossed the strait to make an unsuccessful attempt on Rhégion. Next year a large force came from Carthage to support Magôn; many of the Sikels again joined him. His expedition was mainly aimed at Agyrium; but its tyrant Agyris was firm on the side of Dionysios. The story is not at all clearly told; but a peace between Dionysios and the Carthaginians followed, by which the Sikels were handed over to him, and he was specially allowed to attack Tauromenion. He took it the next year (391); but we have no such account of its taking as we had of his vain attempt to take it.

Dionysios was now at the height of his power in Sicily. We hear nothing more of the movement at Akragas; otherwise all the Greek cities were under his dominion or supremacy. He commanded the whole east coast, and the greater part of the north and south coasts. The Sikel stronghold of Tauromenion he settled with his own mercenaries; the other Sikels were either his subjects or, like Agyrium, his allies. In short Dionysios and Carthage might be said to divide Sicily between them, and Dionysios had the larger share. There was now peace between the two powers for about nine years (392–383), and Dionysios now began to give his chief thoughts to things out of Sicily. In Southern Italy the Rhegines were his enemies and the Lokrians his friends. The other Italiot cities had formed a league to withstand his power. He now, in B.C. 390, planned another campaign in Italy; its object was, if possible, to attack and take Rhégion without any direct hostilities against the other cities. But his new attack on Rhégion was beaten back by the prompt help of the League, favoured by a storm which drove off the Syracusan ships. Dionysios could do nothing till the next year (389), when he was not ashamed to make a treaty with the Lucanians, the barbarian enemies who were pressing on the Greek cities of Italy. They were to attack them by land and himself by sea. The war began by incursions of the Lucanians on the lands of Thourioi, which led the Thourians, without waiting for their allies, to invade the Lucanian territory, where they were entrapped and utterly defeated. The battle was fought near the shore, where the ships of Dionysios were afloat under his brother and admiral Leptinês. Some of the Thourians swam to the ships and were kindly received by Leptinês. But when Leptinês went on further to make an agreement between the Lucanians and the Italiots, by which the war was stopped for a season, that did not at all suit the purposes of Dionysios. He removed Leptinês from his command as admiral, and gave it to his other brother Thearidas. And he determined to make war in person the next year.

So he did (B.C. 389); and he began by attacking the Italiot cities more directly by laying siege to Kaulônia. The Italiots now, Krotôn leading the way, gathered a large army for the relief of Kaulônia, under the command of the Syracusan exile Helôris, as a special enemy of Dionysios. But the tyrant met them on the way; Helôris was slain and his army defeated. The remnant escaped to a strong but waterless hill, where Dionysios and his army watched them from below. The next day they sent a herald asking to be allowed to go away on payment of ransom; but

Dionysios demanded that they should surrender at discretion. To this they could not yet bring themselves; but after several hours more of endurance, they gave way. Dionysios stood with a rod, and reckoned them as they came down, above 10,000 in number. They were in great fear, looking for death or slavery. But Dionysios let them all go free. We are also told that he made treaties with their several cities by which he left them independent. We are not told what cities they were, but Krotôn and Thourioi must have been among them, as we do not find him warring against either of them for some time to come. But he certainly made no peace with Rhégion or with Kaulônia.

Dionysios naturally won much credit by his treatment of the Italiot soldiers. But it was quite of a piece with his general conduct. Dionysios, though he stuck at no crime that served his purpose, had not, like some tyrants, any pleasure in bloodshed for its own sake. He hated the Rhegines; he doubtless hated the Syracusan exile Helôris. But Helôris was dead, and he had no particular reason to hate the men of Krotôn and Thourioi. He saw that he would gain more by winning a reputation for generous conduct than he could gain by selling his prisoners as slaves. There was no wonderful virtue in the act; but it shows that Dionysios did not belong to the very worst class of oppressors, those who delight in wrong simply as wrong.

The Rhegines at all events were none the less afraid of the hatred of Dionysios. Finding themselves without allies, they sent him a humble message, praying for mercy. The siege of Kaulônia was still going on, and he could put off his action against Rhêgion. He spared them for the present, on condition of their giving up all their ships, seventy in number, and putting 100 hostages into his hands. Then he went on to finish the siege of Kaulônia. Here again his different ways of treating different people comes out strongly. He had no special spite against Kaulônia; it simply stood in the way of his plans. So, when he took the town, he destroyed it, and gave its territory to his beloved Lokrians. The citizens he carried to Syracuse, and not only gave them citizenship, but an exemption from taxes for five years. The next year, he did the like to the town of Hippônion, its land and people. Only we do not hear of the exemption from taxes. The men of Hippônion had not endured so long a siege as the men of Kaulônia.

But all this was simply the beginning of what Dionysios had most of all at heart, his attack on Rhêgion. But, as he had so lately made a treaty with Rhêgion, he had to find some excuse for renewing the war. He still had the hostages whom the Rhegines had given; so they were greatly in his power. He first asked them for provisions for his army, promising to send back an equal store from Syracuse, whither he professed to be going. He seemingly hoped that they would refuse, so that he might treat the refusal as a hostile act. They did give him provisions for some days; but, as Dionysios, pleading sickness and other excuses, stayed in their neighbourhood instead of going to Syracuse, they presently stopped the supply. This he affected to treat as a wrong done by the Rhegines; to put himself wholly in the right, he first gave back the hostages, and then besieged the town. The siege of Rhegion was one of the greatest of Dionysios' acts of warfare. He had to use all his forces; for the Rhegines, under their general Phytôn, made a most valiant defence, holding out against all attacks under every possible disadvantage for more than ten months. They had no ships, no allies, and their stock of provisions had been lessened by what they had given Dionysios. The tyrant tried to bribe Phytôn to betray the city, as the generals of several other cities had done. But the general of Rhegion stayed firm in his duty. Dionysios, on his part, took his full share in the work, and was once so badly wounded by a spear that his life was for a while despaired of. At last, under sheer stress of hunger, when many had died for lack of food and the rest had lost all strength, the valiant men of Rhegion were driven to surrender at discretion. Dionysios had gained one of the great objects of his life; he was master of the city which he most hated. And now he showed in a more notable way than ever what manner of man he was. In one way he was really less harsh than many other conquerors had been. It was not very wonderful in Greek warfare to slaughter all the men and sell all the women and children of a captured town. Dionysios made no general massacre. He sent all the people of Rhegion to Syracuse, not indeed to be made citizens like those of Kaulônia. Those who could pay a certain ransom were let go; those who could not were sold. But it was not usual in Greek warfare to put any man to death with torture and mockery. But now Dionysios seemed to gather his whole hatred of the Rhegines into the person of their brave general who had refused his bribes. He exposed Phytôn in mockery on one of his loftiest war-engines; then he told him that he had just drowned his son. And Phytôn answered that his son was luckier than his father by one day. Then he caused Phytôn to be led through the whole army with scourging and insult of every kind. At last Dionysios' own soldiers began to murmur at his cruelty, and he had Phytôn and all his kinsfolk drowned. He appears to have destroyed the town of Rhêgion and to have given its lands, like those of the other cities that he took, to the Lokrians.

It was a memorable year (B.C. 387) for Greece and for Europe in which Dionysios, by the taking of Rhêgion, made himself, beyond all doubt, the chief power, not only in Sicily, but in Greek Italy also. It was the year of the Peace of Antalkidas, which established for a while the power of Sparta in Old Greece and gave over the Greeks of Asia to the dominion of the Persian. It was also the year in which Rome was taken by the Gauls. The presence of these last barbarians in various parts of Italy supplied Dionysios with the means of hiring Gaulish mercenaries. Some of these, as well as Iberians, he sent at a later time, with other troops, to the help of his Spartan allies in the wars of Old Greece. The Peace of Antalkidas supplied patriotic orators with the opportunity of painting Hellas as enslaved at both ends, in the East under the Persian and in the West under Dionysios. So spoke the Athenian Isokratês; so, with more effect, spoke Lysias, once envoy to Dionysios, at the Olympic festival next after the Peace of Antalkidas (B.C. 384). To that festival Dionysios sent a splendid embassy. Lysias called on the assembled Greeks to show their hatred of the tyrant, to hinder his envoys from sacrificing or his chariots from running. His chariots did run; but they were all defeated. Some of the multitude made an attack on the splendid tents of his envoys. He had also sent poems of his own to be recited; but the crowd would not hear them. This was rather out of hatred of the tyrant than for any fault in the poems; for there is no doubt that Dionysios was a poet of some merit. He was now at peace with Athens, and he sent tragedies to be acted there. They gained inferior prizes more than once, and at last one of them won the first prize.

It was said that Dionysios was so annoyed at the ill-fate of his poems that he began to suspect everybody, and to turn his rage against his nearest friends. Whether from this cause or from any other, he certainly banished two of the chief of them, the historian Philistos, to whom he owed his first rise, and his own brother the admiral Leptinês. Leptinês was soon restored; but Philistos remained in banishment till the death of Dionysios. Dionysios, perhaps in his character of poet, affected, like Hierôn, the company of men of letters; but they found that the poet was also the tyrant. The philosophers Aristippos of Kyrênê and Plato of Athens both visited him; but he ill-treated both, and he is said to have caused Plato to be sold as a slave. And his fellow poet Philoxenos he is said to have sent to the stone-quarries for free criticism on his verses.

But however hated Dionysios might be both at home and abroad, he was still strong both at home and abroad. His next field of enterprise was the coasts and islands of the Hadriatic. Here the city of Ankôn or Ancona on the Italian coast was planted by Syracuse exiles trying to escape from his power. Other colonies in those seas he himself founded or helped others to found. Thus the people of Paros, with his help, planted settlements on the islands of Pharos and Issos, and he himself founded Lissos on the Illyrian coast. He then formed alliance with some of the Illyrians and with a banished prince of Molottis named Alketas. Him he was able to restore; but he failed in a scheme of making his way into Greece on this side, and even, it is said, robbing the Delphian temple. This was too much even for his friends the Spartans, and a Lacedæmonian force checked all further advance. He next took up the old Syracusan quarrel with the Etruscans. For a war against them it was easy to find an excuse in their constant piracies. His real object seems to have been to plunder the rich temple of Agylla on the west coast of Italy, whence he carried off spoil in money, slaves, and other things to the value of 1,500 talents. Even at Syracuse he did not fear to plunder the temples; from the Olympicion he carried off the golden robe of the statue of Zeus, saying in mockery that such a garment was too hot in summer and too cold in winter.

The Etruscan campaign might perhaps win back for Dionysios some credit both at home and abroad as a Hellenic champion against the barbarians. He would get more still when, in the year 383, he began another Punic war. At no time in our story do we more lament the lack of a contemporary narrative. Dionysios took advantage of the disaffection towards Carthage felt by some of her dependencies to contract alliances with them. We are not told what cities are meant; some, we may suppose, of the Carthaginian dependencies in Sicily, perhaps the Elymian towns. Carthage, on the other hand, sent, for the first time, a force into Italy to act along with the tyrant's enemies there. A campaign followed, the geography of which is hopeless. Dionysios first won a great battle in which the Shophet Magôn was killed. The Carthaginians then asked for peace; Dionysios refused it except on condition of Carthage withdrawing altogether from Sicily and paying the costs of the war. Such terms needed the consent of the home government of Carthage. A truce was made; while it lasted, the new Carthaginian commander, the son of Magôn, made every preparation for a new struggle. In a second battle Dionysios was defeated and his brother Leptinês killed; the slaughter was among the greatest that Greeks ever underwent at the hands of barbarians. Envoys now came from Carthage with full powers. The terms of peace were now quite the opposite to what Dionysios had proposed just before. He had to pay a thousand talents, and to make the Halykos the boundary between his dominions and those of Carthage. That is to say, he gave up to Carthage Selinous and its territory and part of the territory of Akragas.

Hellas was thus again cut short on Sicilian soil, though not so utterly as had been the case when Dionysios first rose to power. If we had as clear accounts of his later days as we have of the earlier, we should better understand the difference between the two periods. But we have a very meagre account of the war which led to the loss of Selinous, and of the last sixteen years of his reign we know next to nothing. But we can see that about the year 379 both he and the Carthaginians were warring in Italy. They were seeking to set up again some of the towns which he had destroyed; but they had to give up the attempt and go back to Africa on account of a plague and the revolt of their subjects. On the other hand, Dionysios took Krotôn, which had escaped him in his earlier campaign, and robbed the temple of the Lakinian Hêra of a precious robe, which he, oddly enough, sold to the Carthaginians for a huge sum. There is also a story how he planned the building of a wall across the narrowest point of the south-western peninsula. This was, he said, to keep out the Lucanians; but the Greeks north of the proposed wall saw that it was meant only to strengthen his own power in Italy. After this we hear nothing of his doings in Sicily or Italy for about eleven years.

In Old Greece meanwhile, where, from the year B.C. 369 onwards, Athens and Sparta were allies against Thebes, we hear more than once of his sending barbarian mercenaries, Gaulish and Iberian, to help the Spartans. And now (369–367) we find two Attic inscriptions recording the relations of the Athenian democracy with the tyrant. All manner of honours are voted to him and his sons, and in the second an alliance is concluded between Athens and "the ruler of Sicily," without any mention whatever of the people of Syracuse. Each is to help the other in case of attack by any enemy. It is some little comfort to think who the enemies of Dionysios at that moment were.

For, just at the end of his reign, he renewed the greatest exploit of his earlier days, the invasion of the Phœnician possessions in Western Sicily. An excuse for a new Punic war could be easily found in real or alleged Carthaginian encroachments on the dominions of Dionysios. In such a war as this he knew that Greek feeling, in and out of Sicily, would go with him. With a great force, given as 30,000 foot, 3,000 horse, and 300 ships of war, he again marched westward. Carthage was believed to be, as so often happened, deeply weakened by the usual causes, pestilence and the revolt of her African subjects. He was at first successful. He recovered Greek Selinous; he took Entella, now in the hands of the Campanians, and he took Eryx itself for the second time. He then began to besiege the new town of Lilybaion, which had taken the place of his old conquest of Motya. But he found the resistance too strong for him. At sea however he deemed himself so strong that he sent back the more part of his fleet to Syracuse, keeping 130 ships at anchor at Drepana the haven of Eryx. But the Carthaginians, taking heart, made a sudden dash and carried off most of them. Then winter came, and both sides withdrew from the war. This is all that we hear. Before long a treaty was again made between Syracuse and Carthage. We are not told its terms; but as Selinous, when we next hear of it, appears as a Carthaginian possession, the Syracusan conquests were most likely given back to Carthage.

But it was not the elder Dionysios who made the treaty. We have come to the end of the reign and life of a man who had done such great things and had so largely changed the face of the world of his day. In the year 367 Dionysios the tyrant died, after a reign of 38 years. The cause of his death is said to have been a strange one. It was now for the first time that a tragedy of his was thought worthy of the first prize at Athens. The news was brought to him with all speed. His delight was unbounded; he sacrificed to the gods, and indulged in an excess of wine which was unusual with him. A fever followed, and he died. His career had been indeed a wonderful one. He had destroyed the freedom of his native city, but he had made it both the greatest city and the greatest power of Europe. No man had won greater successes over the barbarian enemies of Greece; but no man had done more to destroy Greek cities, and to plant barbarians in his own island. With his great gifts, he might, as a lawful king or as the leader of a free people, have made himself the most illustrious name in all Greek history. As it was, he was a tyrant; he reigned as such, and he was remembered as such. All that we can say for him is that worse tyrants still came after him His reign was unusually long for a tyrant, and he was able to leave his power to his son. He himself had said that he was able to reign so long, because he had abstained from wanton outrages against particular persons. His reign marks an æra in the history of Greece and of the world. He began a state of things which the Macedonian kings continued. It is well to note that when Dionysios died, Philip son of Amyntas was already fifteen years old, and that eight years later he won for himself the Macedonian kingdom.

XI.

THE DELIVERERS.

B.C. 367—317.

[Our chief authorities now are still the narrative of Diodôros and Plutarch's Lives of Diôn and Timoleôn. Plutarch is commonly the fuller. There are also Latin lives of both by Cornelius Nepos. Something may be learned from the letters attributed to Plato, with the cautions already given.]

THE great power of the elder Dionysios, the greatest power, as it is emphatically said, in Europe, now passed to the weaker hands of his son. The father had done great things, even if they were largely evil things. He had changed the whole face of Sicily, and had thereby gone far towards changing the face of the whole Greek world. He had given Syracuse, as the capital of a ruler, a position such as Athens herself had hardly held as a commonwealth bearing rule over other commonwealths. He had done greater things against barbarians in their own land than any Greek leader had done before him. Yet, besides the loss of political freedom in his own and other cities, he had on the whole done more against the

Greek nation than for it. In his very first dealings he had helped the Carthaginians to win more than he could ever win back from them. In Sicily itself he had destroyed some Greek cities and peopled others with barbarians. He had sacrificed several Italiot towns to the advancement of one, and he had decidedly helped towards barbarian advance in Italy. It is only in his most distant enterprises, in his comparatively obscure Hadriatic colonies, that he at all enlarged the borders of Hellas. His career tended, on the whole, to a great lessening, not only of Sicilian freedom, but of Sicilian prosperity. From his time the Sicilian and Italian Greeks began to find that they could not stand alone. The main feature of the times that followed, for about a hundred years beginning with the reign of his son, is the constant intercourse between Old Greece and the Greeks of Italy and Sicily. That intercourse takes a new shape. The Greeks of Italy and Sicily are ever sending to Old Greece for help against domestic tyrants, against barbarian enemies, or against both together. A succession of deliverers go forth, some of them to do great things. But we shall presently have to distinguish between the republican leader who goes out simply to deliver, and the prince who does indeed work deliverance, but who thinks that he has a right to reign over those whom he delivers.

The history of the younger Dionysios illustrates the nature of the Greek tyrannies in many ways. As in many other cases, what the father won the son lost. The tyrant's son, born, as the saying is, in the purple, was commonly a weaker man than his father.

And the elder Dionysios, in his extreme jealousy of everybody, had kept his son shut up in his palace, and allowed him no share in political or military affairs. He was not without ability or without tendencies to good; but he was in every way weaker than his father. Not having his father's strength of purpose, he was easily impressed both for good and for evil. He was less cruel, because less determined, than his father, but, for the same reason, he fell into the vices from which his father was free. It is a characteristic story that the old Dionysios found his son in an intrigue with another man's wife. He rebuked his son, and asked if he had ever heard of his doing anything of that kind. "No; but then your father was not tyrant." "And your son never will be tyrant, if you do such things." The new tyrant was the son of his father's Lokrian wife Dôris, and was about 25 years old at his accession. He was acknowledged, perhaps as general with full powers, by some kind of vote of an assembly which had no will of its own. He then gave his father a splendid funeral, and a tomb, contrary to Greek practice, in the Island. The elder Dionysios, at the time of his death, was at war with both Carthaginians and Lucanians. The new tyrant presently made peace with both. The Halykos again became the frontier between his power and that of Carthage. In Italy he is said to have founded two new towns on the coast of Apulia. Otherwise he simply kept his father's dominion, without extending it or doing anything memorable in any way.

Under a tyranny, above all where the tyrant is

weak and needs guidance, family and personal relations, marriages, and the power of men whom we may call ministers, become of importance, just as they do among lawful princes. Two men specially stand out during the reign of the younger Dionysios. The historian Philistos, who had had so great a hand in setting up the power of his father, was recalled from exile, either at the beginning of his reign or somewhat later. He was now an old man, but he was still vigorous, and he was attached to the system of the elder tyrant. The other was Diôn, the brother of Dionysios' Syracusan wife Aristomachê. His father Hipparinos had had a hand in setting up the tyranny. Aristomachê had two sons, much younger than Dionysios, and two daughters, Sôphrosynê and Aretê—mark the tyrant's choice of names for his children—who were married, the one to her half-brother Dionysios, the other to her uncle Diôn. It was only marriage with a sister by the mother's side which was a sin against Greek feelings. Diôn was enriched and favoured by the elder tyrant, and was largely employed by him in public affairs, specially in embassies to Carthage. He was an able man and a good soldier, stern and haughty in manner, yet capable of winning influence, strict in life, and with a tendency to philosophical speculations. He had had a hand in bringing Plato to Sicily in the days of the elder Dionysios. Now that the younger tyrant had succeeded and he himself stood high in his confidence, he hoped to work great things by the help of his favourite philosophy. He had no thought of restoring the old democratic constitution, which was by no means according to Platonic notions. But he wished to make Dionysios rule well instead of ill, and even to turn him from a tyrant into something like a constitutional king. To this end he persuaded Plato to come again to Syracuse, to act as a kind of spiritual adviser to the tyrant. Not much good was likely to come of this. Plato was a speculator on constitutions, but he had no practical knowledge of affairs. Dionysios listened to the philosopher for a while with pleasure; geometry became fashionable at his court; he talked of making reforms and even of giving up the tyranny. But nothing was really done. Philistos and his party pressed Dionysios on the other side, and set him against Diôn. The peace with Carthage was not yet settled, and Diôn was charged with treasonable dealings with the enemy. He was accordingly suddenly sent away from Sicily, but was allowed to receive the income of his property. His wife Aretê, the half-sister of the tyrant, and his young son Hipparinos, remained at Syracuse.

Dionysios meanwhile kept up a strange kind of friendship for Plato. He was jealous that the philosopher thought more of Diôn than he did of Dionysios. He kept him for a while at Syracuse, and even persuaded him to pay him a second visit. But nothing came of it. Dionysios at last seized Diôn's property and divided it among his own friends. This was during Plato's second visit; after that Plato was very glad to get away. Presently the tyrant took on him to give the wife of Diôn to another man named Timokratês, and he took pains to lead her young son into vice. He also banished one of his chief officers, named

Hêrakleidês, who then passed for a friend of Diôn's. The tyranny in short was getting worse and worse.

All this happened during the first seven years of the reign of the younger Dionysios (B.C. 367-360). Meanwhile Diôn visited several parts of Old Greece, and was everywhere received with honour. At Sparta he received a most special honour, being admitted to full Spartan citizenship, a gift which was most rarely bestowed on any stranger. At Athens he made the acquaintance of Kallippos, one of Plato's followers; indeed he made friends everywhere. He began to plan schemes for upsetting the tyranny of Dionysios, and he met with encouragement in many quarters. Hêrakleidês too was planning for the same object; but he and Diôn did not agree, and each followed his own course. It is certain that no good came of the friendship of Kallippos; as for the rivalry of Hêrakleidês, it is only fair to remember that we have the story only as it was told by the friends of Diôn. At any rate Diôn was ready for his enterprise before Hêrakleidês was. He had gradually raised a small force of mercenaries and volunteers; but of Syracusan exiles, of whom there are said to have been as many as a thousand seeking shelter in different parts of Greece, he could get only twenty-five or thirty to join him. At last, in the summer of the year B.C. 357, ten years after the death of the old Dionysios, he set forth on his errand of deliverance. His force was so small that all could be carried in five merchant-ships.

Diôn and his small fleet did not follow the usual coasting route of ships going from Old Greece to

Sicily. The Italian coast was watched by a force under Philistos. Diôn therefore struck straight across the open sea from Zakynthos to Sicily. His steersman guided him right to the south-east corner and there recommended him to land. But Diôn did not think it wise to land so near Syracuse. Then a wind drove him to the coast of Africa. Thence he was soon able by a change of weather to reach the south coast of Sicily at Hérakleia or Minôa, now, by the late treaty, a border fortress of Carthage and called by the Punic name of *Ras Melkart*. Here the officer in command, Synalos by name, was a Greek in the service of Carthage and a friend of Diôn's. He received him and his followers friendly, and while at Hérakleia Diôn heard a precious piece of news, namely that Dionysios was not at Syracuse, but had gone with the more part of his fleet to look after the towns which he had founded on the Hadriatic. Timokratês, to whom the tyrant had given Diôn's wife, was left in command at Syracuse. As soon as Timokratês heard that Diôn had landed, he sent a letter to Dionysios, but the messenger professed to have lost the letter by a strange accident; so the tyrant only heard the news some days later by common fame. It was a great point for Diôn to reach Syracuse before Dionysios should come back; so he marched with all speed, Greeks, Sikans, and Sikels joining him at every step as he went along. The march was done in three days. The night before the last day they encamped before the hill of Akrai, the inland outpost of Syracuse. There Diôn heard more of the state of things in the city. Epipolai was guarded by some of the barbarian soldiers to whom the elder Dionysios had given Katanê and other towns. Dión cunningly spread a rumour abroad that he was not going to march straight on Syracuse, but on those towns first. The barbarians believed the story, and in spite of all the efforts of Timokratês who came out of the Island to keep them in order, they marched off to defend their own homes. Thus Dión was able to reach Syracuse without opposition. He started from Akrai before daybreak, and reached the crossing of the Anapos just as the sun was rising. He offered sacrifices; the prophets foretold good luck; and the whole army marched on with their sacrificial wreaths on their heads, as if in a religious procession. By this time men could see them from the hill of Syracuse. The whole city rose. The people set on the few mercenaries who were left in the outer city, who contrived to form and encamp on part of Epipolai. Timokratês tried to get back to the Island, but he could not do so for the crowds. He rode away by the northern road. The tyrant's soldiers were thus left without a commander, and Dión was able to enter Syracuse without hindrance.

Meanwhile some of the people set upon the tyrant's spies and other agents. Others went in their best clothes to welcome their deliverer at the gate, the gate of Temenitês, in the new wall of the elder Dionysios. There they saw Dión in splendid armour, leading his troops, with his brother Megaklês and his friend Kallippos on each side of him. When he reached the gate, he announced by sound of trumpet that Dión and Megaklês were come to deliver Syracuse and all the Greek cities of Sicily from the tyrant. Then he marched on through Achradina, the people pressing on him on both sides with wreaths and sacrifices and drink-offerings. At last he was able to mount a tall sundial which the elder Dionysios had made near the gates between Achradina and the Island. There he made a speech as to an assembly of the Syracusan people, and called on them to elect generals. They at once chose Dión and Megaklês generals with full powers. But Dión said that they must have colleagues; so the people chose as many as twenty, some of them taken from among the exiles who had come back with Dión.

SYRACUSE. DIÓN'S TIME.

He then attacked and drove out the barbarians on Epipolai; he set free those who were shut up in the tyrant's prisons, and built a wall of defence between the Island and the delivered parts of the city. Dionysios, owing to the loss of Timokratês' letter, did not come back with his fleet till seven days after Dión's entrance. And then he found that all Syracuse, except the Island, had passed away from his dominion.

Never had any man had such a run of good luck as Dión had up to his time. It was now that his difficulties began. It was always easy to raise suspicion against Dión on account of his long connexion with the house of the tyrants. And in truth, notwithstanding his popular bearing on the day of his entry, it may be doubted whether Dión at any time really thought of restoring freedom to Syracuse in the sense in which most Syracusans would understand freedom. He had not lived in a democracy; he and his friend Plato seem to have dreamed all manner of impossible constitutions. There should be a king with limited powers, or perhaps more than one king, after the manner of Sparta. In short the Syracusans wished to rule themselves, like any other free Greek city; Dión wished to rule them himself or with a few colleagues. He wished no doubt to rule them justly and well; but still to rule them. His haughty manner too helped before long to make him personally unpopular. We hear casually that he had a body-guard, like a tyrant. Dionysios was quite clever enough to know all this, and to make his advantage out of it. His first trick was to try to open negotiations with Dión personally, and not with the Syracusan people. Dión told the tyrant not to speak to him, but to the people. Another message then came; Dionysios, like more modern oppressors, promised to make various reforms. At this the people had the sense to laugh, and Dión told the tyrant's envoys that no offer could be listened to except a complete abdication of the tyranny. If he did this, Dión would, out of old friendship, procure good terms for him personally. Dionysios pretended to agree; he asked that envoys should be sent into the Island to settle terms. But when they came, he kept them there, and sent his mercenaries to make a sudden attack on the wall which now hemmed in the Island by land. A sharp battle followed, in which Dión showed great courage, and received a wound. In the end the barbarians were driven back into the fortress.

Dionysios now sent letters to Dión from his wife and sister whom he still kept in the Island. These Dión read out to the assembly. But one letter was headed "from Hipparinos to his father;" this the people told him to keep to himself; it was too private to be opened publicly. But Dión opened and read it aloud. And it proved not to be from his son, but from the tyrant. Dionysios called on Dión to remember their old friendship, and not to serve an ungrateful people. He did not wish to rule any longer himself; he would willingly give up his power to Dión. If Dión refused this, he would do dreadful things to his sister and wife and son.

It is not perhaps very wonderful that the reading of this letter raised suspicions against Dión among the people. And these suspicions grew stronger when a rival to Dión for the good will of the Syracusans presently came on the field. This was Hérakleidés, who now came with a number of triremes, some say twenty, some only seven, and 1,500 more soldiers. He was skilful in warfare and of more popular manners than Dión; so he easily won the favour of the people. The assembly presently elected him admiral. Then Dión said that this could not be without his own consent; but he presently himself proposed the election of Hérakleidés with a guard equal to his own. This satisfied nobody; men began to call Dión a tyrant, and to say that they had only exchanged a drunken master for a sober one. And presently Hérakleidês was able to do real services which might seem to equal those of Dión.

Dionysios had come back to Syracuse with only part of his fleet; the rest was still off the coast of Italy under the command of Philistos. The historian of Sicily, vigorous in his old age, was now the mainstay of the power of the tyrant. He came from Italy with the ships and troops which had been left there. He failed in an attempt to win back Leontinoi, which had revolted from Dionysios. He next met Hérakleidês in a sea-fight. Some of the crews of the tyrant's ships must have joined the patriots; otherwise Hérakleidês could not have had sixty ships to face the same number which Philistos commanded. The Syracusans had the better, and Philistos, after doing his best for his master, was taken alive. To the disgrace of the delivered commonwealth, the old man was put to death with insult, and his body was dragged into the streets and thrown into the stone-quarries.

With the death of Philistos Dionysios began to lose heart; but he still went on with his tricks to discredit Dión. The victory had naturally made Hérakleidês the favourite. Dionysios now sent another message to Dión, offering to give up the Island on condition of being allowed to withdraw safely to Italy and to keep the profits of a large private estate in the Syracusan territory. Dión again told the tyrant to make his proposal to the people and not to him. At the same time he counselled the assembly to accept the terms. But the people hoped to take the tyrant alive, and refused to hearken. Dionysios now thought mainly of his own personal safety. He contrived to escape by sea, taking with him most of his treasures and furniture, but leaving the best of his mercenaries still in the Island under the command of his son Apollokratês, who must have been young for such a trust. This rather discredited Hêrakleidês, as men said that he ought to have kept better watch. And the story goes that he was thereby stirred up to make yet further attacks on Diôn, setting on men to propose measures which Diôn had to withstand. At last he was able to carry a vote by which Diôn was deprived of his generalship, and twenty-five new generals were appointed, of whom Hêrakleidês himself was one. Hitherto he had not been one of the body of generals, but had held a separate command at sea. And it was further voted to refuse pay to the men who had come from Peloponnêsos with Diôn. These men were not common mercenaries; they had come from zeal in the cause, and had done great things for it; but they could not afford to serve for nothing in a strange country.

The Peloponnesians gathered round Diôn, and prayed him to lead them against the Syracusans. Meanwhile the party of Hêrakleidês tried to win them over by offers of citizenship. There had been a talk of division of lands, and most likely they were to get land instead of their pay. But the soldiers clave to Diôn, and Diôn refused to act against the Syracusans. He accordingly went away with his followers, 3,000 in number. They marched towards Leontinoi; on the road they were followed by the new Syracusan generals with their force. Diôn's men were much better soldiers than the Syracusans, and they easily drove off their assailants, Diôn striving to shed as little Syracusan blood as might be. He and his men were welcomed at Leontinoi and received to citizenship.

The Syracusans had thus (B.C. 356) got rid of their deliverer about nine months after their deliverance. There were faults on both sides; but Diôn undoubtedly had an honest purpose to get rid of the tyranny, whatever kind of government he may have wished to set up in its stead. The Syracusans had now to besiege Ortygia for themselves, without Diôn's help or that of his men. And their prospects grew worse when Dionysios sent a large stock of provisions for his garrison, and an able officer named Nypsios from the Campanian Neapolis or Naples. He came, like Gylippos, at the very moment when the garrison had made up their minds to come to terms with the citizens. The Syracusan generals, who must have been guilty of some negligence in letting Nypsios enter the Great Harbour, repaired their fault by leading out the ships of the commonwealth to attack the mercenaries while they were still busy in getting the provisions on shore. A Syracusan victory followed; but, just as after the greater victory over the Athenians, the night was given up to revelry and drunkenness. Nypsios saw his opportunity; in the dead of the night he sent forth his mercenaries with orders to deal with the citizens as they would. They scaled the wall with which Diôn had hemmed in the Island, slaying the drunken guards. But that night there was little slaughter, save of such as tried to resist; the minds of the mercenaries were bent on plundering the houses and carrying off the women and children. This work went on all night through the lower part of the city. In the morning, those who had come to their senses and had contrived to escape to the parts of the town which the enemy had not reached, held an assembly, and with one voice voted to send to Leontinoi and to pray Dión to come at once to their help with his soldiers.

As soon as the message came, Dión at once held an assembly of his soldiers. He left it to them to say whether they would go and deliver men who had treated them so unworthily. For himself he had no choice; he must go, if only to die in the ruins of his native city. The whole body voted to go with him, and they set out by night. On the way he was met by contradictory messages. At night-fall Nypsios had withdrawn his soldiers into the Island. The enemies of Dión then gave out that there was no longer any need of Dión's help. The gates were shut against him, and a message was sent, bidding him not to come on. But his friends sent another message, bidding him to continue his march. Perplexed between the two messages, he marched on, but with less speed than before. At last, when he was near Megara, about seven miles off, a most pressing message came from Hérakleidés himself, praying him to come with all speed. As soon as Nypsios heard that the gates were shut against Dión, he let out his mercenaries again. This night was yet more frightful than the other. For this time they did not only plunder and carry off, but burned houses and slew all whom they met. Dión's bitterest enemies now felt that their only hope was in him. After this last message, his men came on with all speed. They came up Epipolai on the north side by the gates called Hexapyla. All that part of the city was clear; they had next to carry the wall of Achradina, which Nypsios and some of his men defended. Within the wall, they had to fight their way as they could among the burning houses and the streets choked with dead bodies. But they pressed on; the mercenaries made a last stand near the gate of Ortygia. The more part escaped into the fortress; those who were caught outside, as many as four thousand, were slaughtered.

Dión had thus saved Syracuse a second time, and his second entrance was of a very different kind from the first. His men had to put out the flames and to clear away the dead. As soon as might be, an assembly was held. The more part of Dión's chief enemies had fled; Herakleidés and his uncle Theodotés confessed their fault and craved his pardon. Many of Dión's friends urged him to put them to death, and to free the city from their intrigues. But Dión forgave them, after a somewhat pedantic speech, saying that it was his business as a philosopher to outdo his enemies in virtue. He then repaired the wall which hemmed in the Island; he buried the dead, and ransomed the captives. In another assembly Herakleidés himself proposed that Dión should be made general with full powers by land and sea. But it is said that the sailors who had shared Herakleidés' victory objected; so the command was divided, Herakleidés taking the command by sea. War with Dionysios went on for some while; but each side charged the other with negligence and treason, till Dión and Herakleidês were again formally reconciled through the intervention of a Spartan named Gaisylos, who had come from Sparta to act, if need be, the part of Gylippos. We should like to know something more about his mission; but our account is most meagre in everything but what personally concerns Dión. At any rate Gaisylos behaved thoroughly well, claiming nothing for himself, but binding Herakleidês by the most solemn oaths to be faithful to Dión.

Soon after this came the full completion of deliverance. We do not hear again of Nypsios; but Apollokratês the son of Dionysios found that he could hold out no longer. He sailed away under a truce which he made with Dión, by which he was allowed to take away his mother and sisters, and so much of his goods and treasure as he could take in five triremes. But the fortress and the military stores in it were given up to Dión. And as nothing is said of the mercenaries, it would seem that they passed into Dión's service. Dión now went into the Island and was welcomed by his sister Aristomachê, the widow of the old Dionysios, by his wife Aretê, whom he took back again, and his son Hipparinos.

The joy throughout Syracuse was great; but it was soon damped. Dión went to live in his own house and not in the fortress; but he kept possession of the fortress when men hoped that he would destroy it altogether. We cannot blame him when he refused, what many wished, to destroy the tomb of the elder

Dionysios, and to cast out his bones. But he kept power in his own hands, and kept on his haughty demeanour. He had no thought of restoring the democracy as it had stood before the tyranny began. He was still corresponding with Plato and with friends at Sparta and Corinth, cities used to aristocratic government. Among them they dreamed of another beautiful scheme of government, in which what we may call king, lords, and commons were all to have their proper places. Hérakleidés and his party, whether they knew anything of all this or not, at least knew that Dión had not restored the old Syracusan commonwealth, but kept all power to himself. They naturally complained. And now Dión yielded to his friends who again suggested the death of Hérakleidés. Dión had refused to put him to death when it could have been done, if not by a legal sentence, at least by military execution; he now sank to connive at the secret murder of Hérakleidés. Whatever he had done before, whatever he dreamed of doing, he was now practically tyrant.

As such he was before long to undergo the tyrant's fate. With the position of a tyrant he had not learned to practise the system of caution and suspicion by which tyrants maintained their power. He still put faith in his Athenian friend Kallippos, who all the while was plotting against him. He had warnings and visions, and his son threw himself from a window and was killed. His wife Areté and his sister Aristomaché knew better what was going on. They made Kallippos take the Great Oath, the most solemn of oaths in the name of the great goddesses of Sicily, that he was planning no ill against Diôn. But he cared not for the oath, and he presently compassed the death of Diôn at the hands of some young Zakynthians. These, one would think, must have been men who had followed Diôn when he set sail from their island, but who turned against him now that he was looked on as a tyrant.

Several years of confusion followed the death of Diôn, who had begun so well and had ended so ill. Kallippos kept himself in power for about a year. He gave himself out as a deliverer, and wrote a letter to that effect to his own city of Athens. He threw Aristomaché and Areté into prison, where Areté gave birth to a son. Next one Hiketas, a friend of Diôn, professed to have the two women released and sent to Peloponnêsos, but he had them drowned on the voyage. The child seems to have lived. Presently men began to complain of Kallippos; but for a while he got the better of his enemies, who found shelter at Leontinoi. Then a new claimant appeared, Hipparinos, son of the old Dionysios by Aristomaché, nephew therefore of Diôn. He would naturally strive to get dominion in Syracuse if he could, and he might even give himself out as the avenger of his mother and uncle. When Kallippos was warring against Katanê, Hipparinos contrived to enter Syracuse with his brother Nysaios, and to get possession of the Island. Kallippos had to put up with the tyranny of Katanê instead of that of Syracuse, and Hiketas got hold of the tyranny of Leontinoi. Hipparinos was presently killed in a drunken fit, and Nysaios kept the Island.

Lastly, their elder half-brother, Dionysios himself (B.C. 346), tried his luck again. He had been living at Lokroi, his mother's city, since he had left Syracuse, and had made himself hated there by his cruelty and debauchery. He now saw another chance, and he contrived to drive his brother Nysaios from the Island, which, with his son Apollokratês, he occupied, and was tyrant once more. And all this time Plato was dreaming dreams and writing letters and sketching another constitution for Syracuse, in which Dionysios and Hipparinos and the young son of Diôn should all be constitutional kings at once.

It would seem that none of these tyrants who came in one after the other had occupied all Syracuse; they could have held only the Island. At any rate there were somewhere citizens of Syracuse who were able to act. Besides all these tyrants, the Carthaginians were again beginning to be threatening. Men feared lest, not only freedom but Greek life altogether, should be wiped out in Sicily. They sought for help; they sought it in Old Greece, at the hands of their metropolis Corinth. Hiketas too at Leontinoi was believed to be making plots in concert with Carthage; but he openly joined in the appeal to Corinth, and the free Syracusans chose him general.

And now the purest hero in the whole tale of Sicily, till his likeness came again in our own day, steps on the field. What Diôn had professed to do, what at one time we may believe he really meant to do, Timoleôn did. During our whole story we are struck with the true and generous zeal for the suffering

Sicilian colony which is shown by the Corinthian commonwealth generally. In Timoleôn this zeal reaches its height. He was a noble Corinthian, son of Timodamos, and he first distinguished himself by saving the life of his brother Timophanês in battle. But when Timophanês presently seized the tyranny, after exhorting him in vain to give up his ill-gotten power, he joined with Æschylus the brother-in-law of Timophanês in putting him to death, though he did not himself strike the blow. To slay a tyrant was among the Greeks counted as the noblest of deeds; but some doubted whether it should be done by a brother-in-law and a brother. Men's minds therefore were divided; some honoured Timoleôn as the slayer of a tyrant, while others loathed him as the murderer of a brother. And among these last, to Timoleôn's great grief, was Damarista, the mother both of himself and of his slain brother. According to one account, the Syracusan embassy came very soon after these events, while, according to another, a space of twenty years had passed. In any case, when the Syracusan embassy came to ask help from Corinth, Timoleôn was called to take the command. He was bidden to go forth as a kind of ordeal; his former act should be judged by his acts in his new character.

Just, as in the case of Gylippos, more turned on the man that was sent than on the force that was put under his command. Corinth gave Timoleôn only seven ships, but one of these was specially consecrated to the goddesses of Sicily. For the priestess of Dêmêtêr and Persephonê at Corinth dreamed that the goddesses told her that they were going on a voyage to Sicily with Timoleôn. And he and his men had many signs on the voyage to show that the goddesses were with them. They were further strengthened by human help; for, of the sister cities of Syracuse, Leukas gave one ship, and Korkyra, once more, as in the days of Hippokratês, forgetting her quarrel with her mother, gave two. But the force that went was but small, a few Corinthian volunteers and about 1,200 mercenaries. And these were mostly men of bad repute, who had served with the Phokian leaders who had robbed the Delphian temple. For we must remember that we have come to the days when Philip of Macedon had become a great power in Greece. He had already taken Olynthos, but he had not yet fought the battle of Chairôneia. With such a force as this Timoleôn set forth to drive Dionysios a second time out of his stronghold in the Island of Syracuse. And on the way, when the fleet reached Rhêgion, now again a free city, they found there a Carthaginian fleet of twenty ships, with envoys from Hiketas. He had, he said, defeated the tyrant; he had recovered Syracuse, all but the Island, and there he was going to besiege Dionysios with the help of the Carthaginians. He would be glad to receive Timoleôn himself, and to consult with him as to operations; but the Carthaginians would not allow the Corinthian ships to come to Syracuse. There was more reason than ever to go on, as Hiketas now plainly showed that he was in league with Carthage; but it was hard to go on in the face of the Punic fleet. By a clever trick, planned with the Rhegines, who were zealous in his cause, Timoleôn contrived to get his ships out, and to land at Tauromenion without the knowledge of the Carthaginians.

Timoleôn was now on Sicilian ground, and at Tauromenion he found his first ally. The chief man there, one hardly knows his exact position, was Andromachos, father of the historian Timaios. He had done much for the city, enlarging it and bringing in new settlers. He now joined Timoleôn zealously. But the prospects of the deliverer were dark. Dionysios held the Island, and Hiketas the rest of Syracuse. The other towns, Greek and Sikel, were held by tyrants, all of whom would be against Timoleôn; the Carthaginians meanwhile were strong in the West, besides their fleet in the eastern sea. One Punic trireme was sent to Tauromenion, with envoys, bidding Andromachos drive the Corinthians away. The envoy held the palm of his hand upwards, and said that, if the Corinthians were not sent away, the city of Tauromenion should be turned upside down in the like sort. Then Andromachos turned his hand both ways, and said that, if the Punic ship did not sail away at once, it should be turned upside down in the like sort. The Carthaginians did no more, but sailed away to Syracuse, whither Hiketas called them. Timoleôn was presently invited by the people of Hadranum, at the foot of Ætna, the town which Dionysios the Elder had founded by the temple of the Sikel fire-god. Timoleôn marched thither; so did Hiketas with a larger force. But Timoleôn came suddenly on him and defeated him. He was gladly welcomed by the people of Hadranum; and the tale was told that, while the fight was going on, the doors of the innermost shrine of Hadranus opened of themselves, and the god was seen sweating and brandishing his spear, as having a share in the toil and the victory of Timoleon.

Timoleon now for a while kept his head-quarters at Hadranum. His wonderful success made men believe that he was under the special care of the gods. Allies now began to flock in to him. Several cities joined him, specially Tyndaris, the other foundation of the elder Dionysios on the northern coast. And the tyrant Mamercus of Katanè sought his alliance. And presently a more wonderful message came than all. Dionysios grew tired of being besieged in Ortygia, and he gave up all hope of being able to win back anything beyond Ortygia. And of the two, he liked better to fall into the hands of Timoleon than into those of Hiketas. So he offered to surrender, as it is put, to the Corinthians. He would give up the stronghold and the horses and arms, and the mercenaries, on condition of being sent safely to Corinth with his private property. This offer Timoleon gladly accepted. He sent two Corinthian officers with a small body of men, to take possession of the Island, and Dionysios, with his goods and a few friends, was sent in a trireme to Corinth. There the fallen tyrant lived as a private man for the rest of his days. It was thought the great wonder of the time to see one who had been so powerful living in a private station, more wonderful than if he had been slain or kept as a prisoner. He became the great sight of Corinth, and many stories are told of the sharp sayings that he made to people who came to see him. One may be enough, as it was made to so famous a man. King Philip of Macedon asked him how his father, with so much else to do, had found time to write tragedies. Dionysios answered that he wrote them in the time which himself and Philip and all the rest who passed for happy spent at the wine-cup. His old friend Plato had died before he came to Corinth, or we might have had some reflexions on his fall.

The surrender of Ortygia to Timoleôn happened within fifty days after his landing in Sicily. The Corinthians now thought it worth while to send out a larger force. When they were off the coast of Italy, they were hindered from going on by a Carthaginian fleet; so they spent the time in a work of the same kind as that on which they were sent, namely in helping the people of the Greek town of Thourioi against the neighbouring barbarians. Meanwhile Hiketas went on besieging Ortygia, while Timoleôn still stayed at Hadranum. Thither Hiketas sent two men to murder him, who were hindered in a wonderful way. They sought to slay Timoleôn while he was sacrificing to the local god Hadranus. But a man in the crowd knew one of them as the man who had killed his father, and slew him on the spot. Then the other was conscience-stricken, and confessed his purpose. So Timoleôn was thought more and more to be under the special care of the gods.

Hiketas now prayed the Carthaginian commander Magôn to come to his help with his whole force. The Punic ships now filled the Great Harbour, and, for the first time in all the wars between Carthage and Syracuse, a Punic force was admitted into the Syracusan city. Timoleôn's men in the Island were now in great straits; but he contrived to send them provisions in little boats; and when Hiketas and Magôn went to besiege Katanê, Neôn, the officer in command in Ortygia, made a sudden sally and occupied Achradina. And about the same time the Corinthians in Italy contrived to elude the Punic fleet there and to cross the strait. Timoleôn now took the command, and marched to Syracuse. There Hiketas and Magôn still held all the city outside Ortygia and Achradina, as well as the Great Harbour. But Timoleôn was able to encamp by the Anapos, the old camping-ground of so many armies. Magôn presently grew suspicious of Hiketas, and sailed away. When he reached Carthage, he was so fearful of the punishment of this cowardice that he killed himself, and the Carthaginians could only crucify his dead body.

The gods had thus again fought for Timoleôn. He now planned a threefold assault on those parts of Syracuse which were still held by Hiketas. He himself attacked on the south side of the hill, and other Corinthian officers led on their troops on the north side and from Achradina. All the posts were taken; Hiketas contrived to escape to Leontinoi. All Syracuse was delivered, and it was a real deliverance. Timoleôn did not do this time as Diôn did; he did not give the least suspicion that he wished to keep more than lawful power in his own hands. Diôn had kept possession of the stronghold of the tyrants; Timoleôn called on the Syracusans to come and help with their own hands in destroying it. The whole fortress was swept away, and courts of justice were built on the site. But Syracuse and the other Sicilian cities were in a sad state through all these tyrannies and wars. Some towns were quite forsaken; the tyrants and their mercenaries held the fortresses, while the citizens lived in the country. Stags and wild boars were said to occupy some towns, and in Syracuse itself the grass grew thick in the *agora*. Timoleôn saw that one great need of Syracuse and all Sicily was an increase of citizens. He wrote to Corinth, and at

SYRACUSE.   TIMOLEÔN'S TIME.   ZEUS ELEUTHERIOS.

his request the Corinthians made proclamation at the various games of Greece, and sent messengers to the islands and to many parts of Asia, calling on all banished Syracusans and other Sikeliots to come home again. Many such flocked to Corinth, but the number was by no means so great as was needed. Another Corinthian proclamation invited all Greeks everywhere to take a part in what was in truth a second Corinthian settlement of Syracuse, with Timoleôn as its second founder. Many came at this invitation, and were carried to Sicily under the auspices of the metropolis. Others flocked to Timoleôn of their own accord from various parts of

Sicily and Italy. At last as many as 60,000 returning exiles and new-comers were brought together in restored Syracuse. Two Corinthian citizens, Kephalos and Dionysios, were sent to legislate for what might almost be looked on as a new commonwealth. Citizens of an aristocratic city, they were wise enough to restore the old constitution of the democracy and to enact the laws of Dioklês afresh.

All these reforms took time. And while they were going on, Timoleôn had other work to do. He had to set the rest of Greek Sicily free both from domestic tyrants and from barbarian masters. Of the tyrants the nearest was Hiketas at Leontinoi. Timoleôn marched against him, and, according to one account, he now underwent the only failure that is recorded of him. The walls of Leontinoi were too strong for him. He therefore marched northwards to the inland town of Engyum, and to Apollonia near the northern coast. These were Sikel towns which had by this time fully taken to Greek ways. They were held by a tyrant named Leptinês, a Syracusan by birth, who had murdered Kallippos the murderer of Diôn. He submitted on terms, and Timoleôn sent him to Corinth, that the Greeks of Old Greece might see another fallen tyrant. A little later, it would seem, Hiketas thought it time to submit, to give up his mercenaries to Timoleôn, and to pull down his stronghold at Leontinoi. He was then allowed to live there as a private man.

The Carthaginians were still threatening, and making ready for greater efforts in Sicily. Timoleôn, like Dionysios, thought it well to strike first, the more so as he was in great straits for money to pay his mercenaries. He sent two of his Corinthian officers on a raid into the Carthaginian territory (B.C. 343-342). There they won over several towns to the Greek side, and brought back great spoil, which was useful both for paying the soldiers and for making ready for the greater campaign that was coming.

Before long the great day of trial came. Another huge Carthaginian fleet and army was gathered together at Lilybaion. The numbers were less than in some earlier invasions; but what specially distinguished this expedition was that the need was deemed so great as to call for the presence of the Sacred Band, the hope and defence of Carthage, made up of the noblest and bravest of her citizens. This time then it was not wholly against hirelings that the war had to be waged. The Punic commanders, Hamilkar and Asdrubal, determined at once to march against the Corinthians, that is against Syracuse. Timoleôn's object was to march westwards as fast as he could, and to meet the barbarians before they were able to do damage to any Greek territory. His force was but small, 12,000 at the outside, against 70,000 of the enemy. And just now, when Syracuse and the other Sikeliot cities were in the very act of settling down after the times of confusion, no great force could be drawn from them. A large part of Timoleôn's army was made up of mercenaries. And his march was delayed by a mutiny among them. They demanded their pay at once. Timoleôn won over most of them, but he was obliged to allow a thousand of them to go back to Syracuse.

Yet, after this loss of time, he was able to meet the enemy quite in the western part of Sicily, three times as near to Lilybaion as to Syracuse. He came in time to save Entella from the Carthaginians, and then he met them in the greatest battle in the open field ever fought between Greeks and Phœnicians, the battle by the river Krimisos.

On their march, as they drew near, the Greek army was met by a number of mules laden with the plant called *selinon*, which gave its name to the town of Selinous. This is commonly translated parsley, but it is really wild celery. The soldiers called out that this was a bad omen, as the plant was one used in funerals. But Timoleon, with ready wit, said that it was the best of omens; it was the plant of which the wreath of victory was made in the Isthmian games of Corinth. So he put a wreath of it on his own head, and the officers and soldiers did the like. It was in the forenoon of a June day that they reached the top of the hill by the river, and rested awhile. Hills and plain were covered with clouds and mist; but they heard the hum of a great army below. Presently the sun shone forth, and they saw the enemy crossing the river. First came the war-chariots; then the Sacred Band in heavy armour, with huge shields. Timoleon first sent down the horse to charge them before they had fully crossed the stream and got into order. He himself followed with the phalanx, and led them on with a shout so loud that his men thought that a god was speaking by his voice. But there was hard fighting with the Sacred Band; the Greeks had to do what was a most rare thing for Greeks, to throw away their spears and fight with their swords, like Spaniards or Romans. But at last the whole mass of these brave Carthaginians was cut to pieces. By this time the rest of the Punic army had crossed the river; but now, as men thought, the gods declared openly for their favourite. A fierce storm came on; rain and hail dashed in the faces of the barbarians, and the lightning dazzled their eyes. The Greek victory was complete; well nigh the whole of the great Punic host was killed or taken prisoners or swept away by the river.

As a battle, the fight by the Krimisos ranks along with that of Himera. As an immediate blow to Carthage it was the greater of the two, because of the destruction of the Sacred Band. But it did not give Greek Sicily so long a time of rest as the battle of Himera had done. What men most thought of at the time was the way in which the gods were held to have given visible help to Timoleôn. The spoil was something wonderful. Great gifts were made to the gods, and a special share was sent to Corinth, with an inscription which said how the Corinthians and Timoleôn their general had freed the Greeks of Sicily from the Carthaginians.

Timoleôn had beaten the barbarians; he had still to deal with the tyrants. Mamercus at Katanê had turned against him and had asked for help at Carthage. Just now Carthage could only send a body of Greek mercenaries; but they seem to have set up Hiketas again in the tyranny of Leontinoi, and there was another tyrant Hippôn at Messana. These men gained some victories over some of Timoleôn's mercenaries, men who had had a share in the sacrilege at Delphi. So men said that the gods favoured Timoleôn wherever he went himself, but that they punished his guilty followers when he was not with them. Presently all these tyrants were put down by Timoleôn. Hiketas was taken at Leontinoi and put to death as a tyrant and traitor. His wife and daughters were sent to Syracuse, where the Syracusans condemned them to death in vengeance for the murder of the wife and sister of Diôn by Hiketas. It was held to be the one stain on the character of Timoleôn, that, though he did nothing to promote this cruelty, he did nothing to hinder it. Mamercus surrendered to Timoleôn on condition that he should have a trial before the Syracusan assembly and that Timoleôn should not speak against him. Timoleôn held his peace; when Mamercus saw how strongly the Syracusans were against him, he tried to dash his head against the stone seats of the theatre where the assembly was held. But he failed, and he was put to death as a robber. As for Hippôn, he fell into the hands of the Messanians themselves, who put him solemnly to death, sending for the boys to see, as the punishment of a tyrant was held to be an edifying sight. These things seem harsh to us; but we should remember that all Greeks held that a tyrant who had risen by trampling all law underfoot had lost all right to the protection of law, and that he might be rightly dealt with as a wild beast.

And now peace was made with Carthage. The Halykos was still to be the boundary; so Carthage still kept Selinous and Hērakleia; but those of the inhabitants who chose were allowed to move freely into the Greek territory. And the Carthaginians bound themselves by a clause most unlike their first treaty with Dionysios; they were not to give help to any tyrant. There were still some to put down at Centuripa and Agyrium. The people of the last Sikel town, when set free from their tyrant Apollōniadēs, were admitted to Syracusan citizenship, and they received Greek settlers in their territory. So greatly had the distinction between Greek and Sikel, so clearly marked a hundred years before, now died out. Timoleôn also put an end to the Campanians at Ætna, and he sent fresh settlers to Gela and Akragas. Akragas now again became a place of some importance, though it never rose again to its old greatness. Thus, if not all Sicily, yet nearly all that part of Sicily which had ever been either Greek or Sikel, was now free. It became again a land of free commonwealths, without either foreign masters or domestic tyrants.

Timoleôn's work was now done. He laid down his office of general, and with it all extraordinary powers. He became a private man, and, as a private man, he chose rather to live in the land which he had delivered than to go back to his own Corinth. He sent to Corinth for his wife and children, and spent the rest of his days on an estate close to Syracuse which the Syracusan people had given him. He became blind, and he seldom visited the city or took any part in public affairs. But when the Syracusan people wished for his advice, he was brought in a carriage into the theatre, and he told them what was best. Once or twice men spoke against him; then all that he said was that the wish of his heart was now fulfilled; every man in Syracuse could speak as he pleased. At last, about eight years after his first coming into Sicily, he died (B.C. 336). As a special honour, he was buried within the city, and around his monument in the *agora* was built a range of public buildings called after him the Timoleonteion. So died, and so was honoured, the man of the worthiest fame in the whole story of Sicily, the man who thought it enough to deliver others and who sought nothing for himself.

But though neither Sicily nor any other part of the Greek world ever saw such another as Timoleôn, and though the immediate work of Timoleôn lasted only a short time, yet the example of Diòn and Timoleôn had a great effect. It became the custom now for the Greeks of Italy and Sicily, when they were pressed by any enemies, at once to ask for help in Old Greece. We must remember the state of Old Greece at the time. When Timoleôn sailed for Sicily, Philip of Macedon was fast advancing to the supremacy of Greece, and before Timoleôn died, the battle of Chairóneia in B.C. 338 had actually given him that supremacy. This was a state of things which made many in Greece dissatisfied, and anxious to try their fortunes in the West. Presently came the wonderful conquests of Alexander; and the establishment of Greek kingdoms in Asia and Egypt by his generals stirred up ambitious princes to attempt the like in other lands. There were now no great citizens like Timoleôn or even like Diòn; but several kings of

Sparta and of Epeiros showed themselves eager for western adventure. But even the best of them were not like Timoleôn. They were ready to be deliverers in the sense of driving out barbarians from Greek lands, but they did so to form kingdoms for themselves. A succession of them came, the first even during the life-time of Timoleôn. This was Archidamos king of Sparta, who had played a considerable part in the older state of things in Greece, and who was glad to escape from the new by trying his fortune elsewhere. The Tarantines, pressed by the Lucanians and Messapians, asked help of their metropolis Sparta, just as the Syracusans had asked help of their metropolis Corinth. Archidamos came out to their help; but he was slain (B.C. 338) in a battle with the barbarians at Manduria or Mandurium, on the same day, men said, as Philip's victory at Chairôneia.

We can only guess at the objects of Archidamos. The next who came, the Molottian king Alexander, uncle of the more famous Macedonian of the same name, certainly came to found a dominion for itself over Greeks and barbarians (B.C. 332–331). He began the work with some success; he even made a treaty with Rome, then a strong power in Central Italy, but which had not reached so far south. But he was presently murdered, and his schemes died with him. Neither of these princes actually touched Sicily. But their coming was clearly suggested by the careers of Diôn and Timoleôn, and some of those who came after them on the same errand had directly to do with Sicilian affairs. Meanwhile we have nothing to say about Sicily itself for several years, till a new power arises which brings Sicily into a wider connexion with the world in general than any that came before it.

XII.

THE TYRANNY OF AGATHOKLÉS.

B.C. 317–289.

[We still have the continuous narrative of Diodôros through the greater part of the reign of Agathoklês ; for the latter part we have only fragments. At this time Diodôros no doubt largely followed the History of Timaios of Tauromenion, who was a bitter hater of Agathoklês. There is no other continuous narrative, except the short one in the Latin epitomator Justin. But there are many references to Agathoklês in the later collectors, Polyainos and the like, and we are getting on so far that we get a little help from the Latin historian Titus Livius of Patavium, commonly spoken of as Livy. Polybios himself has some discussion of the acts of Agathoklês, but no narrative of them.]

IT is grievous to think that the freedom and well-being which Timoleôn brought back to Syracuse and to all Greek Sicily lasted hardly more than twenty years. The tyrants could do more lasting evil than the deliverers could do good. Seventeen years after Timoleôn's death we again hear of civil disputes in the Greek commonwealths of Sicily, and of wars between one commonwealth and another. Three years later again there came a tyranny which in some things was worse than any that Timoleôn had overthrown. A man in many things like Dionysios, even more enterprising and far more cruel, made Syracuse again the centre of a great dominion. This was Agathoklês son of Karkinos. About him several things are to be noted. Dionysios was a born Syracusan, and, after all his dealings with Carthage and with other barbarians, he was on the whole a champion of Hellas, and, whenever he showed himself in that character, he was zealously supported by all Greek Sicily. Agathoklês, on the other hand, was not a Syracusan by birth, and, though he did greater things against the Carthaginians than any other Greek, he was never so distinctly as Dionysios the champion of united Greek Sicily. Dionysios too lived before, and Agathoklês after, the great victories of Alexander in Asia. This made a great difference in the position of the two men. Agathoklês saw the Macedonian captains founding kingdoms for themselves, and he made himself a king to match them. And there was a great difference between the kind of tyranny practised by the two men. Dionysios was harsh and suspicious; but, while he stuck at no useful crime, he seldom showed himself wantonly cruel. Agathoklês affected a frank and jovial demeanour, and thus kept the good will of the lower people; but ever and anon he did deeds such as Dionysios never did. Dionysios never wrought a massacre; to Agathoklês it sometimes seems as if a massacre was really a kind of amusement.

The father of Agathoklês, banished from Rhêgion, settled at Therma (the Baths of Himera) on the northern coast of Sicily, then a Greek town under Carthaginian dominion. Warned by an oracle that the child would do great mischief, Karkinos ordered him to be exposed; but his mother saved him and persuaded her brother to bring him up. Afterwards he was received by his father, and when Timoleôn was planting new citizens at Syracuse, the whole family moved thither. There Agathoklês passed his youth in the trade of a potter; but he was strong and handsome, and he specially won the favour of a leading man named Damas, whose widow he afterwards married, and received great wealth with her. He was a valiant soldier, and Damas got him promotion in the army. He distinguished himself in a war with Akragas, and also in an expedition which Syracuse, following the best side of Hierôn of old, sent into Italy to help Krotôn against the neighbouring Bruttians. But the generals Sôsistratos and Hêrakleidês refused Agathoklês the rewards of his valour. They were then the chief men in Syracuse, and a bad report is given of them. They were the leaders of an oligarchic club of 600 men, whom Agathoklês denounced as conspiring to set up a tyranny. Banished, it would seem, he became an adventurer and mercenary captain in Italy. One time we find him defending Rhêgion, the city of his forefathers, against a Syracusan army. Presently Sôsistratos and his party were banished, and Agathoklês was recalled. The banished men sought help from the Carthaginian general Hamilkar, and Agathoklês again distinguished himself in the war against them. Next we hear of a Corinthian named Akestoridês being general at Syracuse, as if he had been another Timoleôn. He seeks the life of Agathoklês, who again escapes.

Another change brings back Sôsistratos and Hêrakleidês, who call Hamilkar to their help, while Agathoklês commands a force from the inland towns, the old Sikel towns which had now taken to Greek ways. But he wins over Hamilkar, and by his mediation, he is again received at Syracuse, on taking a most solemn oath to be faithful to the commonwealth. Presently he was chosen general, and was charged with a special commission to bring about peace among contending parties.

Never did any man more foully betray a trust than Agathoklês did. Some of the party of Sôsistratos had left Syracuse, and were trying to establish themselves in one of the inland towns. Under cover of marching against them, Agathoklês got together his soldiers, and being joined by his partisans in Syracuse, they made a general massacre, which lasted for two days, of the whole party of the six hundred. Then he called an assembly; he congratulated the people on winning back their freedom; he said that, as this was done, he wished to lay aside his office and to live as a private man. They of course again elected him general with full powers, the style under which Dionysios had seized the tyranny. But Agathoklês did not put on the state of a tyrant; he trusted himself to the people, and had no body-guard. Slaughter and banishment ceased till he found it convenient to try them again. So in the year B.C. 317, began the new tyranny over Syracuse and a great part of Sicily.

The object of Agathoklês, even more than that of Dionysios, was to make himself lord of all Sicily, or of as great a part of it as he could. He first brought under his power many of the inland towns—a little time back we should have said the Sikel towns—and he even—with the connivance, it is said, of Hamilkar—carried his arms into the Punic territory. When this was known at Carthage, Hamilkar was recalled; a lucky death saved him from the fate which he might have met at home, and another general of his own name, Hamilkar, son of Gisgon, was sent out to take his place. We hear nothing clearly about the doings of Agathoklês for some time, but about the year 315, we find him warring against Messana, which was saved by Carthaginian help. But he took Abacænum, the Sikel town from whose territory Dionysios had cut off his new town of Tyndaris, and there did a small massacre, only forty of the party opposed to him. All this showed how dangerous he was to all the Sicilian commonwealths. Akragas, above all, ever jealous of Syracuse and now the special shelter of Syracusan exiles, took counsel how best to withstand him.

As had been so often done before, the enemies of Agathoklês sent for a leader from Old Greece, naturally not from Corinth, metropolis of Syracuse, but from Sparta, even now renowned as the head of all Dorian states. Fallen from her old power, she still kept her laws and her kings. As King Archidamos had gone to help the Greeks in Italy against barbarian neighbours, so Akrotatos, son of King Kleomenês, came to help the Greeks of Sicily against a Greek tyrant. They no doubt hoped that he would be as Timoleón; he was not even as Archidamos or as

Alexander. He did nothing in war; he disgusted men by his pride and his luxury, most unlike a Spartan. At last he caused the murder of Sôsistratos the Syracusan exile; and then he had to flee. But, deprived of this expected help, the Akragantines and Geloans lost heart, and under the mediation of Hamilkar, a treaty was made with Agathoklês. Therma, Hérakleia, and Selinous, were to remain Carthaginian possessions; the other Greek cities in Sicily were to be free, but under the overlordship of Syracuse or her master. Messana alone stood aloof, and there the Syracusan exiles were still received. It was thought at Carthage that more favourable terms might have been had, and Hamilkar was greatly blamed.

Messana had been left out of the treaty. About the year 312 we again find Agathoklês warring against that city. He did not take it, but he contrived to get into his hands 600 men from Messana and Tauromenion and slew them. He then marched against Akragas, which was saved by the coming of a Punic fleet; but he went on and ravaged several places in the Punic territory. He was now thoroughly committed to war with Carthage. The Syracusan exiles therefore took the opportunity to pray for a great Punic force to be sent into Sicily. Even in the time of Dionysios we should have called them traitors; but men now felt that the yoke of Carthage was less heavy than the yoke of Agathoklês. But, besides asking for Punic help, they did what they could themselves. Two gallant, but unsuccessful, attempts were made by the exiles to free Centuripa and Galaria, two inland towns which were held by Agathoklês' garrisons. His recovery of them was marked by much slaughter. These successes encouraged him to march against the Punic camp which was pitched on the hill of Eknomos, the hill stands boldly out in the sea by the mouth of the southern Himeras. By sea the Carthaginian fleet made an attack on Syracuse; they sailed into the Great Harbour; but they did nothing but sink an Athenian merchant-ship and cut off the hands of the crew. By land the Punic force did nothing. It was at the moment weaker than the army of Agathoklês, who brought his full strength to the attack on Eknomos. The barbarians therefore refused his challenge to battle, and he went back to Syracuse with such spoil as he could gather in the country round about.

The danger from the advance of Agathoklês was well known at Carthage. It was therefore determined to take to the Sicilian war in good earnest; and Hamilkar was sent forth with another of those great fleets and armies that we have so often heard of. This one was notable for two things. One was the great number of Balearic slingers; the other was that, as in the expedition in Timoleôn's day, an unusual number of Carthaginian citizens, many of them men of high rank, were sent to serve. But a great storm met them on their way and sank many ships, specially those that carried the native Carthaginians. The blow was so heavily felt at Carthage that the walls were hung with black as a sign of mourning. Hamilkar saved what he could of the fleet, and made up his numbers by levies in Sicily, till he sat down again on Eknomos at the head of 40,000 foot and 5,000 horse. This was much smaller than the armies which the earlier Punic generals had commanded; but Punic military skill had grown since then, and Hamilkar no longer trusted to the brute force of multitudes. Agathoklês set out to meet them, and did one of his worst deeds on the road. He cunningly surprised Gela; he slew many, plundered the rest, and marched on. He must have heard on the way that twenty of his ships had been taken by the Carthaginians in the strait of Messana.

He now came to the broad vale of the southern Himeras. As Hamilkar held the hill of Eknomos on the right bank, he occupied another hill on the other side, the river flowing between them. Neither side for a while took courage to cross the stream, for there were old sayings that many men should be slain in that place. At last the battle, one of the greatest battles between Greeks and Phœnicians—we could wish that the Greeks had had a worthier leader—was brought on by chance. The Carthaginian troops were scattered over the dale to plunder; Agathoklês sent down his men to do the like, and planted an ambush of picked men just on his own side of the river. The Greeks ventured close up to the Carthaginian camp, and drove away the beasts of burthen. Punic soldiers came out to follow them, and they were cunningly led to the spot where the liers-in-wait sprang up and cut them in pieces. Then Agathoklês thought the time was come for a general attack. He led his whole force to the Punic camp; the Greeks began to fill up the ditch, to tear up the palisades, and to make their way in. The main body were driven back by the Balearic slingers, who were specially trained with their own weapon, and who met the Greeks with a storm of great stones. Still the Greeks broke in at various points, and the camp had almost again fallen into their hands, when the scale was turned by the landing of a new body of Punic troops. These had doubtless been sent from Carthage to make up for those who had been lost in the shipwreck. They at once set upon the Greeks, who were now hemmed in on both sides and gave way. Agathoklês and his army were now driven to flight. It was the very noon of a hot summer's day; the heat was frightful; some died of the heat and the toil, or of quenching their thirst with the unwholesome waters of the salt river. The battle was utterly lost, the first time that a great battle between the Greeks and Phœnicians had been lost by the Greeks. The Carthaginians had stormed several Greek towns; but Gelôn, Dionysios, and Timoleôn had all had the better in their chief battles. It fared otherwise with Agathoklês.

All the towns of central and eastern Sicily now began to fall away from Agathoklês and to join the Carthaginians. His cruelties had made him generally hated; and Hamilkar took care to act in exactly the opposite way, and to win men and cities over by good treatment. But Agathoklês had a greater plan than all in view. By his cunning stratagems he was able to draw off the Punic forces to Gela; he got safely to Syracuse, and was able to gather in provisions and all that he needed, while he made ready for the most daring enterprise that any man had ever yet thought of.

This was no other than to carry the war into Africa. Agathoklês believed that in no other way could he strike so heavy a blow at Carthage. He might thereby recover his own position in Sicily by drawing the Carthaginians off to the defence of their own homes. The blow would be more than unlooked for; it was something that had never come into men's minds. Since the Phœnicians had settled in Africa, no enemy was known to have attacked them in their own land. That land was fruitful and rich beyond all lands; none offered such a plunder. The Carthaginians were hated by their African subjects, and moreover were not loved by the other Phœnician towns. Agathoklês therefore held that the weak point of Carthage was really in Africa, that a bold attack would at once lead to the revolt of her African subjects, and that, if nothing more came, the Punic forces would be withdrawn from Sicily. He formed his plan therefore, and told it to no man. He made everything ready, including a good deal of extortion, and some slaughtering, among those whom he suspected. But both his mercenaries and the mass of the Syracusans still trusted him, even after his great defeat. When he told them that he was going to sail somewhither for the advantage of Syracuse, they still believed him.

Syracuse was not at this time really besieged; but a Punic fleet watched the mouths of the harbours. Agathoklês had therefore to watch his time to get out. At last, at a lucky moment, he contrived to sail forth with his fleet, taking with him a large force, citizen and mercenary, Greek and barbarian.

He left his brother Antandros to command in Syracuse; his two sons, Archagathos and Hérakleides, went with him. Many guesses were made as to his intended course; but none knew. The next day the whole fleet was frightened by an eclipse of the sun (Aug. 15th, B.C. 310); but all still obeyed, and on the seventh day of their voyage they reached Africa. They landed in the peninsula opposite to Carthage, a little way south-west of the promontory now known as Cape Bon. The Carthaginian fleet had followed them; but the Greeks landed first. Agathoklês then, with a solemn ceremony, burned his ships as an offering to the goddesses of Sicily. The action seemed mad; but, if they were defeated, they could not sail back in the teeth of the Punic fleet, and if they were victorious, the Punic fleet would be theirs.

So the first European army that ever set foot in Phœnician Africa landed under the command of Agathoklês of Syracuse. He led the way, and many others in different ages came after him. For a while he went on conquering and to conquer. The fruitful and well-tilled land, the rich houses and gardens of the great men of Carthage, lay as a spoil before him. Presently he reached the town of Tunis, lying at the end of the lake at whose mouth Carthage stands, and looking out at the great city itself. We are not told how Agathoklês got possession of it; the men of Tunis may well have welcomed him as a deliverer from Carthaginian dominion. At any rate he made Tunis his head-quarters throughout the war. The Carthaginians now made all things ready for defence, and put two generals, Hannôn and Bomilkar, at the head of their army. This was on the strange ground that they were personal enemies, and would therefore each try to excel the other. Hannôn was a brave soldier, and did his duty; Bomilkar was already suspected of aiming at tyranny, and was perhaps in league with Agathoklês. A battle followed between Tunis and Carthage, which reversed the fortunes of the fight by the Himeras. The Greeks won a great victory, putting the Sacred Band of Carthage to flight, and taking the Punic camp. The whole open country was now in the hands of Agathoklês. The Carthaginians could only keep themselves shut up in their city. Their consciences smote them that they had neglected the due honours of their gods. So they sent sacred embassies to their metropolis Tyre, and caused five hundred children of the chief houses of Carthage to pass through the fire to Moloch.

The Carthaginians had one small comfort; they had got hold of the brazen prows of the ships that Agathoklês had burned. These were sent to Hamilkar in Sicily with the true story for his own ear, but with orders to spread abroad a report that Agathoklês had been utterly defeated by land and sea, and that these prows were the spoils. This caused great fear in Syracuse, and Antandros drove out all friends and kinsfolk of the exiles, as dangerous persons at such a time. Hamilkar treated them well; he then marched close up to the walls and called on the city to surrender. Antandros for a moment thought of yielding; but the Aitolian Erymnôn had a stouter heart.

Just at the moment the true tale came. Agathoklês had sent a vessel directly after his victory, which was chased by a Punic ship close to Syracuse in the sight of all the people. By great striving the Syracusan ship came in with the news. There was no more thought of surrender, and an attempt of Hamilkar to storm the walls was defeated. He then (310) went away from Syracuse for several months. He was called on to send part of his army to the defence of Carthage, and he could do nothing against Syracuse till he had gathered fresh troops.

Meanwhile Agathoklês, from his head-quarters at Tunis, was receiving the submission of many African towns, and pressing Carthage hard without actually besieging it. He then carried his arms to some distance; he took Hadrumetum (now Susa) on the coast, and Thapsos, and pressed some way into the interior. This enabled the Carthaginians to attack his camp by Tunis; but he turned back and drove them away. His affairs were also prospering in Sicily, and a ghastly sign of victory was brought to him. One day he rode out in person before the Carthaginian camp and showed them the head of Hamilkar. Even in their amazement and grief, they all bowed in reverence to the head, as if it had been their living commander. The head of Hamilkar told a truer story than the brazen prows had told. After some months waiting (309), Hamilkar, in concert with the Syracusan exile Deinokratês, had got together a great army, Greek and barbarian, for another and more dangerous attack on Syracuse. The plan was to sit down and besiege the city from the Olympieion, as so many had done before. But the soothsayers told Hamilkar that the sacrifices foretold that he should sup in Syracuse the next day. This stirred him up to an immediate attack. The army went round in the night by the same path that Dêmosthenês had gone. They tried in the like sort to climb up Epipolai on the north side, a harder work since Dionysios had built his walls and his strong castle. This attack was badly managed, and was utterly defeated. Hamilkar himself was taken prisoner; he was led through the city, shamefully abused, and at last put to death. His head was sent to Agathoklês, who, as we have seen, knew what to do with it.

A strange mutiny followed in the army of Agathoklês, which shows how dangerous dealings were with mercenary soldiers. A drunken brawl arose between his son Archagathos and an Aitolian officer named Lykiskos, in which Lykiskos was killed. The whole body of mercenaries rose. They demanded the death of Archagathos; they demanded their pay; they chose new generals, and took possession of Tunis, leaving Agathoklês to himself. The Carthaginians, hearing this, offered higher pay and rewards to the soldiers, if they would come over to their service. Many of the officers were inclined to accept the offer; Agathoklês feared that he was about to be handed over to the enemy, when he tried one last chance. He threw aside his general's dress; he harangued the soldiers; he told them of all their exploits; he called on them not to betray him; he would rather die by their hands than by those of the Carthaginians. They were stirred at once; shouts were raised in his favour; he was called on to put on his general's dress again, and to lead them as before. He struck while the iron was hot. The enemy were looking for the mercenaries to join them; but the trumpet sounded the war-note; the Greeks charged, and drove the Carthaginians back to their camp. Two hundred only deserted to the Carthaginians.

Agathoklês was thus strangely successful, and he went on winning successes; but he saw that to take Carthage was still beyond his power. He therefore sought for an ally in Ophellas, the Macedonian officer who commanded at Kyrênê for Ptolemy lord of Egypt. The old kings of Kyrênê, and the commonwealth too, had passed away; the land had become part of Ptolemy's dominion. Agathoklês proposed to Ophellas to join him in the conquest of Carthage. He would leave Africa to Ophellas, and he would then go back to drive the Phœnicians out of Sicily. Ophellas believed him; he gathered an army and many colonists from all parts, and after a march of two months he reached the Syracusan camp at Tunis (307). Agathoklês received them friendly; but after a few days he accused Ophellas of plotting against him, and set upon him with his own men. Then he slew him. The army of Ophellas, not knowing what to do, entered the service of Agathoklês.

Agathoklês had now a stronger force than ever, and about this time news came that all the Macedonian commanders in the East, now that the house of Alexander was extinct, had taken the title of kings. The general or tyrant of Syracuse, carrying on a successful war in Africa, thought he was as great as any of them, and called himself king also. First of Sicilian rulers, he put his name and kingly title on the coin, but he did not go so far as to put his head. Nor did the new king wear the diadem; a sacred wreath belonging to a priesthood that he held was enough for him. In the strength of his kingship he went on to new conquests, taking Utica and other towns which still clave to Carthage, and slaughtering their inhabitants as usual. Carthage was now more closely hemmed in than ever; but there was still no sign of the city being taken.

The kings of that age called themselves simply "King," without adding the name of any particular kingdom. So King Agathoklês did not call himself King of Syracuse or King of Sicily. This last he was far from being; besides the Phœnician possessions, many of the Hellenic and hellenized towns had turned against him. After the defeat and death of Hamilkar at Syracuse, the Akragantines thought themselves strong enough to take up the cause of independence against Agathoklês, without help either from Carthage or from Deinokratês and the exiles. They proclaimed an alliance of all cities that would join under the leadership of Akragas; they were ready to help any that were ready to throw off the dominion of Agathoklês. A crowd of towns, both strictly Greek and those Sikel towns which had become practically Greek, speedily joined them. Gela, metropolis of Akragas, was the first; then came Henna, by this time no doubt reverenced everywhere as the holy seat of the goddesses. Presently others were won, till the lieutenants of the absent Agathoklês seem to have kept nothing for their master beyond the actual territory of Syracuse. Akragas had thus far been in alliance with Carthage; but such an alliance was unnatural, and had been made simply out of common enmity to Agathoklês. Presently the Akragantines and their allies began to deliver the towns that were in bondage to Carthage, among which we can specially see Hérakleia on the south coast, the scene of the legend of Minôs, now known as the Phœnician *Ras Melkart.* Thus there were three wars going on in Sicily at once. The Akragantine alliance was at war both with Carthage and with Agathoklês, and Agathoklês and Carthage were at war with one another. But both of these last were too busy in Africa to do much in Sicily. Punic ships cruised off the harbour of Syracuse to keep cornships from coming in, and that was about all. For about two years (309-307) the Akragantine alliance was able to go on with very little hindrance in the work of deliverance. At last (307), its general Xenodikos ventured to attack the Syracusan territory itself. But he was defeated by Leptinês and Damophilos, the generals of Agathoklês. The Akragantines were so disheartened by this failure that they gave up their great schemes of deliverance, and their alliance fell asunder. Xenodikos remained general of the single commonwealth of Akragas only.

Just after this victory of his generals, Agathoklês, the new king, came back from Africa, leaving his son Archagathos in command there. He sailed to Selinous, and thence struck a blow at Carthage and Akragas at once by seizing the lately freed town of Hérakleia. He then crossed to the northern side of the island, to his own birthplace of Therma, still a Punic possession. There he made some kind of terms; thence he went on and took the hill-town of Cephalœdium with its ancient walls by the sea; thence he struck inland, and failed in an attempt to take Centuripa by treason. He failed in a like attempt on Apollonia, but after two days' fighting he took it by storm. It is important to mark these once Sikel towns, now spoken of without any distinction from the Greek towns, and seeming to be thought of equal importance.

Just at this time the cause of the independence of the Sicilian cities against Agathoklês was again proclaimed, this time by the Syracusan exile Deinokratês. Many flocked to him from all parts; as a private adventurer, he was not so well to be trusted as an established commonwealth like Akragas, but his fellow exiles, tried in warfare, were better soldiers than the levies of Akragas and the other cities. He kept Agathoklês himself in check; he offered battle, which the tyrant did not venture to accept. The cause of the tyrant seemed sinking both in Sicily and in Africa. There Archagathos still held Tunis; but he underwent several defeats from the Carthaginians, and earnestly prayed his father to come to his help. Just at that moment fortune turned in Agathoklês' favour. He himself, with the help of some Etruscan ships, overcame the Punic fleet before Syracuse; he brought in provisions to the city, and had the sea clear for the way to Africa. About the same time Leptinês invaded the Akragantine territory and defeated Xenodikos, who was so blamed by his own people for his two defeats that he withdrew to Gela. Greatly cheered by these two victories, Agathoklês left Leptinês in Sicily and again sailed back to Africa.

But he found that he had no real hope of success there. He himself suffered a defeat in attacking the Punic camp before Tunis. A wonderful night followed in both camps. The Carthaginians burned their choicest captives to their gods. In so doing they set fire to their camp, and they might easily have been set upon and routed in the confusion. But Agathoklês' own camp was in no less confusion. Seeing that success was hopeless, and having a private quarrel with his son Archagathos, he determined to decamp privily with his other son Hêrakleidês and to leave Archagathos and the army to their fate. But the scheme was found out by Archagathos and the soldiers, and Agathoklês was put in bonds in his own camp. But a cry came that the enemy was attacking the camp. At such a moment who could lead them like their old general and king? Agathoklês was brought out in chains; the one cry was to set him free. But the moment he was free, he got away; he found a boat and sailed off with a few companions for Sicily (November, B.C. 307). The soldiers slew his sons and then made peace with the Carthaginians. So the famous African expedition of Agathoklês came to an end in utter discomfiture. He had not strengthened his own power; he had not seriously weakened the power of Carthage. But he had planned and carried out, and for a while succeeded in, the most daring enterprise that man had ever planned. And if he himself came back defeated, he pointed the way to others who came back victorious.

One mourns again that the first man to brave the Phœnician at home should have been such an one as Agathoklês. Soured by disappointment, he came back to Sicily in a more savage mood than ever. He landed at Selinous; he made first for Segesta, the old Elymian city of which we have not lately heard much. It is said to have been in alliance with him; but no barbarian ever treated a city of enemies worse than Agathoklês, in his wrath and disappointment, treated his friends. He demanded a great contribution, and when the people of Segesta were loath to pay it, he charged them with plotting against him. On this ground he slew the great mass of the people, save only the boys and maidens, whom he sold to the Bruttians, in Italy. And he not only slew, but, what the worst Greeks seldom did, he put to death by torture. He is said to have revived the old device of Phalaris; only, instead of a brazen bull, it was a brazen bed, on which he could not only hear but see the sufferings of the victims. Then, having emptied the town of its old inhabitants, he peopled it afresh with a mixed multitude, and gave it the new name of Dikaiopolis—City of Righteousness. But the name of Segesta soon came back, and the new inhabitants took up the old Trojan tradition. But the city never was what it had been before; the great temple, which

TEMPLE OF SEGESTA.

must have been in-building when Agathoklês came, is still unfinished.

It seems to have been while Agathoklês was at Segesta that he heard the news from Africa, the murder of his sons and the rest. In his wrath he sent orders to his brother Antandros, who commanded for him at Syracuse, to put to death all the kinsfolk, young and old, of the men who had served with him in Africa. And the thing was done. It is wonderful that the man who did such deeds as these two last was allowed to live for seventeen years longer, and then did not die in any public outbreak.

The most wonderful thing in the life of Agathoklês is the strange course of ups and downs that he went through. When his power seemed on the point of wholly passing away, it rose up again higher than before. It was so when, just after his great defeat in Sicily, he went on his expedition to Africa; it is so now that he has come back defeated from Africa to find stronger enemies in Sicily than ever. A great part of Greek Sicily was already joined against him under the leadership of Deinokratês. When he came back discomfited from Africa, his own general Pasiphilos, thinking that his power was now at an end, joined Deinokratês, carrying with him a large force and the possession of many towns which he held for Agathoklês. We can see that among these were Therma and Cephalœdium, which he had seized on his first return from Africa. Indeed it would seem that Agathoklês could just now have kept very little beyond Syracuse and its immediate territory. The desertion of Pasiphilos is said to have put the tyrant so utterly out of heart that he thought of giving up all attempts to keep any great dominion. He certainly entered into a negotiation which had very much that look; but it seems far more likely that he was acting in subtlety. He sent to Deinokratês, proposing to give up all dominion at Syracuse. Syracuse should again be a free city, and Deinokratês should come back as one of its citizens. For himself he only asked for two towns, his own birth-place Therma and Cephalœdium, just to live in. This did not at all suit the purposes of Deinokratês. Whatever he had been when he had left Syracuse, he had now put on habits of command; he wished to be a ruler of some kind; he had no mind to go back to Syracuse as one citizen in a commonwealth. It must have been amusing when Agathoklês sent over and over again to beg for his two towns, and Deinokratês kept putting him off with all manner of excuses. But all this while Agathoklês was practising with the followers of Deinokratês till he won many of them to his interests. He then made a treaty by which, to be safe on the side of Carthage, he acknowledged the right of the Carthaginians to all that they had ever held in Sicily. This would take in his own Therma which he had been just asking for himself. In return for his acknowledgement he received a large supply of money and corn, which was very useful to him just then.

Agathoklês now thought it was time to try his luck against Deinokratês. He had much the smaller army of the two, but he knew that many of Deinokratês' men would come over to him. And so they did. The armies met at a place called Torgium, which seems to be the modern Caltavulturo, lying some way inland both from Termini and Cefalù (Therma and Cephalœdium), the towns which just now were most concerned. When the battle began, two thousand men of Deinokratés' army went over to Agathoklés. This still left Deinokratés' force much the stronger, but it was enough to throw everything into confusion. Deinokratés' men gave way; Agathoklés pursued awhile and then made a proclamation. He did not want to do them any further hurt; they had learned by defeat at the hands of a smaller army that it was no use standing against him; they had better go quietly to their own homes. And so most of them did. But there was one body, perhaps Syracusan exiles, who kept together and occupied a strong post in the night. They came to terms with Agathoklés under solemn oaths; but, as soon as they had laid down their arms, his darters shot them to death. Not many tyrants would have done such a deed as this; but it adds little to the shame of the man who had just wrought the massacres at Segesta and Syracuse.

And now a strange agreement was come to between Agathoklés and Deinokratés. There may have been some dealing between them all along; there certainly was some special feeling between them. For Agathoklés at the very beginning of his tyranny, when he slew others, let Deinokratés go; and now men noticed that, while he broke faith with every one else, he always kept it with Deinokratés. Deinokratés now entered the service of Agathoklés, bringing with him the remnant of his army. He perhaps saw that he had no chance of being the first man in Sicily, but that under Agathoklês he might be the second, and as such, more powerful than he could be as a single citizen or magistrate of Syracuse. He became Agathoklês' most trusted general. His first act in that character was to slay Pasiphilos, and to hand over the towns in his possession to his new master.

Thus Agathoklês, baffled in all his attempts in Africa, rose again to a greater position in his own island than he had ever held before. He came nearer to being King of Sicily than any man had done before him. He was master of all the lands and cities east of the Halykos, unless possibly of Akragas. If he did hold Akragas, he was master of all Greek Sicily, from which Sikel Sicily was no longer distinguished. And his dominion seems to have remained unbroken for the remaining seventeen years of his life. As in the case of Dionysios, we know much more of his earlier days than of his later. But we see the undisputed lord or king of Greek Sicily in an altogether new position. Dionysios spread his power into Italy, and even beyond Hadria; but the world had now altogether changed since the time of Dionysios. All Greece and the East, all the Hellenic and *Hellenistic* lands, were now disputed for among the kings who had divided the dominion of Alexander among them. Of those kings, Agathoklês, as we have seen, claimed to be the peer. And in truth his dominion over Greeks and hellenized Sikels had much in common with their dominion over Greeks and other hellenized nations. Now that we have got from commonwealths to tyrants and from tyrants to kings, history becomes more and more personal, more influenced by the alliances and family connexions of particular persons. That in B.C. 304 Agathoklês made a piratical attack on the island of Lipara comes within his usual Sicilian range; that we should find him warring in Italy is only what he had himself done in earlier days; that he should even win for himself a dominion east of Hadria is no more than Dionysios had done. What is special to Agathoklês, what marks his age, is that we find him warring among the Macedonian princes as one of their number. He wins the island of Korkyra, twin-sister of Syracuse, by hard fighting from the Macedonian king Kassandros; he then gives it as a dowry with his daughter Lanassa to the Epeirot King Pyrrhos; when Lanassa tires of Pyrrhos as a husband and of her father as an ally, she offers herself and her island as an acceptable gift to Démétrios the Besieger. Agathoklês himself in his later years, but perhaps before Lanassa's marriage, himself takes a Macedonian wife, seemingly the step-daughter of King Ptolemy of Egypt. His latter years are known only in a most fragmentary way; but we see him several times waging war in southern Italy, and indulging in treachery and slaughter to the last. But all this latter time of his life belongs to lands out of Sicily. Démétrios the Besieger, who would allow only himself and his father to be kings and had nicknames for all the other princes, called Agathoklês the Lord of the

Island. And so he was. After his settlement with Deinokratês, we hear nothing of any wars in Sicily.

At last, when Agathoklês was seventy-two years old and had reigned twenty-eight years, he began to think of his old warfare, and began to plan another expedition against Carthage. To this end he got together a great army and fleet, and had a camp pitched near Ætna, where his grandson Archagathos commanded. But Agathoklês felt himself failing, and thought it time to provide for the succession. For this he chose his son Agathoklês, which naturally gave offence to his grandson Archagathos, the son of his elder son, who moreover had shown greater capacity for command. The old Agathoklês sent orders to Archagathos to give up the command of the army to his uncle. On this he rebelled; he slew his uncle, and began to conspire the death of his grandfather. He is said to have engaged one Mainòn, a special favourite of the old tyrant, whom he had spared in the massacre at Segesta on account of his beauty, to get rid of him by a lingering poison. When Agathoklês felt that his end was coming, he sent away his wife and his young children to the care of King Ptolemy in Egypt, and was quite alone. He held one more assembly of the people. He told them not to continue his power to any one else, and specially to punish the rebellion and impiety of his grandson. And so he died, his body, some said, being put on the pile for burning before he was fully dead.

So in the year 289 B.C. ended the dominion of Agathoklês, the bloodiest of all the tyrants of whom we have to speak, but who seems to have kept the good will of at least the mob of Syracuse through his whole reign. Syracuse and all Sicily, after so many revolutions, had almost lost the power of free government. The death of Agathoklês is followed by a time of utter confusion, till yet another deliverer comes, not a Timoleôn, not an Agathoklês, but a king of heroic stock, and himself as near to a kingly hero as the times allowed. When he had tried and failed, all was over. Sicily had no hope but to fall into the hands of the strongest of her neighbours.

AGATHOKLÊS, WITH NAME OF SYRACUSE ONLY.

AGATHOKLÊS, WITH NAME ONLY.

AGATHOKLÊS, WITH ROYAL TITLE.

XIII.

THE COMING OF PYRRHOS AND THE RISE OF HIERÔN.

B.C. 289-264.

[For the acts of Pyrrhos we have no contemporary narrative, nor any continuous narrative except his Life by Plutarch. We have only fragments of Diodôros, and a fragment or two of Dionysios of Halikarnassos also helps us. Of Livy we have only the Epitomè. But so famous a man of course supplied much material to the compilers and collectors of later times. So there is a great deal of incidental matter about him. In all these latter times, inscriptions, so rare in the early days of Sicily, are getting more and more numerous. And now that we have got into the age of kings, coins begin to be of a new use, as being marked with their heads and names. And towards the end of our period we begin to get again the guidance of a historian of the first rank, though not contemporary. The early acts of Hierôn are recorded in the first book of Polybios.]

ON the death of Agathoklês it is said that the Syracusans restored the democracy. But there is no reason to think that the democracy had been formally abolished. What is meant doubtless is that the special powers which had been granted to Agathoklês were not granted to any one else, and that for the moment no one was able to seize them by force. So there was freedom again, but only for a little while.

Mainón of Segesta, who was said to have poisoned Agathoklês, was banished. He betook himself to the camp of Archagathos; he murdered him, and took the command of the army himself. With that he warred against Syracuse; but the Syracusan general Hiketas withstood him till he made an alliance with the Carthaginians. What became of Mainón we are not told; but Hiketas fled, and the citizens had to submit to give hostages to the Carthaginians and to

MAMERTINI AT MESSANA.

receive their exiles. This seems to mean the barbarian mercenaries of Agathoklês, chiefly Campanians, who had been serving under Archagathos. Things now happened exactly as they had happened nearly two hundred years before, after the fall of Thrasyboulos. The mercenaries and the citizens did not agree; but at last a peaceful settlement was made with the mercenaries, by which they were to leave Sicily and go back to their homes. They set out and reached Messana, where they were received friendly. But, just as their countrymen had done at Entella in the time of Dionysios, they seized on the town, slew the men, and took the women and children to themselves. There they founded a new state, a robber state, which spread havoc through all eastern Sicily. They took the name of *Mamertines*, from the Latin god of war, Mamers or Mars, answering to the Greek Arês. And they called the town of Messana *Civitas Mamertinorum*, which remained its official name for many ages.

The Syracusan general Hiketas must have betrayed his trust ; for we presently find him spoken of as tyrant, in which character he reigned nine years

COIN OF HIKETAS.

(288-279). Other tyrants arose elsewhere, as Tyndariôn at Tauromenion and Phintías at Akragas. This last puts his name on the coin with the title of king ; Hiketas also puts his name, but without the title ; we have not any heads as yet. The old rivalry between Syracuse and Akragas broke forth again ; Hiketas overthrew Phintías in a battle near the Heraian Hybla. But Phintías was supported by Carthage ; the Punic troops pressed Syracuse hard, while Phintías was able to form a large dominion. We read incidentally that Agyrium revolted against him, which shows how far his power had stretched. Thus nearly all Sicily was divided between two Greek and two barbarian powers: Phintías at Akragas, Hiketas at Syracuse, the Carthaginians, and the Mamertines. These last carried their ravages so far as to reach the southern coast and to destroy the city of Gela.

We hear of the cruelty of Phintías, and also how he afterwards mended his ways. But he must have been hated at Akragas; for we find that he was driven out, and that the Akragantines even took in a Carthaginian garrison to keep him from coming in again. Yet in the course of his reign he did at least one good act. When Gela, the metropolis of Akragas, was destroyed by the Mamertines, he built a new town for the homeless citizens. It stood just within the territory of Akragas, at the foot of the hill of Eknomos and by the southern river Himeras, just where Agathoklês underwent his great defeat at the hands of Hamilkar. He called his new town after his own name, Phintiás; but the people still called themselves Geloans, just as the people of Therma called themselves Himeraians. Phintiás was the last Greek city founded in Sicily, and it abides still by the name of Licata.

About the year 279 the power of Hiketas at Syracuse was upset by one Thoinôn. Presently we find Thoinôn commanding a garrison in the Island, while one Sôsistratos commands in the rest of the city. The two quarrelled, and led their soldiers against one another. Yet they do not seem to have been strictly tyrants, such as held parts of the city at the time when Timoleôn came; they were rather mere insubordinate officers. Meanwhile the Carthaginians pressed

Syracuse hard by land and sea, and the Punic fleet entered the Great Harbour. In this strait the rival commanders and all the citizens agreed to ask for help from outside. A cry went up, not only from Syracuse but from all Greek Sicily, calling on the greatest Greek prince of the time to come and help all the Greeks of the island, alike against Carthaginians, Mamertines, and tyrants.

This was Pyrrhos, King of Epeiros, the last and most famous of the men who, from Archidamos onwards, came from Old Greece to help, or to profess to help, the Greeks of Sicily and Italy. He was now in Italy, warring against the Romans on behalf of the Tarantines. He was about forty years old, having been born in 318, just before Agathoklés rose to power. He was the near kinsman of the Epeirot King Alexander who had died in Italy, and he was believed, like him, to come of the heroic stock of Achilleus. Those were wild days in Greece and the neighbouring lands, when each of the kings strove to win all the territory that he could, and many of them arose and fell several times. Pyrrhos had his ups and downs from his childhood. He had been in exile and had come back more than once; he won and lost Macedonia more than once. But he had greatly enlarged his hereditary kingdom, and he was now reigning in honour as the most renowned prince of his time. For though he was as ambitious and as fond of fighting as any of the other kings, he had higher qualities than the rest. He was held after his death to have been the greatest commander after Alexander. And assuredly no man ever was braver or more skilful in battle; but he was too much of a knight-errant to carry out a whole war wisely. He was not treacherous or wantonly cruel; he was beloved by his soldiers and subjects and admired by his enemies. In short he was the very model of a warrior-king, a character as much above Agathoklês as it was below Timoleôn. In 281 he had been asked by the Tarantines to come to their help, and the next year he had gone over himself with a great force of all kinds, including elephants. Since the wars of Alexander, these beasts had been brought into Europe, and now they appeared for the first time in the West.

The war of Pyrrhos with the Romans is one of the most famous in history, through the many stories that are preserved of it. His war in Sicily is not nearly so well known; but it is a memorable tale. The two are really parts of one enterprise. Pyrrhos sought to free the Greeks of the West from all barbarians, Carthaginians, Romans, or any others, and then to set up a great Greek power in the West such as the other kings had set up in the East. Of republican freedom there would be an end; and in truth there was an end already. Pyrrhos, as a king, did not come, like Timoleôn, simply to deliver, but to reign over those whom he delivered. The like had been the aim of the princes who came before him; but he came nearer to success than any of them. If he had succeeded, the whole history of the world would have been changed; Rome, if not altogether conquered, could not have come to be the head even of Italy. As it was, Pyrrhos simply came like a thunderbolt on Italy and Sicily, and did nothing lasting. It must be marked that the Romans and Carthaginians, whom we shall presently find such fierce enemies, are as yet friendly powers, and the coming of Pyrrhos made them allied powers. He had to fight against both. It might seem that, as in the days of Gelôn, two great barbarian powers were leagued against Hellas, Carthage and Rome, as once Carthage and Persia. But Rome, though in the Greek sense a barbarian power, was not like Carthage or Persia. It was a power thoroughly European, ready to take up the championship of Europe against Asia and Africa when Greece could no longer hold it.

It was the two years' warfare of Pyrrhos in Sicily (278-276) which showed that so it must be. In Italy he won two great battles over the Romans; but his victories were so dearly bought, with such hard fighting and with such heavy loss, that they were almost like defeats. When he was prayed to come into Sicily, he was glad to make a truce with the Romans and to try his luck in a new field. In Sicily he had no great battles to fight; but he had hard work none the less. He had to take his whole force, elephants and all, by sea; for the Mamertines held the strait, and were leagued with the Carthaginians to keep him out of Sicily. He avoided them, and landed at Tauromenion, where the tyrant Tyndariôn joined him. He was joyfully welcomed at Katanê; as he came near to Syracuse, Thoinôn came to meet him with a body of ships; he and Sôsistratos gave up to him all their troops, stores, and military engines, and the whole city received him with delight. His fleet, Epeirot and Syracusan, was so strong that the Punic ships in the Great Harbour sailed away without striking a blow. Of the besieging land force we hear nothing. Akragas, it will be remembered, was held by a Carthaginian garrison. Pyrrhos set forth to do his first feat of arms on Sicilian soil by winning the second city in Sicily from the barbarians. On the road he was met by the news that the Akragantines had themselves driven out the Punic troops, and prayed him to come to their help. Sosistratos, now an officer in the King's service, was sent on, and he received the submission of Akragas and of thirty other towns.

Thus, if it was deliverance to be transferred from the fear of barbarians and the rule of domestic tyrants to the rule of a Greek king, all Greek Sicily was delivered without striking a blow. From Tauromenion to Akragas Pyrrhos was as truly king as he was at Passarôn and at Ambrakia. That dominion on both sides of the sea which Agathoklês had begun from the western side was now more fully carried out by his son-in-law from the eastern side. Pyrrhos was spoken of as King of Sicily; he seems almost to have looked on it as a hereditary kingdom. He is said to have designed a division of his dominions, giving Sicily to Alexander, his son by Lanassa and therefore grandson of Agathoklês, and Italy to his other son Helenos. But the King of Greek Sicily would be King of all Sicily; only a very small part of his work was done if the barbarians still held all the north-western part of the island, including more than one subject Greek city. He would do what Pentathlos and Dôrieus and Hermokratês and Dionysios had only tried to do. He first marched against the great Punic stronghold of Herakleia; it fell into his hands, whether by storm or surrender is not said. The subject Greeks of Selinous joyfully welcomed the Greek king. City after city joined him; the new Trojans of Segesta were among them. And now he drew near to a spot trodden by no foot of invading Greek since Heraklês himself had won it. Eryx, on its hill-top above the sea, had willingly submitted to Dionysios; it never saw him as a conqueror. It was now a Punic stronghold, defended by the Punic wall which still abides. The engines were brought up the mountain-side and set to play on the defences; but it was by the hand-to-hand fighting of the King himself and his immediate companions that Eryx was won. Vowing games and sacrifices to Heraklês, Pyrrhos was the first man to plant his ladder against the wall, and to stand victorious on its battlements. The soldiers of Pyrrhos called their king the Eagle; he had now soared to an eyrie worthy of him; the descendant of Achilleus had won back the heritage of Heraklês.

But there was a richer prize to win. From Eryx Pyrrhos marched on into that garden of Sicily of which Hermokratês alone had once for a moment gathered the fruits. We read without details that he took Panormos, that he took her guardian rock of Herktê. We can say no more; but, for the first time of three, the Semitic head of Sicily became European ground. The Roman and the Norman were to come, each in his turn; but it was the man of Epeiros that showed them the way.

But here was the term of his victories. Solous had become his along with Panormos, but the great Phœnician stronghold remained. When Dionysios had entered the barbarian corner, his great blow had been struck at Motya. Motya was no more; but Pyrrhos, on his way to Eryx, had passed by Lilybaion which had taken its place. And while he was winning Eryx and Panormos, the Carthaginians had been making Lilybaion stronger than ever. We are amazed to hear that Pyrrhos needed urging on to attack the great fortress. The Carthaginians offered peace; they would give up all claim to everything else in Sicily, but they would keep Lilybaion. They doubtless hoped, if they kept Lilybaion, to win back all the rest before long. Pyrrhos was disposed to agree to the terms. This is perhaps not very wonderful. He had done enough in Sicily to gratify his love of enterprise; he had done far more than any Greek had done before him; he was needed in Italy, where the Romans were not shut up in one fortress, but were pressing hard on his allies; the state of Macedonia and Greece offered many calls to his ambition. But his officers, above all his Sicilian officers, told him that he must go on. To the Sicilians it was a matter of life and death; now or never the Phœnicians must be driven out of the island, and Sicily must become wholly Greek. The King therefore answered that he would make peace with Carthage on the surrender of everything in Sicily. This was refused, and the siege of Lilybaion began.

Lilybaion was no more to be taken by Pyrrhos than it was by Dionysios. After a toilsome siege of two months he gave up the attempt. It was perhaps now that he won several fortresses from the Mamertines. But he no more recovered Messana than he won Lilybaion. His whole work really went for nothing as long as those two great points were held by the barbarians. He is said to have talked of getting together a great fleet, and carrying the war into Africa like his father-in-law Agathoklês. But he did nothing. He went back to Syracuse as to the capital of his new kingdom, but the man who had hitherto been the mildest and best beloved of generals and kings now, in his disappointment, became cruel and suspicious. He put Thoinôn to death, and Sôsistratos had to flee. The new kingdom began to break up; some towns revolted to the Carthaginians, some to the Mamertines. The King rejoiced when (B.C. 276) a message came from Italy, praying him to come once more to help the Tarantines and the Samnites against Rome. He set out, and made his way into Italy, almost as a fugitive, after hard fighting with Carthaginians by sea and Mamertines by land. In Italy he again began the war with the Romans; but he was defeated in the battle of Beneventum in 275. He went back to Epeiros the next year, and again began to mix in the wars of Macedonia and Greece. In 272 he was killed at Argos; the same year Taras surrendered to the Romans. The work of the deliverers from beyond Hadria in Italy and Sicily was over. Or we may, if we please, say that it stopped for eight hundred or for thirteen hundred years.

When Pyrrhos left Sicily, he is reported to have

said: "What a wrestling-ground I leave here for the Romans and Carthaginians." And so it proved, though not at once. Just at that moment Rome and Carthage had been driven into alliance by common fear of him, and they did not become open enemies for twelve years. After Pyrrhos was gone, one more attempt was made to keep the Greek towns of Sicily, or some of them, together, first as a confederacy and then under a native king. The chief enemies now were the Mamertines. Compared with them, the Carthaginians were beginning to be looked on almost as friends; they were at least a regular government and not a mere band of robbers. They had won back all that Pyrrhos had taken from them, and a good deal more. Akragas was in their hands some years later; so they most likely got possession of it now. But part of the kingdom of Pyrrhos, Syracuse and all the towns of the east coast, and some of the inland towns also, still kept together, and defended themselves against the Mamertines. There was now at Syracuse a certain Hierôn son of Hieroklês, who professed to be a descendant of the famous Gelôn; he might be so through that son of Gelôn of whom we have nothing to say. Many stories were told of him, how he was the son of a slave-woman and was exposed in his childhood, somewhat like Agathoklês, and how a wolf took away his book when he was a boy, like his forefather Gelôn. It is more certain that he was an officer under Pyrrhos and won the king's high esteem and favour. He was still very young when, after Pyrrhos was gone, the soldiers chose him general. The citizens at first objected; but he had powerful friends who gained their consent, and he gradually won general favour. He next strengthened himself by a marriage with the daughter of Leptinês, a leading man in Syracuse, and the beautiful head of Queen Philistis is to be seen on many of the coins of King Hierôn.

But he was not king yet. As general of the Syracusans and their allies, he warred against the Mamertines; he gave help too to the Romans when they subdued and chastised a legion of their Campanian soldiers who had done by Rhêgion just as the Campanians of Agathoklês had done by Messana. He warred too against the Mamertines in Sicily. In one campaign, having taken several towns from them, he distrusted his old mercenaries, and in a battle with the enemy, he left them to be cut in pieces, while he led off the Syracusan citizens in safety. Dionysios had once done the like; so did other commanders, Roman and Carthaginian; there was in truth no other way to get rid of dangerous and mutinous troops. But if we blame Hierôn for this as an act of treachery, we shall find little to blame in him after; he did the best that could be done in a bad time. He next led another army into the Mamertine territory; he defeated the freebooters in a battle by the river Longanos near Mylai, and pressed them very hard. It was thought that he might have taken Messana except for Punic jealousy. Syracuse and Carthage were allied against the Mamertines, but Carthage, aiming at the dominion of all Sicily, did not wish Messana to fall into Syracusan hands. But the Mamertines were now shut up in Messana and shorn of their power of doing mischief. In the general joy at this great success, Hierôn, when he came home was chosen King of the Syracusans and their Allies.

There was thus one more chance for Greek Sicily, under a Greek king, a Sicilian king. But it was too late; if Agathoklês had been such a man as Hierôn instead of what he was, things might have been otherwise. Hierôn did what he could; but all that he could do was to secure well-being, but not freedom,

HIERON II.

for one corner of Sicily. For fifty years he reigned over Syracuse wisely and justly; he was the first native Sicilian ruler to put his head on the coin; in all other things he affected very little of the state of kingship. But in matters of foreign policy he had to shape himself to the time. When he was chosen king, he seemed to have a great career before him; the only fear was how far Carthage, his nominal ally, might stand in his way. Rome too was his ally, and to Rome he had done a great service; nor had Rome any pretence as yet for meddling in the affairs of

Sicily. A very few years later he found that the only way to keep any measure of dominion for himself or of freedom for his people was to become the dependent ally of Rome.

QUEEN PHILISTIS.

XIV.

THE WAR FOR SICILY.

B.C. 264-241.

[Through the whole of this chapter we have a guide second only to Thucydides in the first book of Polybios. He is not contemporary, but he lived near enough to the time to be well informed. He represents Roman traditions. Of Livy we have only the epitome, and of Diodôros only fragments. There is a life of Hamilkar by Cornelius Nepos. The secondary sources are much the same as before. It is a great loss that we have not the history of Philinos of Akragas, who, though a Greek, wrote from the Carthaginian side.]

THE first war between Rome and Carthage is known in general history as the First Punic War. It is spoken of by writers nearer to the time as the War for Sicily. And so it was. It was a war between the two great commonwealths which lay on each side of Sicily for the dominion of the great island which lay between them. That was what things had come to. Carthage, mistress of a great part of Sicily, wished for the rest. Rome, now mistress of Italy, wished for the island that lay so near to Italy. It was Rome's first taste of really foreign dominion out of her own peninsula. Between these two great powers, there was little hope for Hierôn and his independent kingdom of Syracuse. The blow must have come sooner or later; it did come much sooner than any one could have looked for, and it came in a shape by no means honourable to Rome.

It was Hierôn, the Greek king, who was really pressing the Mamertines and threatening altogether to free Sicily from their presence. Carthage was playing fast and loose. Still Carthage, Rome, and Syracuse, were all held to be friendly powers, and Carthage was supposed to be in alliance with Syracuse against the Mamertines. At last, in B.C. 265, Hierôn was pressing the freebooters so hard that they found that they must seek allies somewhere. There was a Carthaginian party among them, and a Carthaginian garrison was admitted into Messana. But the general feeling was for Rome; the head of Italy might be ready to give help to Italians against Phœnicians and Greeks. But Rome had no quarrel with either Syracuse or Carthage; and Rome had just before, with Syracusan help, heavily chastised her own soldiers for doing at Rhêgion what the Mamertines had done at Messana. The Mamertines were therefore for a while afraid to ask for help from Rome. At last however they did. After much debate at Rome, help to the Mamertines was granted. They became dependent allies of Rome, like the towns and nations of Italy; Messana in short became a piece of Italy on the Sicilian side of the strait. But help to the Mamertines meant war with both Syracuse and Carthage. So in B.C. 264 the First Punic War, the War for Sicily, began.

Of that war, simply as a war between Rome and

Carthage, there is no need for the Story of Sicily to speak at any length. The fate of Sicily was decided for her by others; her own people, Greeks and Sikels who had practically become Greeks, could do little indeed. The tale of three-and-twenty years' fighting might be told by saying that, while the rest of Sicily became a Roman province, the Mamertines stayed in the relation of Italian allies, and King Hierôn, after he became the friend of Rome, kept his kingdom of Syracuse as long as he lived, as happy as a good king could make it, and as independent as a state could be which knew that in all foreign affairs it must follow the lead of a greater power. But in this long war a great deal happened in Sicily which is of the deepest local interest to this and that place. Some of the most stirring events that ever happened in Sicily happened during these years. And some of these we must tell, while we leave the general course of the war to those who have to tell the story of Rome and of Carthage. But we may notice that, though a good deal was done by land, yet the characteristic feature of the war was its great battles by sea, and also the number of fleets that were destroyed by storms. All this was off the coast of Sicily. The wonderful thing is that Rome, whose main strength before and after was always by land, could in this war, after many ups and downs, overcome the greatest sea-faring power of the world on its own element.

Very soon after the Romans entered Sicily, in the year 263, they marched with their whole force against the King of Syracuse. They began by taking the sacred town of Hadranum by storm. The slaughter done by a Roman army on taking a town by storm was something to which the Greeks were quite unaccustomed. Several towns were frightened into submission, and Hierôn's kingdom was sadly cut short before the consuls drew near to Syracuse. Then he submitted, and made terms of peace. It was not the interest of Rome to press him hard. He agreed to pay a hundred talents of silver, and to become the ally of Rome. To become the ally of Rome practically meant to become dependent on Rome. Having been thus driven to change sides, Hierôn became the most faithful and zealous ally of the Romans, helping them in every way and receiving all favour and honour back again. The course taken by the war barely touched Syracuse; so the well-being of the city and of the rest of Hierôn's dominions was hardly at all disturbed. Hierôn was the first of many kings whom the Romans called their allies; a new state of things in short began with him. The kingdom left to him took in the old territory of Syracuse and the towns of the east coast as far north as Tauromenion. For the rest of Sicily Romans and Carthaginians went on fighting.

In the next year, 262, it is worth noting that the people of Segesta, who had a Carthaginian garrison in their town, rose and slew them and joined the Romans. Agathoklês had rooted out the old Elymian people of Segesta; but the mixed multitude whom he had planted there did as men always do in such cases; they took up the old traditions of the place. They gave themselves out for Trojans; and it was very convenient for the Romans to greet them as brethren and to deal with Segesta as a favoured ally.

PRETENDED TOMB OF THÉRÔN, AT AGRIGENTUM.

About the same time one of the greatest Greek cities of Sicily came to the end of its history as a Greek city. Akragas was now a Carthaginian possession, and it was determined to make it the great centre of Carthaginian power in Sicily. This led to the great Roman siege of that city. By a strange turning-about of things from what we have been used to see, Akragas was defended by Punic armies. And of course, whichever side succeeded, it meant the dying out of the Greek life of the place. The siege was a long one, with various exploits on both sides. At last the Carthaginian commander Hannibal, finding no hope of holding the place, cut his way out. The city was for a moment left to itself; but the Romans burst in, and all was over. The horrors of a Roman storm followed; those who were not slain were sold into slavery. Akragas, fairest of mortal cities, after rising again, though not to its old greatness, from its first Carthaginian overthrow, finally sinks into the provincial town of Agrigentum. As such it had a third life; but the great city of Theron gradually shrank up into the present town within the old akropolis.

This was in 261. The next year is famous for the first battle by sea won by Romans over Carthaginians, the great victory of Gaius Duilius in the bay of Mylai. This was followed by a great deal of fighting in various parts of Sicily and the taking of many towns by the contending armies. Then Henna was taken, first by a Punic, and then by a Roman, force. The Carthaginians strengthened Drepana the haven of Eryx, and made it one of their chief stations during the remainder of the war. More interesting perhaps is the fact that in 258 the consuls Aulus Atilius and Gaius Sulpicius made, like Hermokratês and Dionysios, an inroad into the land of Panormos. There perhaps Atilius heard enough to enable him before long to repeat the exploit, not only of Hermokratês and Dionysios, but of Pyrrhos himself.

The next year comes the hard-fought sea-fight off Tyndaris, a dearly bought victory for Rome. Then for two years the scene changes to Africa. The tales, true and false, about Marcus Atilius Regulus touch Sicily only in this, that it is plain that his attack on Carthage on African soil was suggested by the invasion of Agathoklês. But the year 254 is one of the most memorable in Sicilian history. The other Atilius, Aulus, had learned his lesson, and now he practised it. We have now for the first time to call up the picture of Panormos with its double haven, the old city with its long street, between the two branches of the sea, and the new city, the peninsula keeping guard between the haven and the outer sea. Besides these it is plain that a fortified suburb had grown up between the southern branch of the haven and the river Oreto. Against this great city, the ancient head of Phœnician Sicily, the consul Aulus and his colleague Gaius Cornelius now led the fleet and army of Rome. The fleet sailed into the haven; the soldiers were landed between the south wall and the river; the New City, attacked by land and sea, was taken by storm, and the Old City presently surrendered in sheer fright. Those of the inhabitants who could pay a ransom were spared;

the rest were sold for slaves. Panormos and the land of Panormos became a Roman possession, save only that the hill of Herkte was not yet taken, but was held by Punic troops as a thorn in the side of its Roman possessors. But, after the fall of Panormos, not a few towns rose against their Punic garrisons and called in the Romans. It is a speaking fact that among them was Phœnician Solous. Carthage was clearly not loved by her subjects, even by those of her own blood.

Thus was the great Semitic city of Sicily for the second time won for Europe. The Greek under Pyrrhos had made his way in for a moment; the Roman was to keep his hold abidingly. Panormos was indeed again to see Semitic masters; but not till nearly eleven hundred years after the entry of Atilius and Cornelius. As a piece of general European history, the taking of Panormos, presently followed by its defence, is the greatest event of the War for Sicily. Strange to say, this great success was immediately followed by a time of great downheartedness among the Romans. They won some successes, as the taking of Therma and of Lipara on its island. Yet they are described as keeping out of the way of the Carthaginian armies, through sheer dread of the elephants. There is something strange in this. The use of elephants in the Punic armies was something new. The elephants of India had been brought into Italy and Sicily by Pyrrhos, and that had led the Carthaginians to tame the elephants of their own continent and to employ them in war in the like sort. They now take the place in the Punic armies which had formerly been held by the war-chariots. But it is not easy to see why the Romans were so specially afraid of them just at this time. It was not the first time that they had met the Punic elephants in Sicily, and before that they had met and overcome the elephants of Pyrrhos at Beneventum. Anyhow the elephants were presently to be put to their trial on a great scale. It was of course the great object at Carthage to win back Panormos, and a failure of the Romans to take Herkté may have raised their hopes higher. The Punic general Asdrubal now (251) set forth to attack Panormos, which was defended by the proconsul Lucius Cæcilius Metellus. The whole campaign was by land; nothing is said of ships on either side. Asdrubal marched from Lilybaion with a great army of the usual kind, and with no less than 120 elephants, the force in which he chiefly trusted. They entered the land of Panormos by the passage in the hills, and found themselves with the river Oreto between them and the city. The plan of Metellus was to keep within the city and to draw on the enemy near to the south wall. Asdrubal was filled with scorn at the supposed cowardice of the enemy, and the captains of the elephants asked specially that they might take the lead in the attack. Metellus had lined the south wall and its ditch with light-armed troops, who, as the elephants drew near, kept up a ceaseless shower of darts and arrows. The beasts presently became unmanageable, and the Punic ranks began to fall into confusion. Then Metellus saw his time; he threw open the gate, and charged with his legionaries. The Punic army was utterly routed; the elephants galloped hither and thither about the plain, with or without their riders. In the end sixty were taken alive and sent to Rome. Panormos was saved for Rome and for Europe.

The Roman despondency now altogether passed away. There now seemed to be a hope of winning those strongholds in the extreme west of the island which were now all that Carthage held in Sicily. As we find Herkté in Roman hands a little later, it was most likely taken soon after the defence of Panormos. But the height of Eryx, the new fortress of Drepana, and the older fortress of Lilybaion, were still held by Carthage. The greatest efforts of Rome were now made to take them. The rest of the war, a space of ten years, gathers altogether round these points, the centre of warfare being the great siege of Lilybaion, which went on all the time. Many stirring deeds were done on both sides; and in the end, though the Romans defeated Carthage in the war, they were no more able to take the great Carthaginian stronghold than Dionysios and Pyrrhos had been.

Of the first year of the siege of Lilybaion we have a minute account, recording many stirring events. It is not quite easy to see why the Carthaginians chose this moment to destroy Selinous, which had long been a Greek town under Punic rule, and to move its inhabitants to the besieged Lilybaion. But this notice marks the end of Selinous as even a subject city. The walls no doubt were slighted; but there is no reason to think that the temples were destroyed, for which there was no motive. At Lilybaion the siege now began by land and sea. The Roman ships were moored off the mouth of the harbour to keep anything from going in: they tried in vain to block up the haven. But Phœnician seamanship was so much better than theirs that for a while skilful captains continued to make their way in. One specially, out of the many bearers of the name of Hannibal, distinguished, we know not why, as the Rhodian, went in and out for a long time as he pleased with his single ship. But he and his ship were at last taken. We are not told what became of Hannibal himself, but his ship became a model to Roman ship-builders, and no one was able to repeat his exploit. By land the Romans strove hard to fill up the great ditch which defended the city, and the Carthaginians tried to burn the Roman engines. In this they at last succeeded. After the first year the long siege seems to have become a mere blockade. We hear but few details. In 249, after the great defeat of the consul Publius Claudius off Drepana by the Punic general Asdrubal, the siege was all but given up; but it still went on.

The defeat off Drepana was followed the next year by a great destruction of a Roman fleet by a storm, after which the Romans sent out no more ships till quite the end of the war. But the consul Lucius Junius struck a bold stroke by land. With the remnant of his fleet he sailed round to the foot of Eryx; he landed; by a sudden blow he seized the town and temple and turned the mountain into a Roman stronghold. Eryx, like Panormos, had been held for a moment by Pyrrhos; now Rome laid a more lasting grasp on the house of the goddess in whom men saw the mother of Æneas. But now the last few years of the war were to be made illustrious by the coming of the greatest man who had as yet had a share in it. Carthage had long been so far advancing in all that makes a power great that even the average of her statesmen and generals is now distinctly higher than that of Rome. She now sent forth a captain greater than any that had been before him, the father of a son yet more famous than himself, though perhaps not of greater gifts. The Punic proper names were so few that it is not always easy to distinguish their bearers : we have now come to the greatest Hamilkar, the father of the greatest Hannibal. Hamilkar, called Barak or the Thunderbolt, was now put at the head of the Punic forces in Sicily. His exploits were wonderful ; but their nature shows what the character of the war had now become. Both the contending commonwealths were nearly worn out with the long struggle. But Rome and her allies had now possession of all Sicily except Drepana and Lilybaion, and of those Lilybaion was blockaded. There was really no room for any enterprises on a great scale ; the question was whether Rome or Carthage could bear up longest, and all that even Hamilkar could do was to try to wear Rome out. He first with his fleet laid waste the shores of southern Italy. He then, by a sudden blow, seized the height of Herkté just above Panormos. The city itself he does not seem to have attacked ; but he occupied a centre from which he could work every kind of annoyance on the

Romans in Panormos and elsewhere.* He fought no pitched battles; he attacked none of the great Roman strongholds; but he defeated every attempt to dislodge his force from the hill, and he laid waste the Roman territory by sea and land.

For three years Hamilkar thus worked hard from his post on Herktê to wear out the Roman power. It might look like a confession of failure when, of his own free will, he left Herktê and chose another point. This time the Thunderbolt fell on Eryx. But he was able to seize only the lower town; the akropolis, with the temple of Ashtoreth or Aphroditê, remained in the hands of the Romans. The combatants were thus close to one another; for two years endless skirmishes went on, without any marked advantage to either side. Romans and Carthaginians alike had to fight for every morsel of food they got. The War for Sicily was now waged on the one height of Eryx, save that outside of Lilybaion there were still Roman besiegers, and inside of it there were still Punic defenders. But they seem to have done little more than watch one another; we hear of no special exploits on either side.

In this way the forces of the two commonwealths which were striving for the dominion of Sicily were both wearing away. The Romans had quite given up all action by sea, and, after the first days of Hamilkar's occupation of Herktê, we hear nothing of any such on the part of Carthage. When Hamilkar had been two years on Eryx, there was no Punic fleet anywhere in Sicilian waters. In the year 241 the Romans, under the energetic consul Gaius Lutatius

Catulus, held that the moment was come for one final attempt by sea which must bring the war to an end one way or the other. Ships were built after the pattern of the famous ship of the Rhodian Hannibal; the crews were well practised, and the fleet set forth. There was no Carthaginian fleet to withstand the Romans. They took Drepana; they renewed the naval blockade of Lilybaion; nothing was left to Carthage save Lilybaion itself and Hamilkar's stronghold on Eryx. For five years naval affairs had been neglected at Carthage; but now it was impossible to avoid fitting out a fleet. It was made ready and manned in haste; it had to carry provisions to Hamilkar on Eryx as well as to meet the Romans off Drepana or Lilybaion. The object of Lutatius was to meet the Punic fleet while it was still laden, before it had reached Eryx. And this he succeeded in doing by going forth in the teeth of a contrary wind. It was perhaps the highest tribute ever paid by enemy to enemy, when Lutatius determined to attack at once in the face of the storm rather than wait for a better wind and allow the Carthaginians to sail round to Eryx. If they did so, they would take Hamilkar and his veterans on board, and Lutatius judged that it was less dangerous to face the storm than to face Hamilkar. The last fight of the war then began off the isle of Aigousa. Even naval skill, the special boast of Carthage, seemed to have gone over to the Roman side. The heavily laden Punic ships could not bear up against the Romans; the War for Sicily was ended by the utter defeat of Carthage on her own element.

The two commonwealths had each thrown its last cast, and Rome had won. Lilybaion and Eryx were not taken; but Carthage was defeated, not only in the battle but in the war. A commission was sent to Hamilkar, empowering him to make peace with the Romans on any terms that he thought good. Lutatius had no such powers, but the two generals agreed on terms, subject to the approval of the Roman people. Carthage was to give up all claim on Sicily, to withdraw all troops from Sicily; to abstain from war with Hierôn, and to pay 2,200 talents within twenty years. At Rome these terms were thought too favourable to Carthage; the money was raised to 3,200 talents, to be paid within ten years. And a clause was added by which Carthage was to give up all claim on the islands between Italy and Sicily. This meant the isles of Lipara; on those islands it was clearly necessary that Carthage should give up all claim. But the words were afterwards construed, strangely and not very fairly, to imply a cession of Sardinia and Corsica. Hamilkar did not refuse, and peace was made. The unconquered garrisons of Lilybaion and Eryx marched out and were carried away to Carthage. The War for Sicily was over, and the island, as far as Carthage was concerned, was left to the dominion of Rome.

With the first appearance of Rome as an actor in Sicilian affairs, all hope of maintaining any real Sicilian independence had passed away. It was plain that the dominion of the island must fall to one or the other of the two great contending commonwealths. At the time men may have doubted whether Rome or Carthage had the better chance. We can see that the advance of Rome could not be checked, and we see further that it was well that it could not be checked. If Greek Sicily could not remain free, if it could not be independent under a Greek king, it was better that it should at least have European masters. The fight of Aigousa determined that Sicily should remain European for 1068 years. In fact it determined that it should remain European for ever; it made the second Semitic occupation something wholly unnatural. The barbarian corner of Sicily was now won for Europe; the Greek subjects of Carthage passed under the less unnatural rule of Rome; the kingdom of Hierón still remained untouched within its own borders, but practically a dependency of Rome. We have still some stirring tales to tell before all Sicily passes under immediate Roman government; but its complete subjection is now only a question of time.

XV.

THE END OF SICILIAN INDEPENDENCE.

B.C. 241–211.

[As we have now come to the great Hannibalian War, the secondary materials, anecdotes, allusions, references of all kinds, are endless. From the beginning of the war we have the continuous narrative of Livy, founded in many parts on Polybios. We have Polybios' own books from the second to the fifth, and fragments of those that follow. Of Diodôros we have only fragments. There is the Life of Marcellus by Plutarch, and the Life of Hannibal by Cornelius Nepos. The Latin poet Silius Italicus wrote a long poem on the war, in which there is much mention of Sicily, and he is very careful in his Sicilian geography. The only actually contemporary materials for this time are some verses of the poet Theokritos, addressed to King Hierôn, and some fragments of the poem of the Italian Ennius on the war.]

THE establishment of the Roman power in Sicily is not only a marked event in the history of the island; it marks a memorable stage in the growth of the Roman dominion, and thereby in the general history of the world. The event of the first war between Rome and Carthage was to give Rome her first province and her first dependent kingdom. Others of both kinds followed in abundance; but Sicily supplied the first of each class. Hierôn, in form a free ally of Rome, was practically dependent. He was perfectly free in the administration of his own kingdom; but he knew that in his foreign policy he had nothing to do but to follow the lead of Rome. The first of his class, he was far better treated than the royal dependents of Rome were in later times. The prosperity and the internal independence of Syracuse were untouched as long as he lived, and if they perished soon after his death, it was through the fault of a foolish successor. The territory of the Mamertines was a piece of Italy on the Sicilian side of the strait. In the rest of the island, the part subject to Carthage, Rome now stepped into the position of Carthage; it became the Roman province of Sicily. That is, it became a land subject to Rome, or rather a possession of Rome, ruled by a Roman governor. The full organization of all Sicily as a land subject to Rome, and the exact relation of all its towns to the ruling commonwealth, did not come yet. But so much of the island as had been under the power of Carthage now becomes Roman provincial soil, the property of the Roman people.

Meanwhile the dominions of Hierôn, so long as Hierôn lived, enjoyed all the advantages that can be had from the government of a good king. And it was well for them that their king lived to be ninety years old, and reigned forty-seven years after he became the ally of Rome. To that character he clave steadily; in all the wars which Rome waged with the Gauls, in the time between the two Punic wars, Hierôn constantly sent help. And after the second, the Hannibalian war, broke out, he was ever zealous in helping his ally with provisions and troops. Syracuse itself was untouched by war; but Hierôn kept up a powerful fleet, and caused the defences of the city to be strengthened, and every kind of military engine to be kept in readiness under the care of his kinsman Archimêdês, the most renowned of mechanical philosophers. He adorned the city with many buildings. Foremost among them was the second temple of Olympian Zeus in the *agora*; then there was the great altar for the feast of Zeus Eleutherios near the theatre, and the repairs of the theatre itself. There Hierôn's name and the names of others of his family may still be read carved on the stone. His rule was mild and just; he observed the old laws and abstained from all kingly pomp. Still he kept the Island as a separate stronghold, the dwelling-place of the king and the place of his treasury and store-houses. He settled the taxation; all land paid a tithe to the state; and the law of King Hierôn remained in force long after his time, when all Sicily had become a province. He was famous among other Greek kings, and kept a strict friendship with the Egyptian Ptolemies, to which it has commonly been thought that the presence of the paper-plant of the Nile in the waters of Syracuse is owing. His bounty reached to Greeks far away; he largely helped the Rhodians when their city had suffered from an earthquake. Like the former Hierôn, he had poets to sing his praises, and the pastoral poems of Theokritos, of which the scene is chiefly laid in Sicily, mark his time as the odes of Pindar mark the time of the old tyrants. Almost the only drawback to his prosperity was the death of his only son Gelôn, a son who walked in his ways, in his life-time.

Towards the end of the good old king's reign, the Hannibalian war began in the year 218. Its early stages barely touched Sicily, and they were marked by one conquest which Rome won from Carthage, that of the island of Melita. But in 216 King Hierôn died, and the good time of his kingdom was over. It was said that Hierôn had wished to restore the commonwealth. That means that he did not wish that the special powers which had been granted to himself should be granted to any one else after him. This is not unlikely. If Gelôn had been alive, nothing could have been better than that he should succeed his father; but there was now no one left but Gelôn's son Hierônymos, a lad of fifteen, who had already begun to show evil tendencies. But the old king was, it is said, talked over by his daughters, who hoped that their husbands, Hadranodôros and Zôippos, might rule in their nephew's name. So he made a will, bequeathing the kingdom to Hierônymos, and putting him under the care of fifteen guardians, among whom were his two uncles. The will had to be confirmed by the Syracusan assembly, which assented, but not very willingly, and the reign of the last king of Syracuse began.

Hierônymos, young as he was, had a will of his own, and that an evil will. Hadranodôros contrived to get rid of his colleagues, and hoped to rule his nephew at his pleasure. Hierônymos gave a certain amount of heed both to him and to Zôippos; but he ruled for himself. He is charged with every kind of cruelty and excess; what seems best proved against him is that, whereas his grandfather and his father Gelôn had lived among the people of Syracuse in the simplest way and had respected all constitutional forms, Hierónymos surrounded himself with the extreme of royal pomp, and never consulted senate or assembly. In short, according to Greek ideas, from a lawful king he became a tyrant. Then came the great political question of the day. Now that Hannibal was winning his great victories in Italy, and Rome seemed almost at the last gasp, it was by no means clear that the Roman alliance was the safest for Syracuse. It was quite possible that help given to Carthage might be rewarded with the possession of all Sicily. Hadranodôros and Zôippos both took the Punic side; another adviser, Thrasón, who pleaded for Rome, was got rid of, and in 215 an embassy was sent to Hannibal, then in Campania after his victory at Cannæ, offering the alliance of Syracuse to Carthage. The envoys were of course gladly received; Hannibal referred them to the government of Carthage for the conclusion of a formal treaty; meanwhile he sent agents to look after Carthaginian interests in Syracuse. These were two brothers, Hippokratés and Epikydés, men of mixed descent, Carthaginian by birth, but grandsons of a Syracusan who had been banished by Agathoklés and had settled and married at Carthage. Hippokratés gained great influence over the young king. Hierónymos fully made up his mind to join Carthage. When the prætor in the Roman province, Appius

Claudius, called on him to keep his faith to Rome, he gave a mocking answer. He sent two embassies to Carthage. The first proposed that he and the Carthaginians should drive the Romans out of Sicily and divide the island between them, with the river Himeras for the boundary. He then rose in his demands, and asked for all Sicily. The Carthaginians consented; it suited their purpose for the time, and Hierónymos became their ally and the enemy of Rome.

But a party in Syracuse was favourable to Rome, and the misrule of Hierónymos had made him many enemies. He set out on a campaign against the Roman province, but was presently killed by conspirators at Leontinoi. Two of the slayers, Theodotos and Sósis, set out at once, hoping to be the first to take the news to Syracuse. But a slave of the king's got there before them, and Hadranodóros, who looked on himself as his nephew's successor, was able to make some preparations for defence. But when Sósis and Theodotos came from Leontinoi, bearing the diadem of Hierónymos and the royal robe stained with his blood, popular feeling broke forth; the soldiers of Hadranodóros would not support him; the rule of the senate and people was proclaimed, and Hadranodóros was called on to submit to the restored commonwealth. He was at first inclined to do so; but his wife Damareta, daughter of Hierón, stirred him up to cleave to power. But he had not strength of mind to take any decided course either way. The next day he went out of the Island, gave up the keys, and made his submission to the new state of things. He was at once elected general, along with Themistos, the husband of Harmonia the sister of Hierónymos. With them were joined several of his slayers. They were of course on the Roman side, and envoys were sent to Appius Claudius to negotiate a renewal of the old friendship between Syracuse and Rome.

Thus far things had gone on the whole quietly; no blood had been shed but that of Hierónymos. But the prospect of renewed friendship with Rome did not at all suit the purposes of Hippokratés and Epikydés. At the time of the death of Hierónymos, they were absent on a military command against the neighbouring Roman garrisons. They tried in vain to keep the news of the king's death from their soldiers, who presently forsook them. They then went to Syracuse; they pleaded that they were officers of Hannibal's, who had come to Syracuse and served Hierónymos only because their own commander had sent them. They wished now to go back to Hannibal, and asked for a guard, as the roads were not safe. The generals granted their request, but foolishly did not send them off at once. They thus had time to intrigue with various kinds of people, largely with the mercenaries and the deserters from the Roman service, against the alliance with Rome. They gave out that the object of the generals was, under cover of the Roman alliance, to bring Syracuse wholly under the power of Rome, and to rule themselves under Roman patronage. Damareta and Harmonia are said to have stirred up their husbands to join in the plot. The other generals professed to have found evidence against them; but, instead of bringing them to trial, they had them murdered at the door of the senate-house, and then got the senate to pass a vote approving the deed. Then they harangued the public assembly, and pretended to carry a vote that the whole house of the tyrants—so the descendants of good King Hierôn were now called—should be put to death. Those who answered to that description in Syracuse were all women. Not only were Damareta and Harmonia slain, but a far more pitiful slaughter was done. Zóippos, the husband of Hierôn's other daughter Hérakleia, was away at Alexandria. He had advised the Carthaginian alliance; but he disapproved of Hierónymos' misdeeds, and, when he was sent to Egypt on an embassy, he chose to stay there rather than come back to Syracuse. His wife and two daughters were left at Syracuse; they were now slaughtered with horrible cruelty.

This was one of the worst deeds in Syracusan history; but it was the deed of the generals, not of the people. When the assembly found out how they had been deceived, orders were sent, but too late, to stop the slaughter. One is rather surprised that the generals who had done such a deed were not deposed, or rather swept away in a burst of wrath. But the anger of the people showed itself only by a strong turn of general feeling towards the Carthaginian side. In this state of mind Hippokratés and Epikydés were chosen generals instead of the two slain men. They still had to dissemble; negotiations were going on with Appius Claudius, and he sent envoys on to the new consul who had come into Sicily, the famous Marcus Claudius Marcellus. The two brothers gave out that there was a plot to give the city altogether up to Rome. And they had the more weight when a Punic fleet came to Pachynos, and when Appius Claudius thought it prudent to bring the Roman fleet to the mouth of the Great Harbour. He came only to watch; but the people were greatly stirred, and they were kept from violence only by the speech of a certain Apollônidês, who persuaded them to keep in the Roman alliance, and to conclude the treaty which was under negotiation with Marcellus.

A new subject of dispute grew out of the terms of the treaty, which shows how the old feelings characteristic of Greek commonwealths still lived on. The treaty provided that all the towns that had been under the rule of King Hierôn should be under the rule of the Syracusan commonwealth. Every Greek knew what that meant. The king might rule in the interest of his whole kingdom; a commonwealth of Syracuse, aristocratic or democratic, would rule in the interest of Syracuse only. In this Hippokratês and Epikydês saw their advantage. They were foolishly sent to Leontinoi with a force of mercenaries and deserters, to get them and their men out of the way. They were after all officers of Hannibal's, who cared for Syracuse only so far as suited the interests of Carthage. They therefore did not scruple, in a style that might have been very becoming in a Leontine patriot, to stir up the Leontines to assert their independence of Syracuse, and also to make inroads into the Roman territory. Marcellus naturally sent to Syracuse to complain of this breach of the treaty which had just been made. The generals answered that Leontinoi was a town subject to Syracuse, and that Syracuse would join with Rome to put down the revolt.

Syracuse might thus even now have remained in the Roman alliance, if Marcellus had not turned all Greek feeling in Sicily against him by an act in which he perhaps thought that he was rather merciful than otherwise. The inland parts of the island had now not seen war for more than fifty years, and now war was going to be waged by Romans. The received war-law of Rome was far harsher than anything to which Greeks were used anywhere. Very bloody deeds were often done even by Greek commonwealths, and worse excesses had now and then been done both by mobs and by tyrants. But nowhere in Greece was there any systematic practice like the indiscriminate slaughter when the Romans took a town by storm. And the bloodiest military executions among Greeks were inflictions of simple death, without the addition of needless pain or mockery. Marcellus now set out for Leontinoi without waiting for the Syracusan contingent which was to join him. A fierce assault carried the town. The usual massacre must have followed for a while, and some plunder was certainly done. But Marcellus stopped it as soon as he could. No citizen of Leontinoi, no soldier who was not a deserter, suffered anything further: the consul even ordered the plundered goods to be restored. In all this Marcellus was certainly acting much less harshly. than Roman generals often did. But there were two thousand men in Leontinoi to whom, by Roman law, he could show no mercy. These were the deserters who were all scourged and beheaded. We may safely say that no such sight had ever been seen in eastern Sicily. The scourging, yet more than the beheading, turned general feeling strongly against the Romans. The story further lent itself to any amount of exaggeration. Hippokratês and Epikydês, who contrived to escape to Herbessus, began to spread reports abroad that the whole people of Leontinoi had been treated in the way in which only the deserters had been.

The result of these falsehoods was that the Syracusan soldiers, citizens and mercenaries, refused to act against either Leontinoi or Herbessus. They welcomed Hippokratês and Epikydês, when they ventured to come out and meet them. The mercenaries were further stirred up by a forged letter from the Syracusan generals to Marcellus, in which they were made to thank him for his treatment of the deserters at Leontinoi, and to pray him to do the like by all the mercenaries in the Syracusan service. The wrath of the mercenaries was naturally great; the generals fled, without waiting to disclaim the letter; Hippokratês and Epikydês had some ado to keep the mercenaries from massacring all the men in the army who were Syracusan citizens. The generals fled to Syracuse; they were followed by a messenger who was sent by the two brothers to repeat all the false tales which had been told to the army. The city was divided; but the more part, specially of the lower people, were now on the Carthaginian side. When Hippokratês and Epikydês came to the Hexapyla, the generals found none who would withstand them.

They fled with their partisans into Achradina; but the wall was stormed; some of the generals and their partisans were slain; others, of whom Sôsis was one, escaped to the Roman camp. An irregular assembly, in which slaves, strangers, and criminals were allowed to take a part, restored the two brothers to their office of general. It is not clear whether any formal vote on behalf of Carthage was passed. But Syracuse was now held in the Carthaginian interest by mercenaries, deserters, and the lowest class of her own people. A large party still clave to Rome, but they were overpowered. The Roman siege of Syracuse (214-212) began.

Marcellus led his troops by a round-about path to the old camping-ground by the Olympieion, leaving the northern part of the city untouched. His object was to act in concert with the fleet in the Great Harbour. He still made two attempts at negotiation. His message was that he did not come to besiege Syracuse; he came to demand the restoration of those Syracusans who had taken refuge in the camp, and the deliverance of those who were now held down by the yoke of strangers. Let the fugitives be restored, let the authors of the massacre be given up, and all would still be well. If not, Rome must appeal to arms. Epikydês heard the envoys outside the gate; he told them that they would find a siege of Syracuse harder than a siege of Leontinoi, and shut the gate in their faces.

The work of the siege now began. It was a siege carried on mainly from the north side. If the camp by the Olympicion was kept up, it was quite secondary to the main Roman post by the Hexapyla, where Appius attacked by land, while Marcellus led the fleet against the cliffs of Achradina. He had many engines and crafty devices on board his ships, towers such as those which were brought against the walls in ordinary sieges by land, a machine too for throwing ladders, by which it was hoped that the walls on the cliffs might be scaled. But there was one within the walls of Syracuse who knew much better how to manage such matters than any one in the Roman camp or fleet. Archimêdês still lived, and he devoted his whole powers to the defence of the besieged city. Hippokratês and Epikydês had the sense to let him have full play; men said that one old man was the soul of Syracuse, and that all the rest were only his body. He pierced the walls with eyelet holes for sharpshooters; he lined the battlements with artillery of every kind for the throwing of stones and all missiles, all proportioned and balanced with wonderful skill. He had iron hands by which the soldiers who drew near to the wall were caught up into the air. He had special devices to meet the Roman devices; the towers and the ladders were useless; the ships that bore them were crushed by stones or huge lumps of lead skilfully aimed, or they were caught up and let fall again with the chance of sinking. Against the skill of Archimêdês the Romans could do nothing by land or sea. If so much as a stick or a piece of rope was seen on the wall, they ran away, crying out that Archimêdês was bringing his engines against them. At last the two Claudii gave up the attack both by land and sea. Appius stayed to watch Syracuse from the old quarters by the Olympieion, and Marcellus set out to recover the other towns which had revolted.

This failure of the great Roman attack on Syracuse went far to change the whole face of the war. Hannibal saw that Sicily must now become its main field. He himself stayed in Italy; there was his special mission; but he wrote to Carthage to plead that strong reinforcements should be sent to Sicily. Himilkôn accordingly came with horse, foot, and elephants. He took Hérakleia and Agrigentum. But he failed in an attempt to relieve Syracuse by land and sea; the Punic fleet which had come with provisions for the besieged town sailed away without giving any further help. But again the Romans helped their enemies by a deed of blood which this time could not be excused even by the Roman laws of war. Lucius Pinarius, who commanded in Henna, had reason, seemingly good reason, to believe that there was a plot to give up the Roman garrison to the enemy; but his way of meeting the danger was to summon the whole people of Henna to their regular assembly, and then to fall upon them and massacre them. Marcellus had not commanded this crime, but he in no way censured it. Such a deed, done too in the holy city of Henna, turned general Sicilian feeling yet more strongly against Rome. Many towns went over to Himilkôn. All that Marcellus could do during the winter (213-212) was to watch, rather than to besiege, Syracuse on both sides. Titus Quinctius Crispinus commanded the post by the Olympieion and the ships in the Great Harbour, while the proconsul himself pitched a camp on the north side, seemingly not far from Thapsos.

There were many Syracusans in the camp of Marcellus, the late general Sôsis among them; and there was still in Syracuse itself a large party which would gladly have returned to the Roman alliance. But the mercenaries and deserters who, under Epikydês, had the upper hand in the town, kept a narrow watch over them. Communications were however opened between the Roman partisans inside and outside the city; the envoys were taken to and fro in a strange way; they were carried in fishing-boats, covered up with the nets. Marcellus offered that Syracuse, on submission, should even now remain a free city governed by its own law. But the plot was betrayed to Epikydês, and, therein showing his Punic breeding, he caused eighty partisans of Rome to be put to death by torture. Still all intercourse did not cease between besieged and besiegers. Conferences went on about the ransom of a Lacedæmonian named Damippos. He had been sent from Syracuse to try to stir up King Philip of Macedonia, who had made a treaty with Hannibal, but had given him no real help. Damippos fell into the hands of the Romans; Rome had just then her own reasons for dealing gently with Sparta, and Marcellus was not disinclined to show him some favour. At a conference held in a tower between the Roman camp and the north wall of Syracuse, a Roman officer marked a point where it would not be hard to scale the wall. He told Marcellus, who did not hurry, but waited for a good opportunity.

Such an opportunity presently came. There was a three days' feast to Artemis kept in Syracuse, when there was every chance that bad watch would be kept and that many would be drunk. As the Romans were not pressing the city at all closely, Archimêdês' engines were not at work; there was nothing to be feared beyond the ordinary risks of war. A chosen party was sent at night under the guidance of the Syracusan Sôsis. They scaled the wall near the Hexapyla, and met with no resistance from the sleepy and drunken guards. Presently the Roman trumpet was blown from the wall; the startled sentinels ran hither and thither; the Hexapyla was opened, and the whole Roman army marched in. They had now possession of the whole open ground of Epipolai; but the older quarters of the city had still to be besieged. Epikydês held Achradina and the Island, and at the other end the castle of Euryalos was still held against them. There was still much to do; but it was something to have got within the wall of Dionysios. Marcellus, a stern man but with a good deal of the hero in him, looked down on the great and famous city, the vastest in all Europe, which he had gone so far to win. He thought of its old glories and of all that it might still have to go through before he had full possession. He looked and wept—there seems no reason to doubt the tale—in mingled joy and wonder and hope and fear.

Marcellus had now, as had been done more than once before in Syracusan history, to besiege the inner town of Syracuse from the outer. He once more offered terms, but the walls of Achradina were manned by deserters, and the herald could not even get a hearing. He turned his mind to the castle on Euryalos, where an Argeian mercenary called Philodamos commanded. Sôsis was sent to negotiate with him, but Philodamos put him off for a while, as he was hoping for relief from Hippokratês. Meanwhile Marcellus pitched a camp on the middle of the hill, between the two later quarters of Tycha and Temenitês, the latter of which had now grown into a *Neapolis* or *Newtown*. Their defences seem to have been much weaker than those of Achradina; the inhabitants presently sent to Marcellus, offering to surrender and begging only for their lives and dwellings. He took them at their word. The two quarters were systematically plundered; but slaughter was forbidden, and the people were seemingly allowed to go back to their empty houses. Soon after, Philodamos, despairing of help, surrendered the castle of Euryalos and was allowed to join Epikydês in the Island. The Romans had now full occupation of the whole hill outside the wall of Achradina. The siege of the inner city of Syracuse now began.

If Philodamos had waited a little longer, he might have given his friends some help. Things looked as if the besiegers were going, like the Athenians, to be themselves besieged by land and sea. Bomilkar brought a Punic fleet into the Great Harbour. Himilkôn and Hippokratês came with a land army, Punic and Sicilian, and occupied a point in the low ground to the south of the camp of Titus Quinctius.

A general attack was made; Epikydês helping with a sally from Achradina. But the Romans beat off their assailants everywhere. For a while all remained watching one another. Marcellus was on the hill; Epikydês was in the inner city; Himilkôn and Hippokratês with their army, and Quinctius with his, were encamped in the lower ground, and the Carthaginian and Roman fleets lay in the harbour. Presently a new and terrible power stepped in.

It was now the autumn of the year 212; and the marshy ground by the Anapos, as ever, became unhealthy. Pestilence broke out among the armies encamped there, as it had done in the days of the former Himilkôn. It did not greatly touch either the besieged or the besiegers within the city; they were in a purer air; but it fell on the army of Quinctius, and still more heavily on the army of Himilkôn. Marcellus was able to help Quinctius' soldiers by moving them to healthier ground on the hill; the Sicilian soldiers who had come with the Carthaginians also found healthy spots in the neighbourhood. But the Punic force was utterly swept away, and with it the two commanders Himilkôn and Hippokratês. The only hope of Epikydês was now in Bomilkar and the Punic fleet. Bomilkar went to Africa to ask for reinforcements. The reinforcements were granted; they came to Sicily, but not to Syracuse. Epikydês went to stir him up; he set sail, but he neither entered the harbour of Syracuse nor met the Roman fleet in battle. He sailed away, it is not easy to see why, to Tarentum.

Epikydês did not come back to Syracuse. He was

really the officer, not of Syracuse but of Carthage, and he may have thought that he could do Carthage better service elsewhere. His absence left Syracuse in the hands of the mercenaries and deserters. These last, in case of Roman success, had nothing to look for but the rods and the axe; all others, citizens and soldiers, might have some hope of making terms. So yet again an attempt at negotiation was made. It began with the Sicilian troops in the neighbourhood. Marcellus said that he was still willing to leave Syracuse a free city, enrolled of course as a dependency of Rome, and paying to Rome the revenue that had been formerly paid to King Hierôn. Envoys were sent to announce these terms to the mercenary captains who now had Syracuse in their power. These captains the envoys contrived to slay, by the help of their friends in Syracuse. An assembly was then held, the last assembly of the Syracusan people. Generals were chosen, who began to treat with Marcellus on the proposed terms. This sounded like a death-warrant to the deserters; they persuaded the mercenaries to share their luck; they slew the new generals, and broke off all communications with the Romans. But presently the ordinary mercenaries began to see that their case and that of the deserters was not the same. The mere mercenaries might make terms, while the deserters could not. A Spanish captain named Mericus entered into communication with Marcellus; great rewards were promised him, and he agreed to betray his post in the Island in the night.

When the appointed time came, a Roman party came by water, and was admitted by Mericus. At daybreak Marcellus made a pretended attack on the wall of Achradina. All the forces in Syracuse went to defend it; larger parties of Romans were admitted by Mericus till the Island was wholly in their power. And now comes the strange part of the story. The deserters contrived to escape; it is implied that their escape was connived at. This looks as if Mericus had made some stipulation for them; if so, Marcellus might shut his eyes to their escape; he could not pardon them, if they came into his hands. But a hard fate fell on the citizens, a large part at least of whom were still inclined to Rome. They came out of the gate of Achradina, asking simply for their lives. The clemency of Marcellus was afterwards much boasted of; but it did not go far beyond forbidding any general massacre. It comes out afterwards that some special enemies of Rome were put to death and their houses and lands were forfeited; but for the mass of the people the rule was the same that had been followed at the entrance of the Romans into Tycha and Neapolis. In truth it would have been impossible to keep the soldiers from the expected reward of their long toils. The houses of Syracuse were given up to plunder; but slaughter and outrage were forbidden, and the inhabitants were allowed to keep their empty houses. Marcellus took possession of the royal hoard for the Roman people; but it proved less rich than had been looked for. And he began that shameless robbery of statues, pictures, and other works of art, which went on constantly from this time. He took away all that he could to adorn his triumph.

Slaughter and outrage were forbidden; but, when

pillage is allowed, some slaughter is sure to follow. And the taking of Syracuse was marked by the slaying of the most memorable man in Sicily. We have heard nothing of Archimêdês since quite the early days of the siege ; indeed, since he drove away Marcellus and Appius, there had been no need of his engines. The story goes that Marcellus sent for him ; was it to lead him in his triumph? When the message came, the philosopher was busy with a mathematical problem ; he asked to be allowed to finish it ; the soldier seemingly misunderstood him, and in his haste drew his sword and killed him. Marcellus is said to have lamented his death and to have shown favour to his kinsfolk. Others were slain by one chance or another ; and those who kept their lives and houses, but had lost all their goods, were in a wretched case. Many had to sell themselves or their children for food. But Rome rewarded those who had served her   Sôsis and Mericus both received Roman citizenship. Sôsis was also given a house in Syracuse and lands in the neighbourhood. Mericus and those who had helped him to let the Romans into the Island received lands elsewhere.

Such was the end of the long history of Syracuse as an independent city, often as a ruling city, the greatest city of Sicily and of Europe. For more than a thousand years it remained, in one shape or another, part of the Roman dominion. Marcellus had now to deal with the other towns which had come under the Roman dominion. The kingdom of Hierôn was swept away ; nor was there any hope of uniting eastern Sicily as a whole or any other shape. Each town was dealt with according to its deserts towards Rome. Those towns which had never fallen away or which had come back before the fall of Syracuse were received to different degrees of favour. Those which had simply come in through fear after Syracuse had fallen Marcellus dealt with as conquered enemies, and as at Syracuse, he portioned out rewards and punishments as he thought good. In these measures we see the beginnings of the different relations in which the towns of Sicily stood to Rome and to one another in after-times.

But it was only in part of Sicily that Marcellus could thus act at pleasure. Many towns still clave to the Punic alliance. Hannôn and Epikydês still held Akragas, and they were now strengthened by Hannibal sending to them a valiant captain of Numidian horse named Mutinês. He was of the mixed breed called Libyphœnicians, who were shut out from honours in the Carthaginian commonwealth, but his merits as a soldier had won him honour and trust in the camp of Hannibal. At the head of his light cavalry he scoured the country unhindered. He harried the lands of the allies of Rome, and became the centre of the Carthaginian party everywhere. But Hannôn envied his exploits, and, having his own commission straight from the Carthaginian government, he despised the officer merely sent by Hannibal. On the other hand, Mutinês cared greatly for Hannibal and Mutinês' soldiers cared greatly for Mutinês; but neither cared much for Carthage and still less for Hannôn. It was therefore not hard for Roman intrigues to shake their allegiance when once they felt wronged. Hannôn and Epikydês marched as far as Phintiás, by the old battle-ground of the southern Himeras. Marcellus marched from Syracuse to meet them; a battle followed; Mutinês was there, and the Romans were driven to their camp. A strange mutiny followed among the Numidians; part rode away to Hérakleia; Mutinês went to bring them back; Hannôn would needs fight a battle while Mutinês was away; the Numidians sent word to Marcellus that they would not fight against him. On the day of battle they stood aloof, and without them Hannôn's army was easily beaten. Marcellus took much spoil and eight elephants, and went back to Syracuse as a conqueror.

This was his last exploit in Sicily. He was succeeded in his command by the prætor Cethegus, and went back to Rome, hoping for a triumph. The conquest of Syracuse was certainly the greatest success that Rome had ever seen; but the war was not over, and Marcellus had come without his army. He was therefore refused the triumph, and was allowed only the lesser honour of the ovation. In that the general walked instead of being drawn in a chariot; flutes were played instead of trumpets, and the sacrifice to Jupiter on the Capitol was a ram and not a bull. But the rich spoil of Syracuse, the plunder of gods and men, the engines of Archimêdês, the captive elephants, made so great a show that the ovation of Marcellus was as splendid as any triumph. At the election of consuls for the next year (B.C. 211–210), he was again chosen with Marcus Valerius Lævinus. All Sicily was frightened at the thought of

Marcellus coming back; embassies went to Rome to beg for mercy; the fright grew greater when the Senate voted that Sicily should be the province of one of the consuls, and when the lot gave it to Marcellus. It seemed, men said, as if Syracuse were going to be sacked a second time. Marcellus talked big, and said that the outcry was raised by the intrigues of his enemies in Rome. But he found the feeling against him so strong that he thought it well to exchange provinces with Lævinus. The Sicilians were then formally heard in the Senate, and set forth their griefs against Marcellus. Many senators spoke strongly against him; but it was not thought expedient to pass any formal censure. His acts were confirmed; but Lævinus was bidden to deal as gently with Syracuse as Roman interests would allow. Then the Sicilians found it expedient to ask pardon of Marcellus and to crave his favour. Marcellus and his house became, according to Roman fashion, hereditary patrons of Syracuse. And lying legends arose about his clemency in Sicily and how much he was beloved there.

While Marcellus was at Rome (210), reinforcements came from Carthage to Akragas; Mutinés still fought, and won over towns for Carthage; Cethegus had much ado to keep his army from mutiny. Presently Lævinus came to his province. He seems to have done something to satisfy the complaints at Syracuse; but the chief work to be done was at Akragas. But Lævinus could do nothing as long as Mutinés rode to and fro unhindered. At last the foolish jealousy of Hannon reached such a pitch that he deprived

Mutinês of his command and gave it to his own son. Then Mutinês held that all ties between him and Carthage were broken, and the Numidians would serve under no captain but Mutinês. He and they sent to Lævinus, offering to betray the town. So they did. A party of Romans were let in by the southern gate; Hannôn, Epikydês, and a few others, startled at the Roman war-shout, were able to make their way out by one of the side-gates; a crowd of others tried to follow them in vain; and Akragas was a second time a Roman conquest. Lævinus came to sit in judgement; he had no commission to be merciful to Akragas, and with a revolted city he dealt yet more sharply than Marcellus had dealt with Syracuse. The mass of the people were sold into slavery; some special enemies of Rome were put to death. But some, the remains doubtless of a Roman party, were left to keep up some shadow of life till, a few years later, they were strengthened by the addition of settlers from other parts of the island. The history of Akragas now ends. There is only provincial Agrigentum.

The work was now nearly done. There were still sixty-six towns in arms against Rome. But the fall of Akragas spread fear everywhere. Some towns surrendered freely; some were betrayed, some were taken by storm. Rewards and punishments were dealt out among their people, according to their merits in Roman eyes. The war, strictly so called, was over. Lævinus could exhort the people of Sicily, now that peace was come, to sit down quietly and till their fields, and grow the corn which was to feed themselves and Rome also. It was rather as a civil magistrate than as a general that he had to put down a gang of robbers that he found at Agathyrnum. Four thousand ruffians of every kind had seized the town, and made it a centre of brigandage. Oddly enough Lævinus found an use for them. He took them over to Italy to defend the lands of Rhêgion against their fellow robbers the Bruttians. He then went on to Rome; he reported to the Senate the peaceful state of his province, and presented Mutinês and his comrades to receive their rewards, in the case of Mutinês that of Roman citizenship. He then went back to Sicily for several years. He and other Roman commanders found the use of the island as the outpost of Europe against Africa. From the havens of Sicily many expeditions were made against the coasts of Africa, which Carthage sometimes threatened to return, but never did. The land was quiet; its corn began to feed the Roman armies and Rome herself.

In the very last stage of the war Sicily becomes at least the scene of greater events. Publius Cornelius Scipio, chosen consul for the year 205, made Sicily the starting-point for his great enterprise. His plan was to go in the path of Agathoklês, to carry the war into Africa, to draw Hannibal out of Italy to the defence of Carthage. All his preparations were made in Sicily; it was from Lilybæum that he set forth, and it was to Lilybæum that he came back. His plan had succeeded. Hannibal came back to Africa, to meet Scipio in arms, to fight his last battle and to undergo his first defeat.

At Hannibal's bidding Carthage accepted the peace by which she ceased to be a ruling city, and became practically a dependency of Rome. The long strife was over; Europe had conquered Africa. Sicily was delivered from all fear of Phœnician rule, but only at the cost of submitting to Roman rule. Sicily has now, for a long time to come, no history but that of a subject province, an appendage to the history of Rome, Old and New. For six hundred years she vanishes from all direct share in the history of the world. This long, and mostly dreary, interval parts off the great times of Sicily through which we have passed from the great times of Sicily which are still far distant. Still it is a time from which we may learn much, and it has some stirring tales here and there. And one change took place greater than all. When Sicily next shows herself as having even a passing share in the great events of the world, it will be a Christian Sicily of which we shall have to speak. The altars of Baal have to pass away from Panormus and the altars of Zeus from Agrigentum. On the day of the victory of Scipio the number of years that part us from the victory of Gelôn at Himera is greater than those that part us from the preaching of Saint Paul at Syracuse.

XVI.

SICILY A ROMAN PROVINCE.

B.C. 201–A.D. 827.

[In this chapter we have to deal with the history of more than a thousand years; but it is only a small part of that time which needs to be treated at any length. It is needless to say that we have no continuous history taking in all that time, and that we have no special Sicilian history at all. Our story, just as at the very beginning, has for the most part to be put together from all manner of casual sources. But for several periods we have the help of good authorities, contemporary or nearly so. Thus for the Slave-wars, besides other notices, we have a good account in Diodôros. He was not actually contemporary, but he was dealing with his own island while the memory of things were fresh. The great speeches of Cicero against Verres are a store of knowledge about Sicily at that time, as, more than six hundred years after, the letters of Pope Gregory the Great are for Sicily in his day. Between them, a pretty full account of the war of Sextus Pompeius may be made out from the histories of Appian and Dion Cassius, and such mention as there is of Sicily in the Vandal and Gothic wars of Belisarius comes from the high contemporary authority of Procopius, the best historian that we have had to deal with since Polybios. Otherwise our authorities are piecemeal. There are of course notices here and there in more general writers, from Suetonius and Tacitus onwards. For the earlier times we have notices of the country from Strabo and the elder Pliny in their general works. In the latter part the Lives of the Saints and other ecclesiastical sources give a great deal of help; but great care must be taken to distinguish legend from fact. But at the very least they are useful for local matters, and sometimes they are of a much higher character. And in the earlier times we have abundant help from inscriptions and coins. The great mass of the Sicilian inscriptions date from the Roman times. We would gladly exchange any of them for a few of earlier days.]

All Sicily was now a Roman province. Part of it, the first province that Rome held, became such when, at the end of the War for Sicily, Carthage ceded to Rome all her possessions in the island. That is, part of Sicily, from being a province of Carthage, became a province of Rome. But the kingdom of Hierôn remained a separate state till his death. Then the second War for Sicily ended in bringing the whole island to the same state of subjection. The system of provinces thus began in Sicily; it went on when the islands of Corsica and Sardinia were ceded by Carthage. It was not till later that Rome took systematically to turning independent lands into provinces. The kingdom of Hierôn was a necessary appendage to the older Sicilian province. Yet it was none the less the first example of a kingdom dependent on Rome, and also the first example of the way in which such a dependency was brought down to a state of subjection.

For subjection it practically was everywhere. Yet we must not think that every inch of ground within a province stood in exactly the same relation to the ruling city. It suited Rome to allow very different degrees of internal freedom to cities all of which, in their external relations, were practically her subjects. One city might have joined Rome as a free ally when its alliance was valuable to Rome. It might keep its old formal alliance, sometimes an alliance on equal terms, though practically it could have no dealings with other powers but such as Rome thought good.

Such a city, though geographically within the bounds of the province, was not strictly part of the province; it was an ally of Rome, not a subject; it held its privileges by virtue of a treaty. Other towns might have privileges above others, not by virtue of a treaty, but by the favour of the ruling city. Such a town might be free in its internal administration; it might be exempt from all tribute to Rome. And, even in the districts which were altogether subject, the towns still kept the character of separate communities with their own magistrates and assemblies, though they could not do anything of importance without leave from the sovereign power. That power was represented in the province by a *proconsul* or other Roman governor, in Sicily by a *prætor*. Practically the prætor or other governor could do pretty much what he chose, subject to the fear of being accused at Rome when he went out of office. And this check was but a slight one; for, besides the power of bribery, the Roman senators and knights were commonly unwilling to condemn their own chief men at the accusation of strangers. The Roman governors were therefore often very oppressive, treating the provinces as fields for their own enrichment. We shall see something of this as we go on.

Examples of all the relations of which we have spoken were to be seen in Sicily. Three towns were allies of Rome (*fœderatæ*). Messana, now officially called *Civitas Mamertina*, kept its place as an Italian ally on Sicilian soil. The other two were Netum and Tauromenium—we may now begin to use the Latin names—which seem to have had more favourable treaties than Messana. They were both in the kingdom of Hierôn, and they must have earned favour by special services during the last war. Their position and that of other allied cities within the provinces was a good deal like that of the republic of San Marino and the principality of Monaco in modern Europe. They remained what the kingdom of Hierôn had been, with the great practical difference, that they were isolated towns and not a considerable territory. Five other towns had the lesser, but not unimportant, privileges of being exempt from tribute to Rome, and of keeping a free local administration (*Civitates liberæ et immunes sine fœdere*). These were Centuripa, Halæsa, Segesta, Halicyæ, and Panormus. The rest of Sicily stood in the simple provincial relation. The towns kept their constitutions as municipalities; but in every province the Roman People was sovereign and landlord. As landlord, it received in Sicily the tithe of the crops by way of rent. Hierôn had also taken the tithe; but that was as a native sovereign to defray the cost of a native government. Now it went out of the country, as tribute to a foreign power. We must also remember that, by the general rule in all cases of Roman allies and dependencies, the different towns, in whatever relation they stood to Rome, stood in no relation to one another. They were quite isolated. A citizen of one town could not hold land in the territory of another, while a Roman could hold land anywhere. Sometimes the same right was granted to specially favoured towns. Thus the people of the old Sikel town of Centuripa might hold land in any part of Sicily. They got great wealth by this privilege, and contrived to oust the people of Leontinoi from nearly the whole of their land.

It is important to remember these differences in the condition of the different towns, and the large amount of separate being which some of them kept under the Roman dominion. Such local independence was a privilege very well worth having; still it was a poor substitute for the full freedom of older times, when each city could itself play a part in the affairs of the world. On the other hand, peace, the Roman Peace, was spread over the land; cities could not make war on one another, as they did in the old time. Whether peace may not be too dearly purchased at the price of freedom and political life is another question.

The Roman Senate and People certainly did not mean to act oppressively towards the lands which their victory over Carthage put into their hands. The fault lay in the system which gave one commonwealth a practically boundless power over another. And it lay still more in the great powers which the Roman officials held in the provinces, and in the way in which they often winked at unlawful acts on the part of other Romans. Yet there was clearly a disposition to do what could be done for the conquered land. Thus when, in the year 146 B.C., Carthage was taken and destroyed by the younger Publius Scipio, he gave back to the cities of Sicily many works of art which had been carried off to Carthage in the various Punic wars. Among these he gave back to Agrigentum a brazen bull which was said, though its claim was very doubtful, to be the real bull of Phalaris. As one effect of the Roman government, we may mark from this time a certain change in the relative importance of the Sicilian towns. Cities like Syracuse, which had been the seat of great independent powers, lost greatly in every way by becoming mere provincial towns. Their trade and wealth lessened, and they began gradually to decay. The process began, though it took a long time fully to carry it out, by which Syracuse shrank up again into its island and Agrigentum into its akropolis, as we see them now. On the other hand, now that the growing of corn became almost the only business of the island, some of the inland towns which were centres of the corn-trade grew greatly in importance. It is needless to say that the distinction between Greeks and Sikels is now quite forgotten. Even the Phœnician towns seem largely to have become Greek. In Cicero's time the whole people of Sicily could be spoken of as Greeks. The truth is that Rome herself came to be so much under Greek influences that she carried somewhat of a Greek element even into her barbarian conquests. Much more then did the Roman conquest help to make a land wholly Greek which was already mainly so.

On the whole, Sicily under the Roman dominion must be spoken of as declining land. Great evils came of the excessive cultivation of corn. Both rich Sicilians and Roman speculators became masters of great estates, which they tilled by gangs of slaves. The endless wars and conquests of Rome led to a vast increase of slavery and the slave-trade, and the corn-growers of Sicily bought captives from all parts. In the slavery of antiquity the domestic slave, above all, the educated slave, such as many were, had a good chance of freedom, and at Rome even of citizenship.

But nothing could be more hopeless than the state of the slaves who worked in the fields. They had no chance of freedom; they were cruelly treated; they were not allowed enough of food and clothing; they were sometimes even mockingly told by their masters that they might supply their wants by robbing on the highway. On the one hand, the whole country was made unsafe; on the other, the wrongs of the slaves at last led them to revolt. The Slave Wars of Sicily form some of the most striking incidents in the otherwise not stirring history of the provincial land

The slaves revolted twice, and both times they cost the Roman government no small trouble before the island could be made quiet again. It must be remembered that most of the Sicilian slaves who tilled the ground were captives taken in war, men well used to fighting. They came largely from Asia, and many of them were Cilician pirates. When therefore they had once taken up arms and made an union among themselves, they were able to make a formidable stand. The first Slave War broke out in the year B.C. 134. It was a time when the slaves rose in several other parts of the world; but it is hard to say whether the Sicilian revolt had anything to do with the others. In Sicily the outbreak took place at Henna. A rich citizen of that town, Damophilos by name, and his wife Megallis, were specially cruel to their slaves, of whom they had a vast number. But their young daughter had always treated the slaves well, and had given them whatever comfort she could under the bad treatment of her parents. Another citizen of Henna, named Antigenês, had a Syrian slave called Eunous, who professed to have the gift of prophecy, and who played various tricks, breathing fire and the like. He gave out that the Syrian goddess had revealed to him that he should be a king. Presently the slaves of Damophilos conspired with the other slaves in Henna. They proclaimed Eunous king; they took possession of the town, and did as they pleased with their former masters and the other inhabitants. Damophilos was put to death with many others; his wife was given to the slave-women, who tortured her and threw her down the brow of the hill. But the slaves remembered her daughter's kindness; to her they did no harm, but sent her under a trusty guard to some friends at Catina. The slaves flocked together from all parts; Eunous was presently at the head of six thousand men, armed with such arms as they could get. Such of the freemen of Henna as were makers of arms they kept alive as prisoners to make them swords and spears. Eunous took on him the state of a king, with the name of Antiochos, after the kings of his own country. He also gave the title of queen to the Syrian slave-woman who lived with him, lawful marriage of course could not be among slaves. King Eunous was nothing great in himself; but he had a wise counsellor in one Achaios. Slaves were often called after their countries, and here was a slave, no barbarian, but an Achaian, a Greek of the leading commonwealth of Greece, who had become a slave, most likely by being kidnapped by pirates. Presently another body of revolted slaves showed themselves under a Cilician named Kleôn. It was thought that he and Eunous would fight against one another; but Kleôn submitted himself to Eunous as king. Kleôn was a good captain; so with him and Achaios the affairs of King Eunous went on very well for a time.

For three years or more this revolt went on. The slave king, or his general Kleôn, was able to defeat more than one Roman prætor with his army. The slaves seem to have had full possession of the open country; but we do not hear of any of the chief towns falling into their hands, except Henna, where the revolt began, and Tauromenium, which they could hardly have taken by force; it must have been betrayed to them. At last in 132 the consul Publius Rupilius overcame them. He besieged King Antiochos and his followers in Tauromenium, where they held out till they were brought to the eating of human flesh. At last Kleôn died fighting masnully in a sally. The town was betrayed to the consul; Eunous or Antiochos escaped with a few attendants, and kept a while in hiding; but he was taken and died of disease in prison. Rupilius stayed in the island as proconsul; and in the next year 131, he put forth a code of regulations by which the province was governed for many years.

The laws of Rupilius however did not put an end to the evils of slavery. These, bad enough in all parts of the ancient world, seem to have reached their highest point in provincial Sicily. A second revolt of the slaves was the consequence. This lasted from B.C. 102 to 99, which was also a time of other revolts of slaves elsewhere. And the time was well chosen in other ways, as it was in the middle of the great war of Rome with the Cimbri and Teutones, when no great heed could be given to the affairs of Sicily. The story is in some things very like that of the first slave-war; but it has perhaps a greater interest, on account of its connexion with some of the ancient sites and religious beliefs of the island. And the way in which the war began throws great light on the nature of ancient slavery. We see how commonly men were kidnapped by pirates, and how they were made slaves in unlawful ways by Roman officers. Whole lands were left almost without inhabitants. The Senate made an order that all slaves in any Roman province who were subjects or citizens of any state in alliance with Rome should be set free. The prætor of Sicily, Publius Licinius Nerva, began accordingly to set free all slaves who came under those terms. So many were thus set free that the slave-owners began to fear that they would lose all their human property. They persuaded or bribed the prætor not to put the law in force, and then the slaves began to revolt in various places. It carries us back to old times when we read that they began with solemn oaths in the temple of the Palici, the old Sikel gods who befriended the slave. Indeed it is said that even in these times no master dared to harm a slave who had taken refuge there. The insurgents carried on the war for some time, having chosen as their king one Salvius, who, like Eunous, had got credit for soothsaying. They fought with success, and were able more than once to defeat such troops as the prætor could lead or send against them. But they could not get hold of any considerable city ; they won a battle before Morgantina ; but they could not get possession of the town. Presently another king arose in the western part of the island about Libybæum and Segesta. This was a Cilician named Athénión, who also laid claim to mysterious powers, but who was withal a good soldier, having most likely been a pirate like Kleôn. Just as in the case of Eunous and Kleôn, men thought that the two would turn against one another ; but Athénión, like Kleôn, submitted to Salvius as king, and acted as his general. Salvius now called himself Tryphôn, after the Syrian king of that name. He assumed all kingly state, and fixed his capital and court in the small but strong town of Triocala, that is most likely either the modern Caltabellotta, or some point in the hills near it. Like Ducetius, he chose the Palici to his special protectors. Not only slaves but many poor freemen joined him, and they met Roman armies in the field. The prætor Lucius Licinius Lucullus, father of the Lucullus who was famous in Asia, defeated them in battle ; but he could not or would not take Triocala. His successor Quintus Servilius did as little. At last the revolt grew so serious that the Senate was driven to treat it as a foreign war, and the consul Gaius Aquillius was sent with his full army. Tryphôn was now dead, and Athénión was king. Athénión was killed in battle with the consul ; the revolt was now thoroughly put down. Many of the slaves were taken to Rome to fight with wild beasts ; but they escaped this fate by slaying one another.

The slave-wars are by far the most striking events in Sicily while it was a Roman province. They are real pieces of Sicilian history, such as it is. We have now little to tell, save the way in which Sicily, as a subject land of Rome, was passively touched by the revolutions of the ruling city, and how much it suffered at the hands of its Roman governors. Thus in B.C. 82, in the civil war of Marius and Sulla, some of the chief partisans of Marius sought refuge in Sicily, and were followed thither and overcome by the famous Gnæus Pompeius. But it concerns us more when we read how one Sthenios, a chief man of Therma, who had done great things for his own city and was honoured throughout all Sicily, was charged before Pompeius on account of his friendship for Marius, but was let go. This comes from our chief source of knowledge of Sicilian matters a little later, namely the great pleading of Cicero against the prætor Gaius Verres, when he was accused for his oppressions in Sicily. Cicero had himself been quæstor in Sicily, and he knew the land well, and we learn a great deal as to its state from his speeches in this famous cause.

Cicero seems to take for granted that there must always be some oppression in a provincial administration. Only the Sicilians, he says, were such good quiet people that they did not complain unless oppression got much worse than usual. This is most likely quite true. The system was bad, specially the farming of the tithe to speculators. The prætor himself might mean to be just, but he could hardly ever keep all his agents in order. But there was a great difference between one Roman officer and another. Thus Sicily suffered a good deal from Marcus Antonius, father of a more famous man of the same name. He was not prætor in Sicily; but having the command at sea, he was able to plunder various provinces, Sicily among them. But the prætor at this time (B.C. 74), Gaius Licinius Sacerdos, is spoken of as a man of blameless character, against whom no charge of oppression could be brought. Then, in 73, came the worst of all the men whom Rome sent to rule her provinces, Gaius Verres—his *nomen* is not known for certain. By ill luck he stayed in the island three years. He heeded no law, Roman or local; he cared nothing for the privileges of the towns or for the rights of particular men. He plundered everywhere; he practised every kind of extortion in collecting the tithe, and in buying the public corn which was needed to be sent to Rome. He committed every kind of excess; he imprisoned and slew men wrongfully. And his hand fell on others besides the provincials; for the crime on which Cicero lays most stress, as the crown of all wickedness, was one that was absolutely unheard of before, the crucifixion of a Roman citizen. There is reason to think that the extortions of Verres really tended to the lasting impoverishment of the island. But the most striking thing at the time was his plunder of the choicest and most sacred works of art. He professed to be a man of taste, and in that character he robbed cities, temples, and private men. And all this while he neglected the common defence of the province, and let pirates sail freely into Sicilian havens. It throws much light on the corrupt state of things at Rome that such a man as this found many supporters among the chief Romans. Every difficulty was put in the way of the Sicilians and their advocate Cicero. In the end they succeeded. The case was so clear that, before sentence was given, indeed before Cicero had finished his pleadings, Verres went into exile at Massilia. This a Roman could always do, and he thus escaped further punishment. In the days of the proscription he was put to death by the younger and more famous Marcus Antonius, for the sake of some of his stolen treasures which he had not given back.

During the civil wars of Rome Sicily becomes at one stage of special importance. In the civil war of Cæsar and Pompeius Sicily played no great part; still it marks the position of the island that when, in B.C. 47, the Dictator Cæsar crossed to his war in Africa, it was from Lilybæum that he set out. Men said that his death in B.C. 44 was foretold, among other signs and wonders, by an eruption of Ætna, and soon after his death Sicily became for a while the great centre of strife. Sextus Pompeius, the younger son of the great Gnæus, had kept on a desultory warfare in Spain since the death of his father in B.C. 48. After the death of the Dictator, his adopted son Gaius Octavius, now known as the younger Cæsar and afterwards as Augustus, was for a moment the professed friend of the republican party against Marcus Antonius. Then Sextus, who was strong at sea, was acknowledged as commander of all

the naval forces of the commonwealth. Presently
Cæsar changed sides, and formed his triumvirate
with Antonius and Lepidus. In the general slaughter
of their enemies that followed, Sextus was set down
among the *proscribed*, though he had no hand in the
death of the Dictator. His fleet became the refuge
of such of the proscribed as could escape; he was
joined by discontented men of all kinds, largely by
pirates and runaway slaves. With this force he was
able to occupy, first Mylæ and Tyndaris, then
Messana, then Syracuse the provincial capital, and
the whole island (B.C. 43). Sicily thus became for
seven years the seat of a separate power, at war with
the powers of Italy and the rest of the Roman
dominion. Not that Sextus had any thought of
founding a distinct Sicilian dominion of any kind.
The position of the island enabled a Roman party-
leader who was strong at sea to hold Sicily for his
own purposes against other Roman party-leaders.

Writers in the interest of Cæsar, as all our authorities are more or less, make a point of speaking of the
war with Sextus Pompeius as a servile war, like those
revolts of the slaves which we spoke of a little time
back. But it is certain that many Romans, some of
high rank, joined him. He showed no remarkable
ability himself, but he was well served by several
freedmen with Greek names, who made excellent
commanders by sea. One suspects that they had
been Cilician pirates. By their help he kept the
dominion of Sicily in the teeth of many attacks for
the space of seven years. He added Sardinia and
Corsica to his dominions, and kept up a plundering

warfare along the Italian coasts. But he seems to have been incapable of any great enterprise, and he did little personally beyond keeping on the defensive in his head-quarters at Messana. But the loss of corn from Sicily brought Rome near to famine. On the other hand, the Sicilians must have lost the market for their corn. We hear next to nothing of the internal state of Sicily during the occupation of Sextus; but shortly afterwards the island is described in a general way as having lost much of its prosperity during his time. His aims seem to have been wholly personal; as to the particular crimes laid to his charge, we must remember that we have only the statements of his enemies. Thus he is charged with the murder of several Roman officers who had come under his suspicion; but the evidence is not very clear.

The first attempt against Sextus was made by the younger Cæsar in B.C. 42. But the officer sent against him, Quintus Salvidienus Rufus, was altogether defeated at sea. Sextus then gave himself great airs, and called himself the son of Neptune or Poseidôn. But he failed to take any advantage of the other wars in which Cæsar was engaged, first along with Marcus Antonius against Brutus and Cassius at Philippi, and then against Lucius Antonius at Perusia. For a moment, in B.C. 40, Sextus made an agreement with Marcus Antonius, but Antonius and Cæsar were soon again joined together against him. Now it was that his valiant freedman Menas won for him the other great islands; but he was more valiant than faithful, and he was already beginning to have dealings with Cæsar. The people of Rome were now feeling the stress of hunger, and they clamoured loudly for peace with Sextus. They showed their zeal in an odd way, by paying special devotion to the image of Neptune, when it was carried round at the games among the other gods. Cæsar and Antonius were driven to make peace with Sextus. In the year 39 the three met at Misenum on the coast of Campania. The two triumvirs entertained Sextus on land, and he entertained them on board his ship. And the story went that Ménas proposed to his master to sail off with Cæsar and Antonius on board, and so make himself master of the whole Roman world. And Sextus is said to have answered: "You should have done it without asking me; Ménas may do such things; Pompeius cannot." By the terms of peace, Sextus was to keep his three islands and to receive the province of Achaia from Antonius. This was the way in which the Roman leaders parted out the world among them. The followers of Sextus were allowed to return to Rome and receive again their rights and properties, save that the proscribed were to receive only a part. Magistracies and priesthoods were to be given to the friends of Sextus; his father-in-law Libo was to be consul the next year along with Antonius, and Sextus himself the year after along with Cæsar. And Sextus' little daughter Pompeia was to be married to Marcellus the little son of Octavia, sister of Cæsar and now wife of Antonius.

The peace was received with universal delight, and many of Sextus' friends went back to Rome. But nothing more really came of it. Each side of course laid the blame of the breach on the other. Antonius failed to make over Achaia to Sextus, and Sextus' plundering warfare began again. Presently Ménas changed sides and went over to Cæsar, taking the islands of Sardinia and Corsica with him. Sextus thus remained master of Sicily only.

There now begins a second War for Sicily, like the war to which that name properly belongs, except that it was not waged by two hostile commonwealths but by two Roman party-leaders. It was a war between Cæsar and Sextus. Cæsar could not as yet persuade the other triumvirs to take any part in it. And the war was unpopular at Rome, where the people wanted corn and therefore peace. Still Cæsar had, both now and in his later war with Antonius, a great advantage from his possession of Rome and Italy. Sextus too never took advantage of any success that he gained. He defended Sicily; elsewhere he did nothing but plunder. Presently Cæsar planned a great attack on Sicily by land and sea. He was himself in southern Italy when the two fleets met off Cumæ (38). The battle was chiefly notable for the meeting in arms of the two freedmen, Ménas, who had now a command under Cæsar, and Menekratés, who led the fleet of Sextus. Their two ships met and fought fiercely. Menekratés was killed; Ménas was disabled by a wound. The Pompeians had greatly the advantage in the battle; but Démocharés, another freedman who took the command, and all under him, were too disheartened by the loss of Menekratés to improve their advantage as they might have done.

What they failed to do, the powers of nature, the power, Sextus would say, of his adopted father, did for them. Cæsar was coming by sea from Tarentum to join his forces on the west side of Italy; Sextus was waiting for him at Messana. Sextus dashed out on the Cæsarian fleet; a fight followed in the strait, in which Cæsar was utterly defeated and escaped with difficulty to land. The next day a storm arose and broke in pieces the ships that had escaped in the battle. The division of Ménas alone was able to find safety, through his knowledge of the coast. And he did Cæsar some service by cutting off a voyage of Démocharês to Africa. Presently he changed sides again, and went back to his former master. Altogether Cæsar's power was so much weakened that he put off all attacks on Sextus and Sicily for more than a year. (B.C. 38-36.)

Meanwhile Cæsar had dealings with the other triumvirs. Antonius gave him 130 ships for Sicilian warfare in exchange for legionaries to help in his Eastern campaigns. He persuaded Lepidus to invade Sicily from the West. Thus Italy and Africa joined together against Sicily. Above all, Cæsar caused his able lieutenant Marcus Vipsanius Agrippa to make all things ready for a great naval expedition. At last, on July 1, B.C. 36—the month was now dedicated to the Dictator as Divus Julius—the great fleet set forth. The Antonian ships were to come from Tarentum to meet it. A great storm arose; Statilius Taurus, who commanded the Antonian ships, put back to Tarentum; Lepidus contrived to land in Sicily and laid siege to Lilybæum; but Cæsar's own fleet, though he had carefully sacrificed to Neptune and the Sea, was so damaged by the storm as to cause thirty days' delay. Sextus now gave himself out more than ever as the son of Neptune, while Cæsar forbade the image of that god to be carried at the games, and said that he would conquer Sicily in spite of him.

Public feeling at Rome was again turning towards Sextus; again men wanted Sicilian corn. Cæsar would gladly have put off any more fighting till next year. He therefore set busily to work to repair his losses, while Sextus, as usual, did nothing to push his advantages. It was ominous that Ménas changed sides yet again, and went back to Cæsar. Cæsar now formed his plans. The main fleet under Agrippa was to attack northern Sicily; the Antonian ships at Tarentum were to join Cæsar in the strait and attack Tauromenium. Lepidus meanwhile was in western Sicily; but Démocharès and the other Pompeian commanders cut off by land and sea the help that was coming to him from Africa. He came back to eastern Sicily in time to meet Agrippa in a sea-fight off the peninsula of Mylæ, in which the Cæsarians had the better. Sextus then hastened to Messana, where he heard that Cæsar was at Tauromenium. He had crossed from Italy with part of his forces, and Sextus was upon him by land and sea before he could send for the rest. Cæsar was again defeated at sea, and escaped to Italy with great difficulty. His land force, under Cornificius, made a march of several days through the inland country, which reminds us of the retreat of the Athenians from Syracuse. They had much difficulty in crossing the lava-covered country under Ætna, and they were constantly beset by the Pompeian horsemen and darters. At last they were met by another force sent by Agrippa to meet them, and they came safely to the north coast.

The war was ended, as far as Sextus was concerned, by another sea-fight. Agrippa won a more decisive victory over the Pompeian fleet off Naulochus, a point between Mylæ and Cape Peloris. Sextus, who had looked on at the battle from the shore, forsook Sicily and sailed with a few ships for Asia. There, after many adventures which do not concern us, he was killed the next year (B.C. 35). Meanwhile both Lepidus and the Pompeian Plennius had come from the West. Plennius still held Messana for Sextus, and was besieged by Agrippa and Lepidus. The forces of Plennius and Lepidus presently joined together and sacked the town. Lepidus was aiming to make himself master of Sicily instead of Sextus. But, when Cæsar came, both armies forsook their generals and entered his service (B.C. 36). Seven years after its first occupation by Sextus, Sicily passed under the dominion of Cæsar.

The later war between Cæsar and Antonius does not concern us. Cæsar was now master of all the West, of Sicily among the rest. He laid a heavy imposition on the island, 1,600 talents, and on his return to Rome, he celebrated an ovation for his Sicilian conquest. Sicily now came back to its former state as a province of Rome. But it had suffered much, and was greatly impoverished, during the war of Sextus. After all the civil wars were over, Cæsar, now Augustus and master of the whole Roman world, began to look to the state of the lands which had practically become his dominions, and, among other things, he tried to do something for the advantage of Sicily. This he did by planting Roman colonies in several of the towns, specially at Syracuse in B.C. 21. Of this last large traces remain. The Roman town seems to have been wholly on the low ground. It took in the Island, and the lower part of Achradina, and an extended *Neapolis*, between the theatre and the Great Harbour. Here we see the remains of several Roman buildings, specially of the amphitheatre; for Roman colonists, in Sicily or anywhere else, could not do without the bloody shows to which they were used at Rome. Other colonies were planted at Tauromenium, Catina, Therma, and Tyndaris, and large remains of Roman buildings are to be seen in modern Catania and among the ruins of Tyndaris. Messana, the Mamertine city, got the Roman franchise, and remained a flourishing town. The lower franchise of Latium was granted to Netum, Centuripa, and Segesta. We may remark that by these changes Messana, Netum, and Tauromenium lost their position as free cities, and became, on different conditions, immediate parts of the Roman dominion. Messana, as getting the full Roman franchise, doubtless gained by this. But Strabo, who wrote in the time of Augustus, describes most of the old towns as having gone to utter decay, and he speaks of the country generally as in a wretched state.

Sicily thus remained a province of the Roman Empire till the Empire began to lose its provinces.

As one of the peaceful provinces, not lying on any dangerous frontier, it was one of those which Augustus professed to put under the rule of the Senate and People, while he kept the more exposed lands in his own hands. For several ages there is but little to record. A province hardly has a history of its own, and the position of Sicily hindered it from being the scene of any of the great events in the general history of the Empire. We come across occasional notices of Sicilian towns, as we do of the other towns of the Empire; we hear for instance of this or that temple being decayed, and perhaps restored by the reigning Emperor. And one at least of the early Emperors, Hadrian, who visited all parts of his dominions, did not fail to visit Sicily also (A.D. 126), and to study the wonders of Ætna. And one or two striking events happened, which sometimes recall past times and sometimes foreshadow times that were to come. There can be no doubt that Sicily lost a great deal by the Roman conquest of Egypt, after which it ceased to be the chief cornfield of the Roman people. We may therefore doubt whether a third revolt of slaves or robbers, of which we hear in the days of Gallienus (A.D. 260–268) was owing to the same causes as the two older and more famous Slave-Wars. Anyhow such an event reminds us of former days, while the next that we have to speak of is an isolated forerunner of what was presently to come. Whatever Sicily had to bear at the hands of Roman masters, she was at least spared the sight of a foreign enemy for several centuries. At last, in the days of the Emperor Probus (276–282), a sudden blow fell. Sicily was again attacked by barbarian invaders. A body of Franks —some say Vandals—who had submitted to the Emperor and had been transplanted by him to new lands by the Euxine, rose in revolt, got possession of ships, and laid waste various parts of Greece, Asia, and Africa. They were driven back from Carthage; but they crossed to Sicily; they seized and sacked Syracuse, and wrought a great massacre of its inhabitants. They then made their way into the Ocean, and sailed safely back to their own land, the *Francia* of those days, on the borders of Northern Germany and Northern Gaul.

These new enemies of Sicily were mere ravagers, not conquerors. But their coming marks an epoch. It was the first appearance of men of Teutonic stock in Sicily or indeed in the Mediterranean waters. The days of Teutonic dominion were not yet; but such an isolated event as this was a forerunner of their coming. Meanwhile another of the great elements of the later life of Europe was making its way in Sicily, as in other parts of the Empire. Christianity was preached in Sicily in very early times. The Acts of the Apostles record a three days' stay of the Apostle Paul at Syracuse. But local legend gathers rather round Saint Peter, who is made to send his disciples from Antioch. Saint Paul, legend tells us, found a bishop, Marcian by name, already at Syracuse, and preached in his church. The story has its local habitation in the undoubtedly very ancient church of Saint Marcian in lower Achradina. Another disciple of Saint Peter was Pancratius of Tauromenium, whose church, made out of a small temple, still remains outside the wall of his own city. Like many other saints, he has conflicts with evil powers, in his case the idols Lyson and Phalkon, in which last we are tempted to see a survival of the old Sikel Palici. Saint Peter is also said to have come to Sicily in person, and a round building of Roman date at Catania is shown as a church which he consecrated to Our Lady while she was still upon earth. Some other legends are yet wilder. The old Sikel town of Agyrium took its later name of *San Filippo d'Argiro* from a Philip who is sometimes made a disciple of Saint Peter and sometimes placed in the reign of the Emperor Arcadius (395–408). In his story we first hear of Ætna as an abode of evil beings. Saint Kalogeros, who is plainly an impersonation of Eastern monasticism, is also made into a disciple of Saint Peter. He gives himself to the discovery of healing springs and vapours, and his memory lives on two hills on the two sides of Sicily, by the Himeræan and the Selinuntine *Therma*, now Termini and Sciacca.

The virgin saints of Sicily are also many and famous. Two especially have had a great name out of the island. Saint Agatha of Catania has in some sort taken the place of the Pious Brethren. After her martyrdom under the Emperor Decius (249-251), her veil, preserved as relic, stops an eruption of Ætna. Saint Lucy of Syracuse, first of several of the name, is martyred under Diocletian (305), whose character is misconceived in the usual way. This Lucy, one of the virgin patronesses of the island, must be distinguished from a matron Lucy, who in the story appears as a personal victim of Diocletian at Rome. That is, the legend forgot that Diocletian's seat of rule was at Nikomêdeia. Presently, under Constantine, came the peace of the Church. By that time we may safely say that the older bishoprics of Sicily, those which claim an apostolic origin, those of Syracuse, Panormus, Catina, Messana, Agrigentum, and Tauromenium, were all in being. We hear of Sicilian bishops attending at councils, and of the island being troubled, like the rest of the West, with the Pelagian heresy. In short, the early ecclesiastical history of Sicily is much like that of any other part of Western Christendom. It was later events which gave it, like its temporal history, a character of its own.

Sicily, it is well again to remember, was the first Roman province, the first land out of Italy possessed by the Roman People. Its position was that of a subject land; its inhabitants were not Romans, except such Romans as settled in the island as colonists or otherwise, and except any natives who were personally admitted to the Roman franchise. After a while the distinction of Romans and provincials was taken away through the Empire by the edict of the Emperor Antoninus, commonly called Caracalla (211–217). By that edict all the free inhabitants of the Empire were admitted to the name and rights of Romans. Under the practical despotism of the Emperors those rights were not worth very much, and it may be doubted whether the provincials found any immediate practical gain in becoming Romans. But the change had its effect nevertheless; the people

of Sicily or of any other province became proud of the
Roman name as opposed to the barbarians outside the
Empire. A kind of artificial Roman nation was formed,
at all events in the West, and no Roman anywhere
willingly submitted to a barbarian ruler. Now that
one land was no more subject than another, the word
province lost its old sense of a subject land, and simply
meant an administrative division of the Empire, whether
in Italy or elsewhere. When the Empire was mapped
out into such divisions by Constantine, Sicily and
Italy were drawn closer together: the *province* of
Sicily became part of the *diocese* of Italy—a formula
which must not be confounded with the ecclesiastical
use of the word. It was governed by a *consular* under
the superior authority of the prætorian præfect at
Rome. In the beginning of the fifth century the
central island of the Mediterranean began to share
in the revolutions which had long touched those
provinces of the Empire which had exposed inland
frontiers. The Teutonic invaders of the Roman
dominions, long known in north-eastern Gaul and in
the South-eastern lands, began to touch Sicily and
other Mediterranean lands in a more lasting way than
the momentary landing of the Franks in the third
century. And we again, as of old, mark the central
position of the island. It can be attacked either from
Italy or from Africa, and conquerors or deliverers can
come from the lands east of the Ionian sea. The
first invasion was threatened from Italy; but it was
only a threat. This was from the West-Gothic king
Alaric, who, after his taking of Rome in 410, designed
an invasion of both Sicily and Africa, and died just

as he was on the point of attempting it. The West-Goth was thus hindered from becoming the first Teutonic master of Sicily. The next enemy was the Vandal king Gaiseric, who in 429 established a Teutonic kingdom in Africa. He made Carthage his capital, and, as soon as that city was once more the seat of an independent power, it sprang again to something like its old position in its Phœnician days. The Vandal king became the great naval power of the Western Mediterranean; he conquered and plundered almost at pleasure. He invaded Italy many times; he sacked Rome itself; he made himself master of Sardinia and Corsica and the Balearic islands. He invaded and plundered Sicily many times; he took and destroyed several towns, and he seems in the end to have established his dominion over the whole island. Besides being, in the speech of the time, barbarians, the Vandals, though Christians, were deemed heretics in religion, having like all the Teutonic nations except the Franks, first learned Christianity in its Arian form.

Towards the end of his days (477) Gaiseric gave up the possession of Sicily to Odowakar on payment of a tribute. Odowakar was a leader of mercenaries who had become master of Italy when the first succession of Emperors in the West came to an end There was now only one Emperor, he who reigned at Constantinople, and Odowakar, practically an independent prince, was held to be his lieutenant with the title of patrician. Sicily thus, without being formally separated from the Roman Empire, really passed under the rule of Teutonic masters. The same was the case when Odowakar was displaced by the great East-Gothic king Theodoric (493). Sicily, as well as Italy, passed under his rule. Theodoric looked carefully after all his dominions, Sicily among the rest, and we have occasional notices of Sicilian matters in the documents of his reign collected by his minister Cassiodorus. We find from them that the people of Sicily were, as we might expect, ill disposed towards Gothic rule, and Cassiodorus is praised by the King for winning them over to his allegiance. We find that corn was now sent from Sicily into Gaul, and that the church of Milan, as we shall presently hear of the church of Rome, held lands in Sicily. There are also some notices of particular places. Thus Syracuse had a Gothic count; the amphitheatre of Catina had fallen into ruins, and the magistrates and citizens were allowed to make use of the stones for the repair of their walls. Theodoric gave one of his daughters in marriage to the Vandal king Thrasimund, and gave him Lilybæum as her dowry. The Vandals thus again got a foothold in Sicily. One thinks of the times when, first Pyrrhos and then the Romans, had won all Sicily except Lilybæum from the Carthaginians. One wonders at Theodoric giving up so important a point to the new masters of Carthage. But Lilybæum must have soon passed back to the Goths, as it was in their hands when we next hear anything about Sicily.

We have thus seen Sicily, in the changes which swept over the Empire in the fifth century, come under the power of barbarians, but still of European barbarians, men indeed of Teutonic race. But we cannot say that the island was wholly separated from the Roman Empire, unless perhaps for a moment under Gaiseric. Presently, under the Emperor Justinian and his great general Belisarius, the Empire began to win back many of the lands which it had lost. Some were won back only for a short time; but Sicily was won back for several centuries. The first land to be won back was Africa. In the year 533 Belisarius came to Sicily, a friendly land under the dominion of the Goths, and made it his starting-point for his expedition against the Vandals. We may thus add his name to the long list of those, from Agathoklês onwards, who invaded Africa from Sicily. He did not however set sail either from Syracuse or from Lilybæum, but from the harbour of Caucana on the south coast. The Romans of Sicily—so we may now speak—received the Imperial general gladly. But after Africa had been won back for the Empire, a special Sicilian dispute arose between the Empire and the Gothic masters of the island. Those who had overcome the Vandals in Africa claimed also their possessions in Sicily, the fortress of Lilybæum ceded to Thrasimund as his bride's dowry. This the Goths refused to restore.

Within two years the question between the Empire and the Gothic king Theodahad came to touch more than Lilybæum; it touched all Sicily and all Italy. In the year 535 began the great Gothic war of Justinian. And it was in Sicily that it began. The consul Belisarius landed at Catina; Syracuse and the towns of Sicily generally submitted willingly. It was only at Panormus, where there was a strong Gothic garrison, that the Imperial forces met with any resistance. It would seem that Panormus had begun to shrink up like Syracuse, and that the suburbs which had grown up north and south of the two arms of the haven were now forsaken. Belisarius sailed into the haven without resistance. The masts of his ships were higher than the walls of the inner city; so he was able to bring the garrison to submission by showers of arrows from a greater height. He went back to Syracuse; while he was there, the year of his consulship came to an end, and he laid down his office with the usual ceremonies at Syracuse instead of at Constantinople. All Sicily was now won back for the Empire, and when Belisarius went on the next year to win back Italy, he left garrisons at Syracuse and Panormus only. The Goths never forgot the ease with which Sicily was lost, and at a later stage of the war we find the Gothic king Totila breathing vengeance against the Sicilians, both for the loss of the island and because Sicilian cornships had come to Rome and helped the defenders of the city to hold out against his siege of it. In 549-50 Totila invaded Sicily; he could not take any of the chief towns, but he ravaged the island and left garrisons in four places which are not named. In 551 the Goths were finally driven out of the island.

Thus Sicily again became an undisputed province of the Roman Empire. We must remember that the seat of the Empire was then at Constantinople, the New Rome, even after the Old Rome and all Italy was won back by Belisarius. A large part of Italy, north and south, was presently torn away again from the Empire by the Lombards. The theological disputes of the eighth century caused the Emperors to lose all practical authority in the Old Rome; and at last in 800 the Empire was finally parted asunder, when the Frank king Charles the Great was chosen and crowned Emperor there. But neither Lombards nor Franks touched Sicily, nor did they ever occupy the whole of Italy. The Eastern Emperors, as we may now distinguish them, the Roman Emperors at Constantinople, kept Sicily and part of southern Italy long after a Western, a Frankish, Emperor was chosen at Rome. The island was governed by a *prætor* or *stratêgos* sent from Constantinople, who commonly held the rank of patrician, the highest rank which did not imply any association in the Empire, and he was often spoken of as Patrician of Sicily. This connexion between Sicily and the Eastern, the Greek-speaking, parts of the Empire no doubt helped largely to strengthen the Greek element in Sicily. Belisarius the Roman consul did in effect repeat the work of Timoleôn and Pyrrhos by winning the island again for the Greek world. Whatever Latin had come in with the Roman colonies gradually died out, as it did in the Roman colonies in the East, of which the New Rome itself was the greatest. The Eastern connexion again was strengthened when, in the eighth century, the Bishops of the Old Rome opposed the course taken by the Emperor Leo in the controversy about images, in return for which he took Sicily out of their ecclesiastical jurisdiction and put it under that of Constantinople, and confiscated their temporal estates in the island. Everything tended to make Sicily, like the rest of the East-Roman Empire, once more part of the Greek world.

It is to the fact just mentioned, that the Bishops of Rome as well as those of Ravenna and Milan, held large estates in Sicily, that we owe a good deal of knowledge of the state of things there during the early part of the connexion of the island with Constantinople. We learn much from the letters of Pope Gregory the Great (590-604) to his officers in Sicily. He writes about all matters public and private, from an appeal to the Empress Constantina, wife of Maurice (582-602) to do something to relieve the burthens of the island, to the smallest matters concerning the property of his church. Many letters are written to prætors and others in authority, many to bishops and other churchmen. As at once Roman Patriarch and a great Sicilian landlord, Gregory looked after everything. Sicily was then full of churches and monasteries; the great majority of the people were Catholics, but there were some heretics, a great many Jews, and still a few pagans. Gregory has a great deal to say about the Jews, many of whom lived on the church lands. They were not to be in any way oppressed, but those who turned Christians were to have their rents lowered. And when the Bishop of Panormus took possession of a Jews' synagogue and turned it into a church, Gregory gave judgement that the act was a wrongful one, that, as the building had been consecrated, it could not be given back to the Jews, but that the Bishop must pay them the value of it. We find also that Sicilian corn was still sent to Rome; the holding of Sicilian lands by the Roman Church would help to keep up the practice. Not very long after Gregory's time we hear a good deal of Saint Zosimus, Bishop of Syracuse. He first, in 646, turned the great temple of Athênê in the island into a church as we see it now; and we gather from his story that Syracuse had now shrunk up into the Island, and that nothing was left on the mainland but scattered churches and houses.

During these ages when Sicily was ruled from Constantinople, the island did not often see its sovereign. But in 665 the Emperor Constans the Second, whose crimes had offended men at both the New and the Old Rome, came to Sicily and dwelled at Syracuse. Some have thought that he came with the purpose of making Syracuse the head of the Empire. But his oppression was great in Sicily also, and in 668 he was killed in a bath. On his death the Sicilians set up one Mezetius—his name is spelled in several ways—as Emperor. But the next year Constans' son Constantine the Fourth (called Pogonatus or the Bearded) came to Sicily, overthrew Mezetius, and won back the island. This may need some explanation. What happened at this time in Sicily had often happened before in other parts of the Empire, but never in Sicily. Nothing was more common than for an ambitious man, most commonly a successful general, to set himself up as Emperor. This happened several times in Britain. His object was to seize the whole Empire, if he could, but at any rate to seize some part of it. If he succeeded in so doing, he went down in history as an Emperor; if not, he was called only *tyrant*. That is to say, the word *tyrant* had now got a meaning which answered exactly, in the changed state of things, to its old use in the days of the Greek commonwealths. It means an usurper or pretender, a man who sets himself up against lawful authority, only now against the authority of a prince and not of a commonwealth.

In the reign of Constantine the Fifth, called Copronymus (741-775), we hear a great deal of the Bishop Leo of Catina and of the magician Heliodôros, who was said, when condemned to death at Constantinople, to have fled through the air back to Catina. Legend also makes him the artist of the lava elephant which is still to be seen there. In the reign of this Emperor, Calabria was made part of the *theme* or province of Sicily. In the reign of Constantine the Sixth, in 781, Elpidius the prætor or *stratêgos* of Sicily set himself up as tyrant ; but he was put down and took refuge with the Saracens in Africa. The Saracens had plundered in Sicily more than once as early as the seventh century ; in the ninth century their invasions began on a greater scale, and before the end of the tenth (827-965) they had complete possession of the whole island.

With their appearance a wholly new period in the history of Sicily begins. The island is gradually torn away from the Roman Empire, and thereby from Europe and from Christendom. It is next, in the eleventh century (1060-1090), won back by the Normans. In all this we have the old history of

Sicily over again. The old struggle between Europe and Africa, between Greeks and Semites, is fought over again, but it is this time made more keen by the religious opposition between Christendom and Islam. One Story of Sicily ended with the Roman conquest of Syracuse; another Story of Sicily begins with the Saracen conquest of Mazzara. The time between is the mere record of a province, a land subject to distant masters. With the coming of the Saracens the island again begins to have a history, and a long history, of its own. But that history will be best told in another volume.

INDEX.

A.

Abacænum, land of, taken for Tyndaris, 181; joins Magôn, 183; taken by Agathoklês, 237
Achaia, province of, 335
Achaios, counsellor of King Eunous, 326
Achradina, outpost of Syracuse, 43; joined to Ortygia by Gelôn, 73; Dionysios' works on, 164; *see also* Syracuse
Adernò, *see* Hadranum
Ægates, *see* Aigousa
Ælian, his history of animals, 29
Æschylus, at Hierôn's court, 83
Æschylus, brother-in-law of Timophanês, 217
Ætna, Mount, 18; legends about, 31, 343; legend of Empedoklês at, 96; eruption of, thought to portend Cæsar's death, 332; visit of Hadrian to, 341
Ætna (town), founded by Hierôn, 84; his death at, 90; men of, support Thrasyboulos, 90; drives out Deinomenês, 92; renamed Katanê, 93, 99; transferred to Inessa, *ib.*; taken by Ducetius, 99; horsemen of Syracuse escape to, 154; joins Syracusan revolt against Dionysios, 158, 159; Dionysios drives away refugee horsemen, 160; Campanians settle at, 175, 229; camp of Agathoklês at, 239

Africa, Phœnician colonies in, 14, 23; campaign of Agathoklês in, 242 *seqq.*; Roman invasions of, 282, 317, 332; Vandal kingdom in, 346; Belisarius's campaign in, 348
Agathoklês, compared with Dionysios, 234, 257; his early life, 235; chosen general at Syracuse, 236; his rise to power, 236; Spartan expedition against, 237; his treaty with Akragas, 238; attacks Messana and Akragas, 238; recovers Centuripa and Galaria, *ib.*; attacks the Punic camp on Eknomos, 239; takes Gela, 240; defeated at the Himeras, 240, 241; his designs on Africa, 242; his African campaign, 243-251; assumes the title of king, 248; returns to Sicily, 249; takes various cities, 250; his treatment of Segesta, 252; massacre ordered by, 254; his dealings with Deinokratês, 255-257; his kingly position in Sicily, 257; attacks Lipara, 258; takes Korkyra, *ib.*; later wars in Italy, *ib.*; called Lord of the Island, *ib.*; plans a fresh Carthaginian expedition, 259; his death, *ib.*
Agathoklês the younger, slain by Archagathos, 259

Agathoklês, defrauds the temple of Athênê at Syracuse, 60
Agathyrnum, centre of brigandage, 317
Agrigentum, bishopric of, 344; *see also* Akragas
Agrippa, M. V., his expedition against Sextus, 337-9
Agylla, temple of, plundered by Dionysios, 191
Agyris of Agyrium, his treaty with Dionysios, 182, 184
Agyrium, Sikel site, 20; Heraklês worshipped at, 31; admitted to Syracusan citizenship, 229; revolts against Phintias, 263; its later name, 343
Aigousa, isles of, 17, 55; battle off, 289
Aiolos, isles of, *see* Lipara
Akestoridês of Corinth, plots against Agathoklês, 235
Akis and Galateia, legend of, 31
Akragas, foundation of, 51; works of Thêrôn at, 89; tyranny of Thrasydaios at, *ib.*; its wealth, 93; banishes Empedoklês, *ib.*; its war with Ducetius, 100; with Syracuse, 101; Athenian envoys at, 111; Selinuntines take refuge at, 143; prepares for Carthaginian attack, 147; siege of, 149; surrender and spoil of, 150; refugees accuse Syracusan generals, 151; subject to Carthage, 154; revolts against Dionysios, 183; re-settled by Timoleôn, 229; withstands Agathoklês, 237; makes terms with him, 238; his fresh attempt on, *ib.*; its alliance against Agathoklês, 248; at war with Carthage, 249; tyranny of Phintias at, 263; drives him out, 264; submits to Pyrrhos, 268; taken by Mamertines, 272; by Rome, 281; known as Agrigentum, *ib.*; taken by Himilkôn, 305; held by Hannôn, 313; reinforcements sent to, 315; betrayed to Lævinus, 316; brazen bull restored to, 323; decay of, 324

Akragas, river, 51
Akrai, outpost of Syracuse, 50
Akrotatos of Sparta, his expedition against Agathoklês, 237
Alaric, king of the West-Goths, 345
Alexander of Epeiros, 231, 265
Alexander the Great, his conquests, 230; their effect on Agathoklês, 234
Alexander, son of Pyrrhos, kingdom of Sicily designed for, 268
Alketas of Molottis, restored by Dionysios, 191
Alkibiadês, supports appeal of Segesta, 113; appointed general, 114; is for attack on Syracuse, 116; charged with impiety, 117; his speech and counsel at Sparta, 120
Alphabet, the, its Phœnician origin, 22
Alpheios, legend of, 37
Amphinomos, 46
Anapios, 46
Anapos, river, 43; battles by, 118, 123
Anaxilas, tyrant of Rhêgion, his action towards Zanklê, 69, 70; his alliance with Terillos of Himera, 74; asks help from Carthage, 78; makes peace with Gelôn, 82; threatens Lokroi, 84; his death, 85; his sons' dealings with Mikythos, 90; their fall, 91
Ancona, *see* Ankôn
Andromachos of Tauromenion, joins Timoleôn, 219
Ankôn, foundation of, 191
Antalkidas, peace of, 189
Antandros, left in command by Agathoklês, 243; hears rumours of his defeat, 244; executes massacre at Syracuse for Agathoklês, 254
Antigenês of Henna, 326
Antiochos, king, *see* Eunous
Antiochos of Syracuse, his Sicilian history, 8, 39, 104

INDEX. 357

Antonius, L., his war with Cæsar, 334
Antonius, M., the elder, plunders Sicily, 331
Antonius, M., the younger, puts Verres to death, 332; one of the triumvirate, 333; his agreement with Sextus, 334; joins Cæsar against him, *ib.*; makes peace with Sextus, 335; sends ships against him, 337
Apollokratès, commands in Ortygia, 209; his truce with Diôn, 213; re-enters Ortygia, 216
Apollôn, statue of, taken from Gela to Tyre, 153
Apollôn Archêgetês, his altar at Naxos, 41
Apollonia, submits to Timoleôn, 224; taken by Agathoklês, 250
Apollôniadès, tyrant of Agyrium, 229
Apollônidès, his speech at Syracuse, 300
Aquillius, G., sent against the slaves, 329
Archagathos, accompanies Agathoklês to Africa, 243; mercenaries demand his death, 246; left in command, 249; prays his father for help, 250; Agathoklês plans to desert him, 251; his death, *ib.*
Archagathos, the younger, conspires against his grandfather, 259; slain by Mainôn, 262
Archias, founder of Syracuse, 42, 59
Archidamos, king of Sparta, slain at Manduria, 231
Archimêdês, kinsman of Hierôn II., 294; at the siege of Syracuse, 304; his death, 312; his engines in Marcellus's ovation, 314
Archônidès I., Sikel king, helps Ducetius to found Kale Aktê, 101, 161; ally of Athens, 108, 124; his death, 124
Archônidès II., Sikel king, founds Halæsa, 161

Aretê, daughter of Dionysios, and wife of Diôn, 200, 201; given in marriage to Timokratês, 201; taken back by Diôn, 213; suspects Kallippos, 214; his treatment of, 215: her death, *ib.*
Arethousa, fountain of, 37, 42
Argos, sends contingent to Athenian army, 114; Pyrrhos slain at, 271
Aristippos of Kyrênê, Dionysios' treatment of, 191
Aristomachê, wife of Dionysios, 165, 200; welcomes Diôn's return, 213; suspects Kallippos, 214; his treatment of, 215; her death, *ib.*
Aristôn of Corinth, improves Syracusan naval tactics, 128
Aristos of Sparta, supports Dionysios, 160
Asdrubal, his defeat at the Krimisos, 225-7
Asdrubal, his attack on Panormos, 284; his victory off Drepana, 286
Ashtoreth, worshipped at Eryx, 14, 27
Assinaros, river, Athenian slaughter at, 136
Athènagoras, his speech at Syracuse, 115
Athêniôn, general under Salvius, 329; succeeds him as king, *ib.*; killed, *ib.*
Athens, her relations to Sparta, 105; her alliances in Sicily, 106, 108; helps to found Thourioi, 106; Sikeliot appeals to, 107, 108; generals accept peace of Gela, 110; embassy to Sicily 422 B.C., 111; Segesta appeals to, 112; story of the envoys, 113; expedition to Sicily voted, 114; action of Nikias, 117; battle by the Anapos, 118: Nikias asks for reinforcements, 119; beginning of siege of Syracuse, 121; second expedition voted, 127; defeat at sea, 128, 131; coming of Dêmosthenês,

129; last battle and retreat, 132-6; end of the invasion, 137; Sikeliots, imprisoned by, 139; decrees in honour of Dionysios, 180, 194; reception of Dionysios' tragedies at, 190, 194; her alliance with him, 194

Atilius, A., invades Panormos, 146, 282; takes it, 282, 283

Augusta, see Xiphonia

Augustus, see Cæsar, G. O.

B

Bacchiads of Corinth, 58

Balearic Isles taken by Gaiseric, 346

Barbarians, meaning of the name, 21

Belisarius, his expedition against the Vandals, 348; wins back Sicily, 348, 349; effect of his conquest, 350

Beneventum, battle of, 271

Boeo, Cape, see Lilybaion

Bomilkar, in command against Agathoklês, 244

Bomilkar at the siege of Syracuse, 308; seeks reinforcements, 309; goes to Tarentum, *ib.*

Bruttians, war of, with Krotón, 235; Segestans sold to, 252

C

Cadiz, 23

Cæsar, G. J., at Lilybæum, 332; his death foretold, *ib.*

Cæsar, G. O. (Augustus), his war with Sextus, 333-5; makes peace with him, 335; his second war with Sextus, 336-9; master of Sicily, 339; his Sicilian ovation, *ib.*; plants colonies in Sicily, 340

Calabria part of the *theme* of Sicily, 353

Caltabellotta, said to be site of Kamikos, 33; whether identical with Triocala, 329

Caltavulturo, see Torgium

Campanian mercenaries, under Hannibal, 141; help Dionysius, 159; take Entella, *ib.*; settle at Ætna, 175; Timoleón's dealings with, 229; in the camp of Archagathos, 262; seize on Messana, *ib.*; take the name of Mamertines, 263; ravage Rhégion, 273; chastised by the Romans, 273, 277

Canaan, gods of, worshipped in Sicily, 21, 26

Caracalla, Emperor, his edict, 344

Carthage, origin of the name, 23; her dependencies in Sicily, 24, 66; war with, to avenge Dorieus, 74; her alliance with Persia, 77; invades Sicily under Hamilkar, 77-81; *Shophetim* of, 79; treaty with Gelón, 82; cult of the goddesses at, 82, 180; Athenian embassy to, 120; second invasion of Sicily, 140 *seqq.*; spoil from Akragas sent to, 150; treaty with Dionysios, 154; his embassy to, 166; Sicilian Greeks rise against, *ib.*; sends Himilkón, 171; victory off Katanê, 175; besieges Syracuse, 176-179; defeat of, 179; invasion of, under Magón, 183; makes peace with Dionysios, 184; first war in Italy, 192; fresh peace with Dionysios, *ib.*; robe of Lakinian Hera sold to, 193; fresh war with Dionysios, 194; makes peace with his son, 195, 199; Hiketas in league with, 216, 218; envoys at Tauromenion, 219; admitted into Syracuse by Hiketas, 222; crucifies Magón, 222; war of, with Timoleón, 225-227; defeat at the Krimisos, 227; supports the tyrants, 227; makes peace with Timoleón, 228; recalls Hamilkar, 237; treaty with Agathoklês, 238; help sought by Syracusan exiles, *ib.*; naval losses, 239; victory at the Himeras, 240, 241; her position in Africa, 242; expedition of Agathoklês against, 243-251; Akragas throws off her alliance, 249; defeats Archagathos, 250; peace made with, by the Greek soldiers, 251; treaty of Agathoklês with, 255; Mainôn's alliance with, 262; supports Phintias, 263; besieges Syracuse, 264; her alliance with Rome, 267, 272; withstands Pyrrhos, 267, 271; fortifies Lilybaion, 270; alliance with Hierôn, 273, 277; wars of, with Rome. 276-290, 295-317; makes peace with Rome, 290; embassy of Hierônymos to, 296; second peace of, with Rome, 318; taken by Scipio, 323; under Gaiseric, 346

Cassibile, *see* Kakyparis

Cassiodorus, his notices of Sicilian matters, 347

Castrogiovanni, origin of the name, 20

Catania, plain of, 17, 18, *and see* Katanê

Catulus, G. L., his victory off Aigousa, 289; makes terms with Hamilkar, 290

Caucana, Belisarius sets sail from, 348

Centuripa, Centorbi, Sikel site, 20; tyrants at, 229; held by Agathoklês, 238; attacked by him, 250; position of, under Rome, 322, 340; specially favoured as regards land, 322

Cephalœdium, Cefalù, Sikel site, 20; betrayed to Dionysios, 182; taken by Agathoklês, 250; joins Deinokratês, 254; Agathoklês negotiates for, 255

Cethegus, Prætor, 314, 315

Chaironeia, battle of, 230

Chalkis, metropolis of Naxos, 40, 41; of Zanklê, 48; its treatment by Athens, 119

Charles the Great, crowned at Rome, 350

Charôndas, his code of laws, 57, 65; story of his death, 65

Charybdis, tale of, 30

Chersikratês, founder of Korkyra, 42

Chna, land of the Phœnicians, 21

Christianity preached in Sicily, 342

Cicero, his speeches against Verres, 319, 330-332

Cilician pirates enslaved in Sicily, 325

Citizenship, right of, in old commonwealths, 58

Claudius A., Roman prætor, 296; Syracusan negotiations with, 298, 299; with the fleet at Syracuse, 300; at the siege of Syracuse, 304

Claudius P., defeated off Drepana, 286

Colonies, nature of, 10, 11

Constans II., Emperor, at Syracuse, 352; killed, *ib.*

Constantina, Empress, appeals to Gregory the Great on behalf of Sicily, 351

Constantine IV., Emperor, wins back Sicily, 352

Constantine V., Emperor, 353

Constantine VI., Emperor, 353

Constantinople, seat of the Empire, 349; its connexion with Sicily, 350

Corinth, her colonies and their relations, 41, 42; mediates between Syracuse and Hippokratês, 71; Ducetius sent to, 100; Syracusan embassy to, 120, 160; embassy of Dionysios to 176; Syracusan appeal to, 216; sends Timoleon, 217; Dionysios the younger sent to, 220; sends settlers to Syracuse, 223; Leptinês sent to, 224; Carthaginian spoil sent to, 227

Corn, Sicily the market of, for Rome, 19, 317, 324, 334, 338, 351; for Gaul, 347

Cornelius G. takes Panormos, 282

INDEX

Cornificius, Q., his retreat before Sextus, 338
Corsica, possible Syracusan settlement in, 98; claimed by Rome, 290; ceded by Carthage, 320; taken by Sextus, 333, 334; confirmed to him at Misenum, 335; joins Cæsar, 336; taken by Gaiseric, 346
Crete, independent cities in, 14; settlers from, at Gela, 49
Crispinus, T. Q., commands at siege of Syracuse, 305, 308; pestilence in his army, 309
Cumæ, battle off, 336, *and see* Kymé
Cyprus, compared with Sicily, 5; Phœnicians in, 22

D

Daidalos, story of, 32
Damarata, wife of Gelôn, 74; marries Polyzélos, 83; her tomb destroyed by Himilkôn, 177
Damareta, wife of Hadranodôros, 297; put to death, 299
Damarista, mother of Timoleôn, 217
Damas, promotes Agathoklês, 235
Damippos, as to his ransom, 306
Damophilos, defeats Xenodikos, 249
Damophilos of Henna, his treatment of his slaves, 325; killed by them, 326
Daphnaios, Syracusan general, before Akragas, 149
Darius I., King of Persia, 69; receives Skythês of Zanklê, 70
Darius II., his alliance with Sparta, 137
Demokratês, joins Hamilkar, 245; withstands Agathoklês, 250, 254; negotiates with him, 255; his defeat, 256; Agathoklês' treatment of, *ib.*; slays Pasiphilos, 257
Deinomenês, father of Gelôn, 71
Deinomenês, son of Hierôn, King of Ætna, 84, 90; driven out of Ætna, 92

Delphi, designs of Dionysios on, 191
Demagogues at Syracuse, 94
Démêtêr and Persephonê, legend of, 29, 35; temple of, at Syracuse, 83, 176; temples of Carthage, 82, 180; solemnity of oath by, 214; Corinthian ship consecrated to, 217; Agathoklês offers up his ships to, 243
Démétrios the Besieger, 258
Démocharês, in command under Sextus, 336, 337; cuts off Lepidus' reinforcements, 338
Democracy, origin of, 58; defined by Athenagoras, 115
Demos of Athens, 59
Démosthenês, appointed general, 114, 127; his plan of attack, 129; counsels retreat, 130; surrenders, 134; put to death, 136
Dexippos, commands at Akragas, 147; suspected of bribery, 149, 150; commands at Gela, 151; sent back by Dionysios, 152
Dikaiopolis, *see* Segesta
Diodôros, his Sicilian history, 8, 31, 76, 104, 140, 156, 319; his version of the battle of Himera, 80; gives the kingly title to Gelôn, 82
Dioklês of Syracuse, his code of laws, 138; negotiates with Hannibal, 143; marches back to Syracuse, 144; banished from Syracuse, 146
Dion, Life of, by Plutarch and Cornelius Nepos, 156, 197; favoured by Dionysios the elder, 200; persuades Plato to revisit Syracuse, 201; banished, *ib.*; treatment of his property and wife, *ib.*; receives Spartan citizenship, 202; his expedition against Dionysios the younger, 202 *seqq.*; enters Syracuse, 204; chosen general, 205; drives out the mercenaries, *ib.*; negotiations of Dionysios with, 206; Dionysios' letter to, 207; charges against, *ib.*;

counsels acceptation of Dionysios' terms, 208; deprived of his generalship, 209; retires to Leontinoi, *ib.*; his return, 211, 212; his treatment of his enemies, 212; reconciled to Hérakleidés, 213; recovers the Island, 213; refuses to destroy tomb of Dionysios, *ib.*; connives at murder of Hérakleidés, 214; plots against, *ib.*; his death, 215; Plato's schemes for his son, 162

Dionysios the elder, escapes the fate of Hermokratés, 146; his speech in the assembly, 151; chosen general, *ib.*; his conduct at Gela and Leontinoi, 151, 152; established as tyrant, 152; his marriage, *ib.*; empties Gela and Kamarina, 153; treatment of his wife, *ib.*; recovers his power at Syracuse, 154; his treaty with Himilkôn, *ib.*; greatness of his power, 157, 184; fortifies Ortygia, 158; his Sikel wars, 158, 161; revolt against, *ib.*; his policy to his besiegers, 159; his alliance with Sparta, 160; his treatment of Naxos and Katanê, 161; extends the Syracusan fortifications, 164; founds Hadranum, *ib.*; his war with Rhégion and Messana, 165; his double marriage, *ib.*; his preparations against Carthage, 165, 175, 176; his speech, 166; besieges Eryx, 168; and Segesta and Entella, 170. 171; defeated off Katanê, 175; his embassies to Peloponnésos, 176; calls an assembly, 177; defeats the Carthaginians, 178; his agreement with them, 179; Attic decrees in his honour, 156, 180, 194; his settlements, 181, 182; his defeat at Tauromenion, 183; defeats Magón, *ib.*; makes peace with Carthage, 184; takes Tauromenion, *ib.*; his wars in Italy, 184-189; takes Rhégion, 188; his embassy to Olympia, 190; his tragedies at Athens, 190, 193; his treatment of men of letters, 190, 191; his Hadriatic and Etruscan campaigns, 191; fresh war with Carthage, 192; terms of peace, *ib.*; takes Krotôn, 193; wall planned by, *ib.*; invades Western Sicily, 194; his death, 195; effect of his reign, 195, 197; his tomb in Ortygia, 199, 213; his sun-dial, 205; compared with Agathoklês, 234, 257

Dionysios the younger, compared with his father, 198, 199; acknowledged by the assembly, 199; makes peace with Carthaginians and Lucanians, *ib.*; his marriage, 200; his friendship for Plato, 201; his treatment of Dión, *ib.*; banishes Hérakleidés, *ib.*; his negotiations with Dión, 206, 208; his letter to Dión, 207; escapes from Ortygia, 209; sends Nypsios to Syracuse, 210; re-occupies Ortygia, 216; surrenders to Timoleon, 220; sent to Corinth, *ib.*

Dionysios of Corinth, 224

Dorian settlements in Sicily, 41, 46, 49

Dórieus of Sparta, his expedition to Western Sicily, 66; war to avenge him, 74

Doris of Lokroi, wife of Dionysios, 165

Drepana, haven of Eryx, 194; stronghold of Carthage, 281, 285; Roman defeat off, 286; taken by Rome, 289

Ducetius, helps to drive out Deinomenés, 92; union of Sikels under, 98, 99; founds Menænum, 99, 102; and Palica, 99; takes Etna, *ib.*; his war with Akragas and Syracuse, 100; throws himself on the mercy of the Syracusans, *ib.*; sent to Corinth, *ib.*; founds Kalè Akté, 101; his death, *ib.*

Duilius, G., his victory off Mylai, 281

E

East and West, their strife in Sicily, 4, 354
Ebbsfleet, compared with Naxos, 41
Egypt, Roman conquest of, its effect on Sicily, 341
Eknomos, Punic camp on, 239, 240
Elba, 98
Elephants first used in the West, 266; use of in the Punic armies, 283-285
Eleutheria, feast of, at Syracuse, 91
Elpidius, Sicilian tyrant, 353
Elymians, hold Segesta and Eryx, 13, 20; as to their Trojan origin, 20, 30, 31
Empedion of Selinous, 143
Empedoklês, his Life by Diogenês Laertios, 87; legend of, 96; refuses tyranny of Akragas, *ib.*; banishment and death, *ib.*
Empire, Eastern, its connexion with Sicily, 350
Empire, Roman, Sicily a province of, 339, 340, 344, 349; division of the empire, 350
Engyum, submits to Timoleôn, 224
Entella, taken by the Campanians, 159; besieged by Dionysios, 170: taken by him, 194; saved by Timoleôn, 226
Epicharmos, at Hierôn's court, 83
Epikydês, his mission to Syracuse, 296; intrigues against Rome, 298, 299; chosen general, 299; stirs up the Leontines, 300; spreads falsehoods about Marcellus, 302; re-enters Syracuse, 303; his answer to the Roman envoys, *ib.*; puts Roman partisans to death, 306; holds Achradina, 307, 309; asks for re-inforcements, 309; leaves Syracuse, *ib.*; holds Akragas, 313; escapes from it, 316
Epipolai, *see* Syracuse

Ergetion, conquered by Hippokratês, 68
Erineos, river, Athenian halt by, 134
Erymnôn of Aitolia, withstands Hamilkar, 244
Eryx, temple at, 14, 27; Phœnician remains at, 27; attempted foundation of Dôrieus on, 67; Athenian envoys at, 113; joins Dionysios against Carthage, 168; taken by Hamilkôn, 171; retaken by Dionysios, 194; won by Pyrrhos, 269; taken by Rome, 286; lower town seized by Hamilkar, 288; prolonged strife for, 288-290; garrison marches out, 290
Eryx, epônymos hero overthrown by Hêraklês, 31
Etruscans, Hierôn's victory over, 85; war of, with Syracuse, 98; help Athens, 120, 131; war of Dionysios with, 191
Euboia, island, independent cities in, 14
Euboia in Sicily, a settlement of Chalkis, 46; its treatment by Gelôn, 73
Eumêlos, the poet, settles at Syracuse, 59
Eunous the slave, King of Henna, 326; calls himself Antiochos, *ib.*; defeats the Romans, 327; his death, *ib.*
Eupatrids of Athens, origin of, 59
Euphêmos, his speech at Kamarina, 119
Euryalos, occupied by the Athenians, 121; Dionysios' castle at, 164; surrendered to Marcellus, 308
Euryleôn, founds Hêrakleia, 67; his tyranny and overthrow at Selinous, *ib.*
Eurymedôn, commander of second Athenian expedition, 127; joins in attack on Epipolai, 129; counsels retreat, 130; dies in the sea-fight, 131

INDEX. 363

Euthydêmos, Athenian general, 127; joins in attack on Epipolai, 129

F

Faro, Capo del, *see* Pelôris
Fiumare, 18
Floridia, 133
Franks invade Sicily, 342

G

Gadeira, Gades, 23
Gaiseric, King of the Vandals, his African kingdom, 346; invades Sicily and Italy, *ib.*; gives Sicily up to Odowakar, *ib.*
Gaisylos of Sparta, 213
Galaria, held by Agathoklês, 238
Galateia, legend of, 31
Gamoroi of Syracuse, 59; political disputes among, 60; driven out of Syracuse, 62; restored by Gelôn, 72
Gaul, corn sent to, from Sicily, 347
Gauls, their wars with Rome, 189, 293; take service under Dionysios, 189, 194
Gaulos, island of, 17
Gela, foundation of, 49; founds Akragas, 51; secession to Maktôrion from, 67; tyranny of Kleandros, 68; of Hippokratês, 68–71; of Gelôn, 72; metropolis of new Kamarina, 91; makes peace with Kamarina, 109; congress at, *ib.*; peace of, 110; joins Gylippos, 124; asks for help from Syracuse, 151; siege and forsaking of, 153; tributary to Carthage, 154; resettled by Timoleôn, 229; makes terms with Agathoklês, 238; taken by Agathoklês, 240; joins Akragas against him, 248; destroyed by the Mamertines, 264
Gelas, river, meaning of the name, 49

Gellias of Akragas, his death, 150
Gelôn, son of Deinomenês, his treatment of the sons of Hippokratês, 71, 72; becomes tyrant of Syracuse, 72; his dealings with oligarchs and commons, 73; enlarges Syracuse, *ib.*; grants citizenship to strangers, 74; allies himself to Therôn, *ib.*; alleged treaty with Carthage, 75; embassy from Greeks of the Isthmus to, 78; his victory at Himera, 80, 81; honours paid to at Syracuse, 81, 83; his treaty with Syracuse, 82; his gifts and temples, 83; his death, *ib.*; his tomb destroyed by Himilkôn, 177
Gelôn, son of Hierôn II.; his death, 295
Gêryonês, his oxen, 31
Girgenti, *see* Akragas
Gongylos of Corinth, 124
Gorgias of Leontinoi, teacher of rhetoric, 94; his embassy to Athens, 107
Goths, their rule in Sicily, 347–349
Gozo, island of, *see* Gaulos
Greeks, independent political system of, 9; national migrations of, 10; their settlements in Sicily, 11, 14, 39 *seqq.*; compared with the Phœnicians, 22; ask Gelôn's help against Xerxes, 78; Sikel attempt against, in Sicily, 98; share of Sicily in their wars, 105 *seqq.*, 160
Gregory the Great, Pope, Sicilian notices in his letters, 351
Gylippos, sent to Syracuse, 121; collects contingents, 124; 126; his proposals to Nikias, 125; his forts and wall, *ib.*; urges attack on the fleet, 127; takes Plêmmyrion, 128; blocks the roads, 133; takes Nikias and his army prisoners, 136; pleads for Athenian generals, *ib.*

H

Hadranodôros, uncle of Hierônymos, 295; supports Carthage, 296; hopes to succeed Hierônymos, 297; elected general, *ib.*; put to death, 298
Hadranum, foundation of, 34, 165; Timoleôn's victory at, 219; attempted murder of Timoleôn at, 221; taken by Rome, 278
Hadranus, Sikel fire-god, 29, 34, 35
Hadrian, Emperor, his visit to Sicily, 341
Hadriatic, the, settlements of Dionysios on, 191
Hadrumetum taken by Agathoklês, 245
Halæsa, foundation of, 161; position of under Rome, 322
Halikyai, Halicyæ, Sikan town, 106; position of, under Rome, 322
Halykos, river, 18; boundary between Syracuse and Carthage, 193, 199
Hamilkar, son of Hannôn, invades Sicily, 79-81; his defeat and sacrifice, 80, 81; his death avenged by Hannibal, 143
Hamilkar, his defeat at the Krimisos, 225-227
Hamilkar, Syracusan generals seek help of, 235, 236; won over by Agathoklês, 236; his recall and death, 237
Hamilkar, son of Gisgon, succeeds his namesake, 237; his treaty with Agathoklês, 238; fresh expedition under, 239; his victory at the Himeras, 240, 241; his policy towards the Sicilians, 241; his attempts on Syracuse, 244, 245; his death, 246; head exposed by Agathoklês, 245, 246
Hamilkar Barak, sent against Rome, 287; takes Herkte, *ib.*: and lower Eryx, 288; makes peace with Rome, 290

Hananiah, meaning of name, 21
Hannibal, meaning of name, 21
Hannibal, son of Giskon, his hatred of Greeks, 141; besieges and takes Selinous, 142; takes and destroys Himera, 144; his second invasion, 147; his death, 149
Hannibal, Carthaginian commander, at the siege of Akragas, 281
Hannibal, son of Hamilkar Barak, Syracusan embassy to, 296; sends envoys to Syracuse, 298; pleads for reinforcements in Sicily, 305; sends help to Akragas, 313; his war with Scipio, 317; makes peace with Rome, 318
Hannibal the Rhodian, at the siege of Lilybaion, 286; his ship copied by Rome, 286, 289
Hannôn, in command against Agathoklês, 244
Hannôn, holds Akragas, 313; his jealousy of Mutinês, 313, 315; his victory and defeat at Phintiás, 314; deprives Mutinês of his command, 315; escapes from Akragas, 316
Harmonia, wife of Themistos, 298; put to death, 299
Hebrew tongue same as Phœnician, 21
Heliodôros the magician, 353
Helôris, of Syracuse, his advice to Dionysios, 158; whether the same as the Rhegian general, 182; his death, 185
Helôron, outpost of Syracuse, 50
Helôros, river, battle of, 70
Henna, Sikel site, 20; its modern name, *ib.*; legend of the goddesses at, 35; attacked by Dionysios, 161; betrayed to him, 182; joins Akragas against Agathoklês, 248; taken by Carthage and by Rome, 281; massacre at, 305; revolt of the slaves at, 325
Hérakleia Minôa, founded by Euryleôn, 67; destroyed by the

INDEX.

Carthaginians, 75; Diôn lands at, 203; held by Carthage. 203, 229, 238; delivered by Akragas, 249; seized by Agathoklês, 250; taken by Pyrrhos, 269; taken by Himilkôn. 305
Hêrakleia, daughter of Hierôn, put to death, 299
Hêrakleidês, of Syracuse, banished by Dionysios the younger, 202; plots against him, *ib.*; elected admiral at Syracuse, 207; defeats Philistos, 208; his attack on Diôn, 209; appointed general, *ib.*; sends to Diôn for help, 211; Diôn's treatment of, 212; reconciled to him, 213; secret murder of, 214
Hêrakleidês, Syracusan general, denounced by Agathoklês, 235; banished, *ib.*; seeks Hamilkar's help, 235, 236
Hêrakleidês, son of Agathoklês, 243, 251
Hêraklês, legends of, 31
Herbessus, besieged by Dionysios, 158; Hippokratês and Epikydês at, 302
Herbita, attacked by Dionysios, 161
Herktê, rock of, 25; taken by Pyrrhos. 269; held by Carthage 283; taken by Rome, 285; recovered by Hamilkar, 287
Hermokratês of Syracuse, his speech at Gela, 109, 110; his speech at Syracuse, 114; and at Kamarina, 119; appointed general, 119; driven back from Euryalos, 121; deposed, 124; advises attack on fleet, 127; his stratagem, 132; pleads for mercy to Athenian generals, 136; his action in Asia, 137; his banishment, 138; his dealings with Pharnabazos, 138, 145; occupies Selinous, 145; his war with Motya and Panormos, 145, 146; enters Syracuse and is killed, 146; his daughter marries Dionysios, 152

Herodotus, on Sicilian history, 57; his account of Gelôn, 76, 78; of the battle of Himera, 80
Hierôn I., son of Deinomenês, 72; his victories commemorated by Pindar, 76, 83; his helmet, 76, 85; his dialogue with Simonidês, 76; succeeds Gelôn, 83; his war with Thêrôn, *ib.*; reconciled to him, 84; founds Ætna, *ib.*; sends help to Lokroi and Kymê, 84, 85; his death, 90; his tomb at Ætna destroyed, 93
Hierôn II., stories of his ancestry and birth, 272; chosen general at Syracuse, *ib.*; marries Philistis, 273; his war with the Mamertines, 273, 277; his rule in Syracuse, 274, 293, 294; his alliance with Rome, 279; position of his kingdom under Rome, 293; strengthens and adorns Syracuse, 294; his law as to tithe, 294, 322; his death, 295; slaughter of his descendants, 299
Hierônymos, son of Hierôn II., kingdom of Syracuse bequeathed to, 295; his character, 295, 296; joins Carthage, 296, 297; killed at Leontinoi, 297
Hiketas, puts Aristomakê and Aretê to death, 215; tyrant of Leontinoi, *ib.*; in league with the Carthaginians, 216. 218, 219, 221; defeated by Timoleôn, 219; besieges Ortygia, 219, 221; his plots against Timoleôn, 221; besieges Katanê, 222; escapes to Leontinoi, *ib.*; submits to Timoleôn, 224; set up again by Carthage, 227; put to death, 228
Hiketas, Syracusan general, withstands Mainôn, 262; tyrant of Syracuse, 263; defeats Phintias, *ib.*; overthrown by Thoinôn, 264
Hill towns in Sicily, 20
Himera, founded by Zanklê, 50;

its hot baths, 51; held by Théron, 78; battle of, 79-81, 227; betrayed by Hierôn to Théron, 84; Pindar's odes to the citizens, 87; refuses Athenian alliance, 117; joins Gylippos, 124; vengeance of Hannibal on, 143, 144; Hermokratés at, 146
Himeras, river, 18; battle of, 240, 241; proposed boundary of Hierônymos, 297
Himilkôn, colleague of Hannibal, besieges Akragas, 147, 150; sacrifices his son, 149; besieges Gela, 153; his treaty with Dionysios, 154; tries to defend Motya, 170; recovers Western Sicily, 171; founds Lilybaion, *ib.*; destroys Messana, 173; founds Tauromenion, *ib.*; his victory off Katanê, 175; besieges Syracuse, 176; plunders temples, *ib.*; and destroys tombs, 177; his defeat, 179; makes terms with Dionysios, *ib.*
Himilkôn, Carthaginian general, his expedition to Sicily, 305; besieges Marcellus at Syracuse, 309; his death, *ib.*
Hipparinos, father of Diôn, 200
Hipparinos, son of Diôn, 201; his alleged letter to him, 207; welcomes his father back, 213
Hipparinos, son of Dionysios, takes Ortygia, 215; killed, *ib.*
Hippo, Phœnician colony, 23
Hippokratés, tyrant of Gela, his conquests, 68; his dealings with Zanklê, 69, 70; his war with Syracuse, 70; refounds Kamarina, 71; his death, *ib.*; Gelôn's dealings with his sons, 71, 72
Hippokratés, of Carthage, his mission to Syracuse, 296; intrigues against Rome, 298, 299; chosen general, 299; stirs up the Leontines, 300; spreads falsehoods about Marcellus, 302; re-enters Syracuse, 303; joins Himilkôn against Marcellus, 308; his death, 309
Hippôn, tyrant of Messana, 227; put to death, 228
Hippônion, Dionysios' treatment of, 187
Holm, A., his *Geschichte Siciliens*, 8
Hybla, Sikel goddess, towns called after, 33; temple of, at Paternò, 34
Hybla the Greater, *see* Megara Hyblaia
Hybla, Galeatic, worship of the goddess at, 34; unsuccessful Athenian attack on, 117
Hybla Heraia, called after the goddess, 33; death of Hippokratés at, 71
Hyblon, Sikel prince, helps Megarian settlers, 47
Hykkara, taken by Nikias, 117
Hypsas, river, at Selinous, 51; at Akragas, 53

I

Iapygians defeat the Tarentines, 85
Iberian mercenaries under Dionysios, 189, 194
Illyrians, alliance of Dionysios with, 191
Inessa, name changed to Ætna, 93; Syracusan garrison at, 108
Inscriptions, Sicilian, mainly Roman, 320
Ischia, *see* Pithékoussa
Isokratés, on the Athenian siege, 104; on the Peace of Antalkidas, 190
Issos, island settlements from Paros on, 191
Italy, wars of Dionysios in, 184, 193; Punic invasions of, 192, 193; intercourse of, with old Greece, 198; campaign of Pyrrhos in, 267, 271; designed for his son Helenos, 268; under

J

Jehohanan, same as Hananiah, 21
Jews in Sicily, dealings of Gregory the Great with, 351
John, origin of the name, 21
Junius, L., takes Eryx, 286
Justinian, Emperor, Sicily recovered by, 348, 349

K

Kadmos of Kôs, 79
Kakyparis, river, guarded by Syracusans, 133
Kalè Aktè, proposed Greek settlement at, 69; settlement at by Ducetius, 101
Kallimachos, his mention of Henna, 35
Kallipolis, Chalkidian settlement, 46; conquered by Hippokratès, 68
Kallippos, his friendship with Diôn, 202; enters Syracuse, 204; plots the death of Diôn, 214; his rule at Syracuse, 215; turned out, *ib.*; murder of, 224
Kamarina, outpost of Syracuse, 50; its war with Syracuse and destruction, *ib.*; refounded by Hippokratès, 71; destroyed by Gelôn, 73; Pindar's odes to, 87; set up again by Gela, 91; allied with Athens, 108; makes peace with Gela, 109; refuses Athenian alliance, 116, 120; debate in the assembly, 119; joins Gylippos, 126; emptied by Dionysios, 153; tributary to Carthage, 154
Kamikos, built by Daidalos, 32; its probable site, 33
Karkinos, father of Agathoklès, 234
Kasmenai, outpost of Syracuse, 50; occupied by the *Gamoroi*, 62, 72
Kassandros, King of Macedôn, 258
Katanê, Catina, Catania, foundation of, 45; legends of the lava at, 46, 343; Charondas makes laws for, 65; enforced migration and repopulation by Hierôn, 84; name changed to Ætna, *ib.*, *see* Ætna; its old name restored, 93; joins Athenian alliance, 116; Athenian headquarters at, 116, 118, 121; camp at, burnt, 119; war of, with Syracuse, 140; treatment of, by Dionysios, 161; sea-fight off, 175; Kallippos, tyrant of, 215; welcomes Pyrrhos, 267; Roman colony at, 340; Saint Peter at, 343; bishopric of, 344; amphitheatre at, 347; Belisarius lands at, 348; stories of Heliodòros at, 353
Kaulônia, siege of, 185-187
Kephalos of Corinth, 224
Kleandros, tyrant of Gela, 68
Kleôn, general under Eunous, 326, 327; his death, 327
Knidos, metropolis of Lipara, 55; Athenian victory at, 180
Kôkalos, King of Kamikos, 32
Korax, teacher of rhetoric, 94
Korkyra, colony of Corinth, 41, 42; mediates between Syracuse and Hippokratès, 71; asks help of Athens, 106; sends contingent to Athenian expedition, 114; meeting of Athenian fleet at, 115; sends help to Syracuse, 218; won by Agathoklès, 258; dowry of his daughter, *ib.*
Kossoura, island, 17
Krimisos, river, 18; battle of, 226
Krotôn, at war with Sybaris, 66; sends help to Kaulônia, 185; makes treaty with Dionysios, 186; taken by Dionysios, 193; at war with the Bruttians, 235
Kyana, legend of, 36, 43
Kydippè, wife of Terillos, 74
Kyklôpes, 30
Kymè, foundation of, 40, 42; settlers from, at Zanklè, 48; delivered by Hierôn, 85

Kyrênê, 247

L

Lævinus, M. V., chosen consul, 314; his exchange with Marcellus, 315; Akragas betrayed to, 316; his dealings with the brigands, 317
Laistrygones, 30
Lamachos, appointed general, 114; is for attack on Syracuse, 116; his plan carried out, 121; killed in battle, 123
Lamis, his attempt at settlement in Sicily, 46; his death, 47
Lanassa, daughter of Agathoklês, 258
Land tenure in Sicily, under Rome, 322
Landowners of Syracuse, *see* Gamoroi
Latin tongue, akin to Sikel, 12, 27
Leo, Bishop of Catina, 353
Leo, Emperor, deprives the Popes of jurisdiction in Sicily, 350
Leontinoi, Lentini, plain of, 17, 18; foundation of, 45; its war with Megara, 63; taken by Hippokratês, 68; peopled from Naxos and Katanê, 84; its treaty with Athens, 106; wars with Syracuse, 107; asks help of Athens, 107, 112; absorbed by Syracuse, 111; Athenians attempt to restore, *ib.*; Akragantine refugees settled at, 151; independent of Syracuse, 155; treatment of, by Dionysios, 161; given to his mercenaries, 181; revolts against Dionysios the younger, 208; welcomes Diôn, 210; Hiketas, tyrant of, 215; Hiketas escapes to, 222; Timoleôn's attempt on, 224; Hierônymos slain at, 297; revolts against Syracuse, 300; taken by Marcellus, 301
Lepidus, M. Æ., invades Sicily, 337-339; his designs on Sicily, 339
Leptinês, commands Dionysios' fleet, 175, 177; Attic decrees in his honour, 180; his treatment of the Thourians, 185; banished by Dionysios, 190; his death, 192
Leptinês, tyrant of Engium and Apollonia, 224
Leptinês, general of Agathoklês, defeats Xenodikos, 249, 251
Leptinês, father of Philistis, 273
Leukas, sends help to Syracuse, 218
Libyphœnicians, 313
Licata, *see* Phintias
Libo, father-in-law of Sextus, 335
Lilybaion, its geographical position, 16; foundation of, 25, 171; besieged by Dionysios, 194; Carthaginian fleet at, 225; besieged by Pyrrhos, 270; besieged by Rome, 285, 288, 289; garrison marches out, 290; Scipio at, 317; Cæsar sets out for Africa from, 332; besieged by Lepidus, 337; marriage portion of Theodoric's daughter, 347; Imperial claim to, 348
Lindioi, akropolis of Gela, 49
Lipara, 17; Knidian settlement on, 55; Himilkôn at, 173; attacked by Agathoklês, 258; taken by Rome, 283; ceded to Rome by Carthage, 290
Lissos, founded by Dionysios, 191
Lokroi, delivered by Hierôn, 84; Thrasyboulos retires to, 90; its union with Messana, 108; refuses peace of Gela, 110; gives a wife to Dionysios, 165; Messana repeopled from, 181; lands given to Dionysios, 187, 189; Dionysios the younger at, 216
Lombards in Italy, 350
Longanos, river, battle near, 273
Lucanians, their treaty with Dionysios, 185; wage war on Tarentines, 231
Lucullus, L. L., defeats Tryphôn, 329

Lykiskos of Aitolia, 246
Lysandros, Spartan envoy to Syracuse, 160
Lysias, Attic orator, 156; his embassy to Dionysios, 181; his speech against Dionysios, 190
Lyson, idol, 343

M

Maccaluba, mud volcano of, 33
Macrobius, on the Palici, 29
Magón, defeated by Dionysios, 183; his death, 192
Magón, comes to help of Hiketas, 221; kills himself, 222
Mainón, of Segesta, said to have poisoned Agathoklés, 259; banished, 262; murders Archagathos, *ib.*
Maktórion, secession from Gela, 67
Malta, *see* Melita
Mamercus of Katané joins Timoleón, 220
Mamertines at Messana, 262; destroy Gela, 264; withstand Pyrrhos, 267, 271; wars of Hierón II. with, 273, 277; alliance of Syracuse and Carthage against, 273, 277; seek help from Rome, 277
Mamercus, tyrant of Katané, asks help from Carthage, 227; his death, 228
Manduria, battle of, 231
Marcellus, M. C., 299; negotiates with Syracuse, 300; takes Leontinoi, 301; his treatment of the deserters, *ib.*; falsehoods about, *ib.*; besieges Syracuse, 303-7; takes the outer city, 307; continues the siege, 308; Syracusan negotiations with, 310; his treatment of Syracuse, 311; of other Sicilian towns, 313; his victory over Hannón, 314; his ovation, *ib.*; re-elected consul, *ib.*; Sicilian feeling against, 315; his exchange with Lævinus, *ib.*; patron of Syracuse, *ib.*

Marcellus, M. C., betrothed to Pompeia, 335
Marius, C., his war with Sulla, 330
Marsala, *see* Lilybaion
Massilia, Verres in exile at, 332
Mazaros, river, Selinuntine outpost on, 51, 142
Megaklés, brother of Dión, enters Syracuse, 204; elected general, 205
Megallis, her treatment of the slaves, 325; killed by them, 326
Megara, Old, its colonies in Sicily, 46-48; trial and execution of Thrasydaios at, 89; Empedoklés buried at, 96
Megara, Hyblaia, foundation of, 33, 48; metropolis of Selinous, 51; its war with Leontinoi, 63; its treatment by Gelón, 73
Melita, island of, 17; won by Rome, 295
Melkart, his relation to Héraklés, 31
Menænum, temple of the Palici near, 34; founded by Ducetius, 99, 102
Menandros, Athenian general, 127; joins in attack on Epipolai, 129
Ménas, freedman of Sextus, 334; his proposal at Misenum, 335; joins Cæsar, 336; wounded at Cumæ, *ib.*; returns to Sextus, 337; changes sides again, 338;
Menekratés, killed off Cumæ, 336
Mercenaries, Sikeliot, decree as to their settlement, 92; *see also* Campanians
Mericus, betrays Syracuse to Marcellus, 310; his rewards, 312
Messana, Messéné, Messina, name of Zanklé changed to, 92; its shifting politics, 108; attacks Naxos, *ib.*; its union with Lokroi, *ib.*; refuses Athenian alliance, 116; independent of Syracuse, 155; joins Syracusan revolt against Dionysios, 158; makes peace with Dionysios, 165; destroyed by

Himilkôn, 173; repeopled by Dionysios, 181; puts Hippôn to death, 228; war of, with Agathoklês, 237; refuge of Syracusan exiles, 238; attacked by Agathoklês, *ib.*; massacre at, by mercenaries, 262; called *Civitas Mamertina*, 263, 321; Carthaginian garrison in, 277; its alliance with Rome, 321; occupied by Sextus, 333; Cæsar defeated at, 337; gets full Roman franchise, 340; bishopric of, 344
Messapians, their wars with the Tarentines, 85, 231
Messenia, settlers from, in Sicily, 92, 181, 182
Metellus, L. C., defends Panormos, 284
Metropolis, relations of, to the colony, 10, 11
Mezetius, set up as Emperor in Sicily, 352
Mikythos, his rule at Rhêgion, 85, 90; his retirement and death, 90
Milan, church of, holds lands in Sicily, 347, 351
Milazzo, *see* Mylai
Milesians share in the Samian expedition to Sicily, 69
Milêtos, Tissaphernes' castle at, 137
Mineo, *see* Menænum
Minôa, foundation of, 32, *see also* Hêrakleia Minôa
Minos, King of Crete, 32
Misenum, peace of, 335
Monaco, principality of, 322
Morgantina, battle of, 329
Motya, Phœnician settlement of, 24; Hannibal at, 142; war of Hermokratês against, 145; besieged by Dionysios, 168-71; won back by Himilkôn, 171; forsaken for Lilybaion, *ib.*
Motyon, taken and lost by Ducetius, 100
Mutinês, his exploits in Sicily, 313, 314; deprived of his command, 316; betrays Akragas to Rome,

ib.; receives Roman citizenship, 317
Mylai, said to be site of *Thrinakiê*, 30; outpost of Zanklê, 48, 50; attacked by Athens, 108; seized by Rhêgion, 182; won back by Messana, *ib.*; Roman victory off, 281; occupied by Sextus, 333; sea-fight off, 338
Myletids, banished from Syracuse, 60

N

Naulochus, sea-fight off, 339
Naxos, island, gives its name to Sicilian Naxos, 41
Naxos, Sicilian, foundation of, 41, 42; analogy with Ebbsfleet, *ib.*; conquered by Hippokratês, 68; people of, moved to Leontinoi, 84; attacked by Messana, 108; joins Athenian alliance, 116; Athenian fleet at, 118; war of, with Syracuse, 140; destroyed by Dionysios, 161
Neaiton, Netum, outpost of Syracuse, 50; its position under Rome, 321, 340
Neptune, Sextus claims him as father, 334, 338; devotion to, at Rome, 335; Cæsar's edict against, *ib.*
Neôn, 222
Nerva, P. L., sets free the slaves, 328
Nikias, opposes Sicilian expedition, 113; appointed general, 114; counsels return, 116; his delays, 117, 123, 125; his stratagem, 118; asks for horsemen and money, 119; in sole command, 123; sends ships to meet Gylippos, 124; his letter to the Athenians, 126; refuses to retreat, 130; his energy during the retreat, 133; surrenders to Gylippos, 135, 136; put to death, 136
Nikotelês, of Corinth, 160
Norman kingdom in Sicily, 6, 353
Noto, *see* Neaiton

Numidians under Mutines, 313, 314
Nypsios, holds Ortygia for Dionysios, 210-212
Nysaios, in possession of Ortygia, 215; driven out, 216

O

Odowakar, 346
Odyssey, sites for, sought in Sicily, 16, 30, 48; mention of Sikels in, 39
Olympia, embassy of Dionysios to, 190
Olympieion, temple at Syracuse, 43; Himilkôn's head-quarters at, 176; robbed by Dionysios, 191
Ophellas of Macedonia, 247
Orethos, river, 18
Ortygia, story of Arethousa at, 36, 42; *see also* Syracuse
Ostracism, meaning of, 94

P

Pachynos, Promontory of, 16
Palazzuolo, *see* Akrai
Palermo, Semitic and Norman capital of Sicily, 26; Phoenician tombs in museum, 27; *see also* Panormos
Palica, founded by Ducetius, 99; destroyed by the Syracusans, 102
Palici, their lake and worship, 34, 99; temple of, refuge for the slaves, 328; protectors of King Tryphôn, 329; whether they survived in god Phalkon, 343
Panaitios of Leontinoi, 63
Panormos, harbour of, 17, 26; Phoenician settlement at, 26; Semitic head of Sicily, 26; Hamilkar lands at, 79; invaded by Hermokrates, 146; taken by Pyrrhos, 269; taken by Rome, 282; attacked by Asdrubal, 284; position of, under Rome, 322; bishopric of, 344; withstands Belisarius, 349; *see also* Palermo
Pantagias, Pantakyas, river, 46

Pantellaria, *see* Kossoura
Papyrus at Syracuse, 294
Paros, settlements of, 191
Pasiphilos, joins Deinokrates, 254; slain by him, 257
Passero Cape, 16
Paterno, *see* Hybla Galeatic
Peithagoras, tyrant of Selinous, 67
Pellegrino, *see* Herkte
Pelôris, 16
Pentathlos, counted as founder of Lipara, 55
Pergus, Lake, 35, 36
Persephone, *see* Demeter
Persia, its alliance with Carthage, 77; invades Greece, 78
Petalism, instituted at Syracuse, 95
Phalaris of Akragas, his forged letters, 57; stories of, 64; his bull, 64, 323
Phalkon, idol, 343
Pharakidas, Spartan admiral, 177, 178
Pharnabazos, his dealings with Hermokrates, 138
Pharos, Parian settlement on, 191
Philinos of Akragas, 276
Philip of Macedon, his conquests in Greece, 218, 230; interviews Dionysios, 221
Philistis, wife of Hierôn II., 273
Philistos, Sicilian historian, 8, 76, 140; takes part in the war against Athens, 104; his friendship with Dionysios, 151, 158; banished by him, 190; recalled, 200; in command against Diôn, 203, 208; taken by Herakleides and slain, 208
Philodamos of Argos, 308
Philoxenos, treatment of, by Dionysios, 191
Phintias, tyrant of Akragas, 263; defeated by Hiketas, *ib.*; driven out of Akragas, 264; town founded by, *ib.*
Phintias (town), foundation of, 264; battle of, 314
Phoenicians, their political system,

9; plant colonies in Sicily, 11, 14, 21 28; origin of the name, 21; their tongue the same as Hebrew, *ib.*; their relations with the Greeks, 21, 22; their Mediterranean colonies, 22, 23, 26; alphabet taught to Greeks by, 22; hold the west of Sicily against Greeks, 24; remains of their walls at Motya, 25; tombs of, in Palermo Museum, 27; their coins, *ib.*; their wars with the Greeks, 66
Phyton, Rhegian general, 188; Dionysios' treatment of, 189
Pinarius, L., his massacre at Henna, 305
Pindar, notices of the goddesses in, 35; refers to Phalaris, 57; Sicilian references in his odes, 76, 83, 87; entertained by Hierón, 76, 83; gives Hierón title of king, 82
Pious Brethren, legend of, 46
Pithékoussa, island, 85
Plato, his alleged letters on Syracusan affairs, 156, 196; treatment of by Dionysios, 191; visits the younger Dionysios, 201; his constitutional schemes for Syracuse, 214, 216
Plemmyrion, peninsula, 42; occupied by the Athenians, 125; recovered by Gylippos, 128; Himilkón's fort on, 177
Plennius, 339
Polichna, early Greek outpost, 43; occupied by Syracuse, 125; Himilkón's camp on, 176
Pollis, king of Syracuse, 62
Polyphémos, legend of, 31
Polyxenos, brings help from Old Greece to Syracuse, 177
Polyzélos, son of Deinomenés, 72; marries Damareta, 83; Hierón's plots against, *ib.*
Pompeia, daughter of Sextus, 335
Pompeius, G., in Sicily, 330
Pompeius, S., his war in Spain, 332; his war with the Triumvirs, 333; charges made against, 334; claims divine origin, 334, 338; his agreement with Antonius, 334; makes peace with Cæsar and Antonius, 335; proposal of Ménas to, *ib.*; his second war in Sicily, 336-339; his death, 339
Porcari, *see* Pantagias
Probus, Emperor, 341
Province, Roman system of, 320, 344, 345
Ptolemy, King of Egypt, his friendship with Agathoklés, 258, 259
Punic Wars, *see* Carthage
Pylos, won back for Sparta, 139
Pyrrhos, King of Epeiros, marries Agathoklés' daughter, 258; Greek Sicily seeks his help, 265; his wars against Rome, 265, 266, 267, 271; withstood by the Mamertines, 267; lands at Tauromenion, *ib.*; received at Syracuse, 267; wins Akragas, 268; his title of King of Sicily, *ib.*; his campaign in North-west Sicily, 268, 269; takes Panormos, 146, 269; besieges Lilybaion, 270; fails to recover Messana, 271; leaves Sicily, *ib.*; defeated at Beneventum, *ib.*; killed at Argos, *ib.*

R

Ragusa, *see* Hybla Heraia
Ras Melkart, *see* Hérakleia Minóa
Ravenna, church of, holds lands in Sicily, 351
Regulus, M. A., his attack on Carthage, 282
Rhégion, tyranny of Anaxilas at, 69, 70; rule of Mikythos at, 85, 90; sons of Anaxilas at, 90, 91; treaty with Athens, 106; asks help of Athens, 107; Athenian fleet at, 115; joins Syracusan revolt against Dionysios, 158; makes peace with Dionysios, 165; refuses him a wife, 165, 181; seizes on Mylai,

182; attacked by Dionysios, 184; sends embassy to him, 186; siege and taking of, 188; destruction of, 189; Timoleon at, 218; ravaged by Agathoklés. 235; by the Campanians, 273; defence of, by Lævinus, 317

Rhodes, her settlements in Sicily, 49, 53, 55; bounty of Hierón II. to, 294

Roman Peace in Sicily, 323

Rome, Romans, Sicily the granary of, 19, 317, 324, 334, 338, 351; war of Pyrrhos with, 265-7. 271; allied to Carthage, 267, 272; dealings of, with the mercenaries, 273; wars of, with Carthage, 276 290, 295 317; Hierón's alliance with, 279; establishment of her power in Sicily, 292; Hieronymos revolts against, 296; war-law of, 301; uses Sicily as an outpost against Africa, 317; relations of, to subject cities, 320; state of Sicily under, 321-323, 330-2; enactment as to slaves, 328; colonies of, in Sicily, 340; rights of, extended by edict of Caracalla, 344; taken by Alaric, 345; besieged by Totila, 349

Rome, Church of, deprived of jurisdiction in Sicily, 350; estates therein, 351

Rome, New, *see* Constantinople

Rufus, Q. S., sent against Sextus, 334

Rupilius, P., takes Tauromenium, 327; his laws, *ib.*

S

Sacerdos, G. L., Prætor in Sicily. 331

Sacred Band of Carthage, destroyed at the Krimisos, 225-227

Saint Agatha of Catania, 343
Saint Kalogeros, 343
Saint Lucy, Matron, 343
Saint Lucy of Syracuse, Virgin, 343

Saint Marcian, bishop of Syracuse, 342
Saint Pancratius of Tauromenium, 342
Saint Paul, at Syracuse, 342
Saint Peter, legends of, at Syracuse, 342; said to have been at Catania, 343
Saint Zosimus, Bishop of Syracuse, 352
Salvius, king of the slaves, 328; calls himself Tryphón, 329; his revolt against Rome, *ib.*
Samians, take Zanklé, 69; treaty of Hippocratés with, 70; turned out by Anaxilas, *ib.*
Samnites, pray Pyrrhos for help against Rome, 271
San Filippo d'Argiro, 343; *see* Agyrium
San Marino, republic of, 322
Saracen invasion of Sicily, 4, 353
Sardinia, ceded by Carthage to Rome, 290, 320; taken by Sextus, 333, 334; confirmed to him at Misenum, 335; joins Cæsar, 336; taken by Gaiseric, 346
Sciacca, hot springs near, 33, 343
Scipio, P. C., his expedition against Hannibal, 317
Scipio, P. C., the younger, restores to Sicily spoil from Carthage, 323
Segesta, Elymian site, 13, 20; wars of with Selinous, 55, 112, 141; with Dórieus, 67; its treaty with Athens, 106, 108; appeals to Athens, *ib.*; trick played on Athenian envoys, 113; helps Athens, 120; alliance of, with Carthage, 141; besieged by Dionysios, 170; siege raised, 171; treatment of, by Agathoklés, 252, 279; joins Pyrrhos, 269; joins Rome, 279; position of, under Rome, 322, 340
Selinous, foundation of, 51; wars with Segesta, 55, 112, 141; tyranny of Peithagoras and

Euryleon at, 67; her relations to Carthage, 74, 82, 154, 220, 238; promises help to Hamilkar, 80; joins Gylippos, 124; sends help to Greece, 137; taken by Hannibal, 139, 142; fortified by Hermokrates, 145; recovered by Dionysios, 194; origin of the name, 226; welcomes Pyrrhos, 269; destroyed by Carthage, 285

Selinous, river, 51

Servilius, Q., his war with the slaves, 329

Shophetim of Carthage, 179

Sicily, its historical importance, 1, 2; its geographical position and character, 3, 9, 15 *seqq.*; strife between East and West for, 3, 26, 354; compared with Cyprus and Spain, 5; Norman kingdom of, 6, 353; Phoenician colonies in, 11, 14, 21-28; Greek colonies in, 11, 14, 39 *seqq.*; older inhabitants of, 11-14; becomes practically Greek, 16, 324; its triangular shape, 16; sites for Odyssey sought in, 16, 30, 48; mountain and rivers of, 17-19; chief granary of Rome, 19, 317, 324, 334, 338, 351; hill towns of, 20; legends of, 29 *seqq.*; Hamilkar's invasion of, 77 81; independence of its cities, 87 *seqq.*; share of, in the wars of Greece, 104 *seqq.*, 160; Athenian expedition to, 114 *seqq.*; second Carthaginian invasion of, 140 *seqq.*; effect of the reign of Dionysios on, 197, 198; new settlement of, 223; freed by Timoleon, 229; position of Agathokles in, 257; war of Pyrrhos in, 265 271; a wrestling ground for Rome and Carthage, 272, 276 *seqq.*; given up by Carthage, 290; becomes a Roman province, 292, 320, 339, 344; main battlefield of Hannibal, 305; outcry in, against Marcellus, 315; an outpost of Europe, 317; Scipio's starting point for Africa, 317; relation of its cities to Rome, 320 322; Roman Peace in, 323; increase of slavery, 324; slave wars of, 325 329, 341; Cicero's account of, 330; Julius Cæsar's starting point for Africa, 332; occupied by Sextus, 333 *seq.*; war between Cæsar and Sextus for, 336-339; Cæsar master of, 339; Roman colonies in, 340; Hadrian's visit to, 341; Frankish invasion of, 342; Christianity in, 342 344; effect of the edict of Caracalla on, 344; part of the *diocese* of Italy, 345; Teutonic invasions of, 345 *seq.*; under Theodoric, 347; won back by Belisarius, 348-349; its connexion with the Eastern Empire, 350; lands of the Roman Church in, 347, 351, 352; Constans II. in, 352; Mezetius Emperor in, 352; recovered by Constantine IV., *ib.*; Saracen invasions in, 353; won back by the Normans, 353

Sidon, probable settlement from in Sicily, 24; its hatred towards the Greeks, 77

Sikania, name of Sicily, 11; mentioned in Odyssey, 39

Sikans, the, 11-13, 27; hill towns, characteristic of, 20; remains of, in Sicily, 27; traditions of, 32

Sikelia, 11; subject to Carthage, 154

Sikeliots, distinguished from Sikels, 41

Sikels, the, 11-13; gradually become Greek, 13; language of, akin to Latin, 12, 27; hill-towns of, 20; remains of, in Sicily, 27; tale of their migration from Italy, 29; their beliefs and traditions, 33-37; mentioned in Odyssey, 39; driven out of Syracuse, 45; Theokles'

INDEX.   375

dealings with, 47 ; war of, with Skythes, 69 ; their union under Ducetius, 98 ; help Naxos, 108 ; help Athens, 120 ; guaranty of their independence, 155
Simonides, Sicilian references in his poems, 76 ; entertained by Hierón, 76, 83 ; said to have reconciled Hierón and Thérôn, 84
Skylla, tale of, 30
Skythes of Zanklé, his war with the Sikels, 69 ; Hippokratés' treatment of, 70 ; escapes to Asia, *ib.*
Slaves, increase of, in Sicily, 324 ; wars of, 325–330 ; Roman order for their liberation, 328 ; third revolt of, 341
Solous, Solunto, Phœnician settlement of, 25 ; taken by Pyrrhos, 270 ; joins Rome, 283
Sophrosynê, daughter of Dionysios, 200
Sôsis, slays Hierónymos, 297 ; takes refuge with Marcellus, 303, 306 ; leads the Romans into the Hexapyla, 307 ; rewarded by Marcellus, 312
Sôsistratos, denounced by Agathoklés, 235 ; banished, *ib.* ; seeks Hamilkar's help, 235, 236 ; his death, 238
Sôsistratos, in command at Syracuse, 264 ; welcomes Pyrrhos, 267 ; takes service under him, 268 ; flees from Syracuse, 271
Spaccaforno, *see* Kasmenai
Spain, compared with Sicily, 5 ; Phœnician colonies in, 14, 15, 23, 26
Spanish mercenaries of Dionysios, 179
Sparta, compared with Athens, 105 ; Syracusan embassy to, 120 ; her alliance with Darius, 137 ; Pylos won back for, 139 ; supports Dionysios, 160 ; embassy of Dionysios to, 176 ; objects to settlement of Messenians by Dionysios, 181 ; Dionysios sends help to, 180, 194 ; checks his advance, 191 ; admits Dión to citizenship, 202 ; sends help against Agathoklés, 237
Sthenios of Therma, 330
Stesichoros, 64
Strabo, his description of Sicily, 39, 340
Sulla, L. C., his war with Marius, 330
Sulpicius, G., invades Panormos, 282
Susa, *see* Hadrumetum
Sybaris, its war with Kroton, 67
Symaithos, river, 18
Synalos, receives Dión at Hérakleia Minôa, 203
Syracuse, foundation of, 42 ; her relations to Corinth, *ib.* ; importance of her topography, 43 ; her outposts, 49, 50 ; her war with Kamarina, 50 ; champion of Europe against Africa, 56 ; *Gamoroi* of, 59-62 ; war of Hippokratés with, 71 ; tyranny of Gelón at, 72 *sqq.* ; enlarged by him, 73 ; temples at, built by Gelón, 83 ; drives out Thrasyboulos, 90 ; feast of the *Eleutheria* at, 91 ; exclusion of the new citizens, *ib.* ; demagogues at, 94 ; institution of petalism, 95 ; her wars with Akragas, 96, 101 ; with Etruscans, 98 ; with Ducetius, 100 ; with Leontinoi, 107, 111 ; attacks Naxos, 108 ; Athenian expedition against, 114 *sqq.* ; debate in the assembly, *ib.* ; embassies to Peloponnésos, 120 ; beginning of the siege, 123 ; coming of Gylippos, 124, 125 ; improvement of naval tactics, 128 ; Athenians surrender to, 134, 136 ; treatment of prisoners, 136 ; sends help to Greece, 137 ; threatened by Hannibal, 144 ; feeling towards Hermokratés, 145-6 ; sends help to Akragas, 149 ; generals accused

of treason, 151; recalls the exiles, 151; Dionysios tyrant at, 152, 156; revolt of the horsemen, 153; return of Dionysios, 154; subjection to Dionysios guaranteed by Carthage, 155; fortification of the Island, 158; revolts against Dionysios, *ib.*; fortified by Dionysios, 164; besieged by Himilkon, 176; Olympicion plundered by Dionysios, 191; her treaty with Carthage, 195; position of, under Dionysios, 197; delivered by Dion, 203–5; Island held by Dionysios the younger, 205, 207; treatment of Philistos by, 208; gets rid of Dion, 209; prays him for help against Dionysios, 211; Dion's entrance into, 212; Plato's schemes for, 214, 216; tyrannies in, on Dion's death, 215–6; embassy to Corinth, 217; delivered by Timoleon, 220–2; second Corinthian settlement of, 223; treatment of Hiketas' family, 228, of Mamercus, *ib.*; massacre at, by Agathoklês, 236; his tyranny at, *ib.*; Carthaginian attack on, 239 *seqq.*; Hamilkar retires from, 245; his first attack on, 246; wars of with Akragas, 249, 263; Hiketas tyrant of, 263; prays Pyrrhos for help against Carthage, 265; welcomes Pyrrhos, 267; allied with Carthage against Mamertines, 273, 277; Hieron's kingdom of, 274, 278–9; prosperity of, under Hieron, 293, 294; misrule of Hieronymos in, 297; negotiates with Appius Claudius, 298, 300; slaughter of Hieron's descendants, 299; Leontinoi revolts against, 300; effect of Marcellus' treatment of the deserters on, 301–2; Roman siege of, 303, 311; Marcellus, hereditary patron of, 315; gradual decay of, 324, 352; occupied by Sextus, 333; Roman colony at, 340; sacked by the Franks, 342; SS. Peter and Paul at, *ib.*; bishopric of, 344; Gothic count of, 347; submits to Belisarius, 348; temple of Athênê turned into a church, 352; Constans II. at, *ib.*

T

Taormina, *see* Tauromenion
Taras, Tarentum, helped by Mikythos, 85; asks help of Sparta, 231; helped by Pyrrhos against Rome, 265, 266, 271; submits to Rome, 271; head-quarters of Antonian ships, 337, 338
Tauromenion, foundation of, 173; defeat of Dionysios at, 183; taken by him, 184; Timoleon lands at, 219; Punic envoys at, *ib.*; men of, slain by Agathoklês, 238; Pyrrhos lands at 267; its alliance with Rome, 321; taken by the slaves, 327; Roman siege of, *ib.*; Cæsar at, 338; Roman colony at, 340; church of Saint Pancratius at, 342; bishopric of, 344
Taurus, S., in command under Antonius, 337
Tegea, Mikythos dies at, 90
Telemachos of Akragas, 65
Telines of Gela, 68
Temenites, outpost of Syracuse, 43; taken into the city, 119
Tenea, settlers from, at Syracuse, 59
Terillos, tyrant of Himera, 74; driven out by Thêron, 78
Termini, *see* Thermai of Himera
Terranova, *see* Gela
Teutonic invaders of Sicily, 342, 345
Thapsos, peninsula, 43; Megarian settlement at, 47; Athenian station at, 121; taken by Agathoklês, 245
Thearidas, admiral of Dionysios' fleet, 185
Themistos, elected general, 297; put to death, 298

Theodahad, king of the East Goths, 348
Theodoric, king of the East Goths, 347
Theodôros, denounces Dionysios, 177
Theodotés, Dión's treatment of, 212
Theodotos, slays Hierónymos, 297
Theoklês of Chalkis, founds Naxos, 40; and Leontinoi, 45; his dealings with the Sikels and Megarians, 47
Theokritos, his verses to Hierón II., 294
Therma, Thermai, of Himera, 51, 343; colony of Carthage at, 33, 147; becomes Greek, 147; subject to Carthage, 154, 238; Agathoklês born at, 234; taken by Agathoklês, 250; joins Deinokratês, 254; Agathoklês negotiates for, 255; taken by Rome, 283; Roman colony at, 340
Thermai of Selinous, 343
Thêrón, tyrant of Akragas; his alliance with Gelón, 73; drives out Terillos, 78; his share in the battle of Himera, 80, 81; his war with Hierón, 83; reconciled to him, 84; his works at Akragas and death, 89; destruction of his tomb, 149
Thespia, sends contingent to Syracuse, 126, 129
Thoinón, of Syracuse, overthrows Hiketas, 264; welcomes Pyrrhos, 267; put to death, 271
Thourioi, foundation of, 106; treatment of by Leptinês, 185; makes treaty with Dionysios, 186; helped by Corinth, 221
Thrasimund, king of the Vandals, 347
Thrasón, adviser of Hierónymos, 296
Thrasyboulos, son of Deinomenês, 72, 83; his tyranny at Syracuse, 90; withdraws to Lokroi, *ib.*
Thrasydaios, his oppression at Himera, 84; his tyranny at Akragas, 89; put to death at Old Megara, *ib.*
Thrinakiê, 16, 30
Timokratês, Dión's wife given to, 201; left in command at Syracuse, 203; his letter to Dionysios, 203, 205
Timoleón, his share in Timophanês' death, 217; sent to help Syracuse, *ib.*; lands at Tauromenion, 219; defeats Hiketas at Hadranum, *ib.*; Dionysios surrenders to, 220; plots against, 221; takes Syracuse, 222; re-founds it, 223; repulsed at Leontinoi, 224; Leptinês and Hiketas submit to, *ib.*; his war with Carthage, 225; his victory by the Krimisos, 227; his treatment of the tyrants, 227, 228; makes peace with Carthage, 228; sends settlers to Gela and Akragas, 229; ends his days at Syracuse, *ib.*; the Timoleonteion built in his honour, 230
Timophanês, of Corinth, his tyranny and death, 217
Tisias, teacher of rhetoric, 94
Tissaphernes, his alliance with Sparta, 137; withstood by Hermokratês, *ib.*
Torgium, battle of, 255
Totila, king of the Goths, invades Sicily, 349
Trinacia taken by Syracuse, 107
Trinakria, 16, 30
Triocala, capital of King Tryphón, 329
Trotilon, first Megarian settlement at, 46
Trojan traditions at Segesta, 13, 252, 269, 279
Tryphón, *see* Salvius, 75
Tunis, head-quarters of Agathoklês, 243; victory of, over Carthage, 244; taken by the mercenaries, 246; Ophellas slain at, 247
Tycha, quarter of Syracuse, 92, 165

Tyndarión, his attempt at tyranny at Syracuse, 94
Tyndarión, tyrant of Tauromenion, 263; joins Pyrrhos, 267
Tyndaris, foundation of, 182; joins Timoleón, 220; Roman victory off, 282; occupied by Sextus, 333; Roman colony at, 340
Tyrants, use of the name, 62, 353; Greek view as to slaying of, 217, 228
Tyre, probable settlements from in Sicily, 24; its hatred towards Greeks, 77; the Geloan Apollôn sent to, 153; Carthaginian embassies to, 244

U

Utica, Phœnician colony. 23; taken by Agathoklês, 248

V

Vandals, alleged invasion of Sicily by, 342; in Africa, Italy, and Sicily, 346; Belisarius' campaign against, 348

Verres, G., Cicero's speech against, 319, 330, 332; his oppression in Sicily, 331; goes into exile, 332; put to death, *ib.*
Volcanic mountains and lakes in Sicily, 33, 34

X

Xenodikos of Akragas, defeated by Leptinês, 249, 251
Xerxes, invades Greece, 78
Xiphonia, peninsula, 43, 46

Z

Zanklê, foundation of, 48; founds Himera, 50; ruled by Skythês, 69; seized by the Samians, *ib.*; its army enslaved by Hippocratês, 70; occupied by Anaxilas, *ib.*; name changed to Messana, 70, 92; rule of Mikythos at, 85, 90; sons of Anaxilas at, 90, 91; *see* Messana
Zöippos, uncle of Hierônymos, 295; supports Carthage, 296; sent to Egypt, 299; slaughter of his family, *ib.*

www.ingramcontent.com/pod-product-compliance
Lightning Source LLC
Chambersburg PA
CBHW031412230426
43668CB00007B/282